everyday DEBATE & DISCUSSION

A Guide to Socratic Conversation, Informal Discussion, and Formal Debate

by Shelly Johnson, PhD

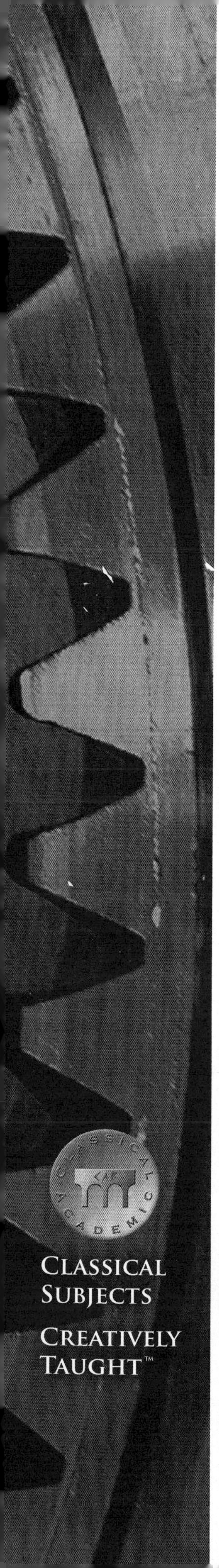

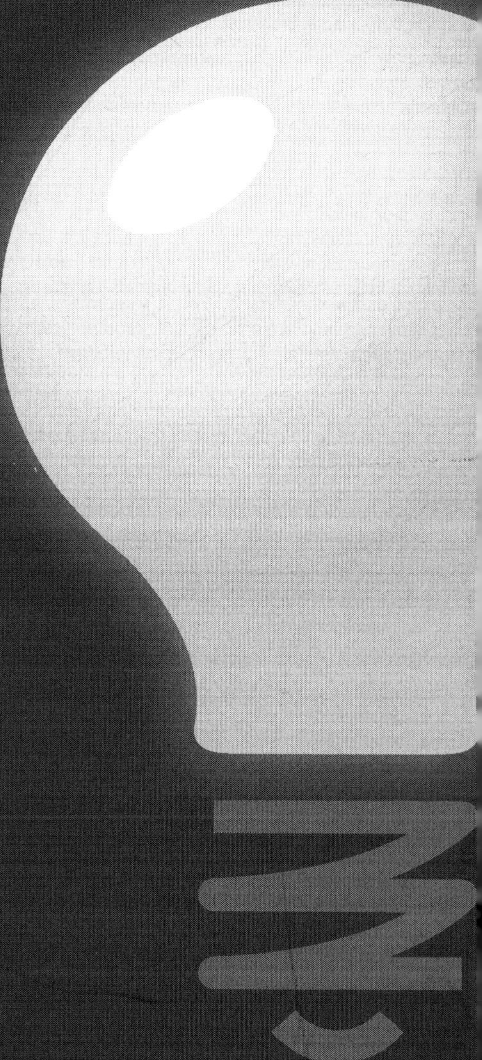

CLASSICAL SUBJECTS CREATIVELY TAUGHT™

Everyday Debate & Discussion
© Classical Academic Press, 2016
Version 1.0

ISBN: 978-1-60051-293-3

All rights reserved. This publication may not be reproduced, stored in a retrieval system, or transmitted, in any form or by any means, without the prior written permission of Classical Academic Press.

Classical Academic Press
2151 Market Street
Camp Hill, PA 17011

www.ClassicalAcademicPress.com

Editor: Janet Dixon
Illustrations: Jason Rayner
Book design: Lenora Riley

PGP.04.16

I would like to dedicate this book to my nephews and niece:

Andrew, Joshua, Eli, and Amelie.

May they grow up to be critical thinkers and lovers of wisdom.

Table of Contents

Unit V: Arrangement

Unit VI: Presentation and Debate Possibilities

To Students: Introduction

You may not know it, but you debate all the time. A debate is simply a discussion in which two or more people present their arguments for a particular view and critique each other's views. If you have strong opinions about certain issues (and who doesn't?), and if you try to convince other people of your opinion (and who hasn't?), you are very likely engaging in a debate. You may debate your family members over dinner or debate your friends on Facebook. You may debate your classmates informally during class discussion or debate other students formally in a setting like a debate tournament.

Debates can happen every day, at any time, and in any place. When they are handled well, debates can be very enjoyable, and the people involved learn a great deal. On the other hand, when debates are handled poorly, they can be an exercise in frustration in which people talk quite a lot but learn very little. I want your debate experience to resemble the former rather than the latter kind of debate. That is why I have written *Everyday Debate & Discussion.*

In *Everyday Debate & Discussion*, you will learn to develop good arguments by using good logic and the resources available in your own thinking, as well as in the world around you. You will learn how to appeal to people's emotions in the proper way and to strengthen your credibility with other people through methods such as the effective use of humor and thoughtful quotes. You will also learn how to critique the opposing view in a debate and develop good skills for organizing your own arguments. In addition to all of this, you will learn how to use these skills in both informal as well as formal debate settings so that whenever you find yourself debating, be it over tea or in a tournament, you will have the tools you need to be an effective debater.

Welcome to *Everyday Debate & Discussion*!

Let's get going.

Objectives:

1. Keep debate front and center in our minds
2. Grow skills, knowledge, confidence in making use of debate.
3. Grow the frequency and quality of debating activity on our hallway, growing the quality of our dialectic* classrooms.

* meaning?

Chapter 1

Welcome to Debate! An Introduction and Overview

> ALL MEN BY NATURE DESIRE KNOWLEDGE.
> —ARISTOTLE[1]

Introduction

What would you do if you were having a conversation with a friend and realized that you completely disagreed with her point of view? What if your friend wanted to debate you about this issue? Would you welcome such a challenge as an adventure, or would you shrink from it as a threat? All human beings have a fight-or-flight response that kicks in when we face any kind of danger or challenge. Unfortunately, when it comes to debate and disagreement, the "flight" response often kicks in rather than the "fight" response. Usually, this is because people don't really understand the nature of debate or disagreement. They automatically assume that it is a hostile, combative activity. Other times people avoid debates because they are afraid of being overwhelmed by the force of another person's arguments. They are not sure how to respond effectively, or how to craft powerful arguments themselves. More commonly, people view debate either as an extremely intellectual activity in which only university professors engage, or as the attention-seeking self-service often found in political or presidential "debates." To many people, these debates seem especially rancorous and interminable. Therefore, they decide that while such an activity might be fine for those who make a living by being intellectual, it isn't necessary or helpful for the normal, everyday person.

If you are one who feels fearful about—or even disgusted by—debate or disagreement, I hope that this book changes your mind, giving you debating confidence and opening your eyes to the benefit of debate, disagreement, and discussion in your day-to-day life. While it is true that some people conduct themselves in such a way as to make their debates disagreeable and unprofitable, participating in debates and discussions conducted in a thoughtful and civil manner can be one of the most rewarding experiences in life. Who knows? By the end of this book, you may find yourself jumping willingly into the debating fray and experiencing quite a few successes along the way.

Whether or not you decide to participate in formal debate, such as in a debate club, or in the kind of informal debate that you might experience in a coffee shop or around your dining room table with your family, this book presents you with tools for success along each step of debate. Furthermore, you will learn techniques that will help you develop a debater's mind, which is an invaluable asset for your everyday life. Even if you choose not to debate on a regular basis, developing a debater's mind will help you think more critically about the world around you, enabling you to understand others' viewpoints better, and to cut through all of the facts and words to find the truth or error in people's arguments. If you are already curious and excited about debate, this book gives you empowering information. In

1. Susan Ratcliffe, ed., *Oxford Dictionary of Quotations by Subject*, 2nd ed. (Oxford: Oxford University Press, 2010), 266.

addition, this book will supply some suggestions about finding or starting a formal debate club.

Definition

Before we proceed any further, it is wise to make sure that we have a clear definition of the term "**debate.**" Its first definition can seem intimidating. After all, the word "debate"[2] comes from the Latin word *battuere*, which itself means "to beat." However, after looking at several possible definitions of debate, this etymology may become a little less intimidating.

One definition of debate is "to turn over in one's mind."[3] It is important to realize that a person can debate with herself. She might do this by first considering several different possible answers, ideas, or strategies for a plan she is considering; then contemplating the strengths and weaknesses of each option; and finally choosing what she believes is the correct answer. In this case, it is as if she were "beating" her thoughts into the proper form, working out kinks and inconsistencies (similar to a metal worker beating a piece of metal into the correct shape) in order to arrive at the best possible answer.

Another common definition of debate is "to contend in words" or "to discuss a question by considering opposed arguments."[4] This second definition presents a picture of debate that people commonly think of when they hear the word "debate": two people verbally wrestling over the opposing sides of a topic in order, hopefully, to determine which side is correct. (Of course, it is true that a person might debate merely to win or to prove himself correct, rather than to seek the truth.) However, in the best sense of this definition of the word "debate," people are also "beating" their own and one another's logic into proper shape, hammering it out, finding weaknesses and flaws, in order to achieve the best argument. Note that this type of debate can take place anywhere—in a home, in a restaurant, on a street corner, or in an auditorium.

A third type of debate is a formal debate between two people or teams. This debate is regulated by a certain set of procedures or guidelines established ahead of time.[5] Webster's further defines this type of debate as a "series of formal spoken arguments for and against a definite proposition."[6] If you are unfamiliar with the word "**proposition**," it is, simply, a statement that can be proven true or false. When people debate, they argue for or against a statement (proposition) that can be proven true or false, right or wrong, good or bad.

As you can see from these definitions, debate can be both formal and informal. A **formal debate** can be defined as one that takes place before a judge or judges, and follows a set of rules. People might participate in this type of debate in a classroom or as a part of a debate team. Formal debates usually have a very specific kind of format. For example, one common form of debate is organized in the following manner:[7]

First Speaker—Affirmative Team (5 minutes)

First Speaker—Negative Team (5 minutes)

Second Speaker—Affirmative Team (5 minutes)

Second Speaker—Negative Team (5 minutes)

Rebuttal Speaker—Affirmative Team (3 minutes)

Rebuttal Speaker—Negative Team (3 minutes)

As you can see, this is a highly regulated debate format with a specific speaking order and time allotment for each part of the debate. There are several other common formal debate formats that you will examine later. People engage in these structured debates in the classroom or in a formal debate club. The presidential debates that occur before elections are also formalized debates. Some people love this type of debating contest. If you are one of them, there is information in this book that will help you start, join, or prepare for this type of debating organization. Formal debate can be excellent training in thinking and speaking, and it is a great way to explore important topics.

However, even if you never participate in a formal debate, this book is helpful for you because every human

2. *Webster's Ninth New Collegiate Dictionary*, s.v. "debate."
3. Ibid.
4. Ibid.

5. J. Scott Wunn, "Debate," in *World Book Encyclopedia* (Chicago: World Book, 2011), 63–65.
6. *Webster's Ninth New Collegiate Dictionary*, s.v. "debate."
7. Kate Shuster and John Meany, *Speak Out! Debate and Public Speaking in the Middle Grades* (New York: International Debate Education Association, 2005), 48.

being participates in informal debates regularly in life, whether we realize it or not. **Informal debate** happens all the time. In this type of debate, two people discuss an idea to figure out truth or a plan or simply to entertain themselves intellectually. There is rarely any kind of deliberative body or previously established rules in an informal debate. Friends debate and discuss whether the latest movie is worth watching. Families debate whether they should get a cat or a dog, or even a pet at all. As you continue reading this book, you will notice that there can be similarities between debate and discussion. *Webster's Ninth New Collegiate Dictionary* defines the word "**discussion**" as "an investigation by reasoning or argumentation."[8] Another way to think of discussion is as "a discourse or conversation between two people in which a specific problem or idea is explored." When people discuss an issue, they identify a problem they want to explore, and they discuss various views and methods for addressing and solving the problem. It is important to note that when people discuss something, they can be on the same side of an issue. For instance, two parents from a school may discuss how they can best raise money for their children's end-of-the-year field trip. Or they may discuss how they can handle a problem with bullying in their children's class. These two parents could agree, essentially, on the general methods for raising money or dealing with bullies. However, they could discuss several different options, and consider the various strengths and weaknesses of each option. The parents might not adopt opposing sides in an argument, but they still could debate the correct choice among several possible "competing" choices.

As a different example, if these same two parents were debating about fund-raising—say, at a meeting of a parent-teacher group—the process would look a little different. In this case, these two parents could believe in two different methods of fund-raising. One might believe in children going door-to-door, selling candy bars. The other parent might believe in holding a schoolwide event, such as a silent auction. In this scenario, one parent would present her idea of the children selling candy bars, and she would likely discuss the strengths of this plan. Then the other parent would speak, critiquing the idea of selling candy, and then proposing a plan for a schoolwide silent auction instead, discussing the strengths of her idea. After she'd speak, the other parent would have the chance to critique the auction idea as well. As you can see, in this scenario the parents disagree about the means and methods for obtaining an objective. They are debating the best method for raising funds. In order to do this, each must present her ideas for what she believes is best, as well as critique the opposing idea. Be assured that the skills that you learn from this book will help you with all forms of debate, discussion, and disagreement.

8. *Webster's Ninth New Collegiate Dictionary*, s.v. "discussion."

Why Debate?

Although you are now familiar with what debate is and with its different definitions, you may still wonder why anyone would really *want* to debate. After all, debating takes time, preparation, and energy. Wouldn't it just be easier to live and let live, as the saying goes? Furthermore, a lot of people feel nervous about debating or disagreeing with others, especially people who hold strongly opposing views. We often feel nervous or frightened when we have conflict with other people. Remember the fight-or-flight reflex mentioned at the beginning of this chapter? When we are in situations of emotional or physical danger, human beings have a natural tendency to gear up to fight or to get away as fast as we can. Some people love a good fight, while others want to flee tense situations. Believe it or not, learning debate skills can help you in these emotionally tense situations when you find that you disagree with someone (and we all have those times in life). These skills can be very helpful because they can teach you how to prove your point, critique the opposing point, or search for further truth without getting too emotionally involved in the process, and without hurling insults.

It is safe to say that since humans first had different ideas about things they have had debates. Why have we always felt the need to share our views, discuss the relative merits and problems of our respective views, all in an attempt to discover a right answer? Philosophers, sociologists, lawyers, politicians, psychologists, theologians, and others who study humans and their motivations, ideas, and behaviors all agree that humans have always pondered the big questions of the universe: What is the nature of this world I live in? What's my purpose in life? Why is there suffering in the world? How can we fix the suffering? How can I find happiness?

Everyone thinks about these issues, but we may think about them in slightly different manners. For instance, when a teenage girl wonders, "What college will be the best place for me to pursue learning more about philosophy?" or "What summer job should I take?" she is asking questions about the pursuit of happiness. A college student may wonder, "What are the causes of poverty and inequality in my city?" and this could prompt her to major in sociology or social work. When she asks such a question, she is pondering questions about her purpose in life and the means for achieving happiness and peace. A father asks himself, "How can I raise my children to have a positive impact on their world?" or "How can I care for the earth responsibly so that I can give my children a clean, safe world in which to live?" Another adult may look around her neighborhood and ask, "Why has crime increased in my neighborhood over the past few years? What can I do to stop it?" or "How can I show kindness and compassion to my neighbor who is suffering from mental illness?" As you can see, these questions are aimed at personal happiness, purpose in life, and the question of suffering in the world.

Many people ask these big questions about things that immediately pertain to their lives, their families, and their neighborhoods. This is natural, as these will always be the most important things in a person's life. However, at some point most people begin to ask these questions as they pertain to society and the world at large. For instance, people ask questions such as, "How can we help developing nations overcome major health issues such as the AIDS pandemic?" or "Should America be the police of the world?" Today, many people ask questions such as, "How far should science be allowed to go in its manipulation of human genes?" or "Is abortion ever permissible?" or "To what extent is human behavior negatively impacting our environment?" Although not all people will become professional scientists, philosophers, and politicians whose job it is to answer such questions, it is valuable for all of us to learn to debate important issues, because they eventually affect all of us through the influence of laws, education, our neighborhoods, and the people we know. It is important to realize that whenever we pursue and discuss questions such as those mentioned previously, we are being politicians and philosophers. That is, we are people who are searching for truth and wisdom, people who are concerned with the welfare of our families, friends, and nation.

As you learn the skills of everyday debate, you will engage in a process that will positively impact your life, as well as the lives of those around you. Before we jump into learning these skills, it is important for you to gain perspective on the role debate and discussion has played throughout world history, and especially in your own country. The following chapters will help you better understand the significance of discussion and debate, as well as the role it plays in shaping culture and society, and it will help you understand why debate is such a worthwhile pursuit.

Review Exercises

List

debate – literally "to beat" but as in to mold

Give three possible definitions of the word "debate."

1. to turn over in one's mind
2. to contend in words by considering opposed arguments
3. series of formal arguments for and against

Explain

1. Explain how a person could express the etymology of debate (from the Latin word *battuere*, "to beat") in a positive light (i.e., not as just "beating" one's opponent).

Like a metal worker shaping a piece of metal into a beautiful piece of jewelry.

shaping words into understanding and truth – law #6 speaking and writing new ideas into truth

2. Explain the difference between formal and informal debate. Make sure you explain where each kind of debate is likely to take place.

Formal debate takes place before a judge and has a pre-determined structure.

Informal can happen almost anywhere even inside one's own head

Define and Relate

What is definition of the word "discussion"? How is discussion related to debate?

A discussion is a conversation between two people in which a specific problem or idea is explored. A discussion can involve two or more people considering the best options for something.

Everyday Debate

List

Think back over the last couple of weeks or months of your life. List three controversial topics that you have heard people discussing or debating. They can be small or large. They can be in day-to-day life or on TV. They can also be topics that pertain just to your family or the culture at large.

Trump v Clinton
abortion
Black Lives Matter
Voter ID

Develop

Pick one of the topics you mentioned in the "Everyday Debate" section that your class could debate without much research. Now, sum up that topic in a proposition (i.e., a statement that can be proven true or false). For instance, if you wanted to debate the topic of capital punishment, you could write the following proposition: "Capital punishment is inhumane and ought to be prohibited by the federal government." Once you choose a topic, your teacher will divide the class into two teams. One side is the affirmative side, which means that team will argue *for* the proposition. The other side is the negative side, which means that they will argue *against* the proposition. (The affirmative and negative sides are discussed further in chapter 5.) It's OK to be on a side that doesn't necessarily reflect your actual belief (i.e., you may personally agree with the proposition but actually end up on the negative side for the purpose of the class debate). It's good practice to argue against a proposition you believe, or to argue for a proposition you do not believe; this exercise helps you learn how to examine topics from all sides.

Once the class has been divided into teams, make sure that everyone on your team has at least one argument that she can make for or against the proposition. Everyone should have a key point that supports or critiques the proposition, and each person should also have some facts that develop that point. Each argument doesn't have to be long—a few sentences will suffice.

In addition, think of the potential arguments that the other side may bring against you and how you could counteract those arguments. There are several basic ways to disprove (or rebut) an argument: prove it is based on faulty information; prove it is a misinterpretation of the information; or prove that the reasoning behind the argument is faulty. Don't worry if you aren't sure how to go about rebutting an argument right now. Just keep these points in mind. Once you have spent some time talking through this with your team, your teacher will tell you how to debate.

Learning from the Masters

Discuss

The Great Debaters, starring Denzel Washington, is a movie that is based on a true story and details the adventures of the first African American debate team to debate with Harvard College.[9] Watch the movie and answer the following questions:

1. What role did debate play in the lives of the main characters in this movie?
2. What skills did these students need in their debates?
3. What are some things that the debate coach did to improve their debate abilities?
4. In what ways were the main characters on the debate team especially effective debaters?
5. In what way did these students effect change in their world through debate?

9. Todd Black, et al, *The Great Debaters*, directed by Denzel Washington (2007; New York: Weinstein Co., 2008), DVD.

Chapter 2

Why Debate?

> DARE TO KNOW! HAVE THE COURAGE TO USE YOUR OWN REASON!
> —IMMANUEL KANT[1]

Introduction

If you have any doubt about how powerful debate and discussion can be, all you have to do is look at history to see how they have radically changed, and often improved, our world and culture. Most of the major breakthroughs, discoveries, and decisions in history have happened because of debate and discussion. Sometimes the format was formal debate that took place in universities, parliament, congress, or before church councils. Other times this important historical debate was much more informal, having taken place between friends as they debated science or theology, as they learned from each other's thoughts and discoveries. Sometimes it took place in people's letters or in books they wrote in response to previous ideas. When we debate and discuss ideas with others, even if it can be tense at times, we often come away with a clearer understanding of the topic at hand.

Definition

We can say that history is the history of **dialectic**. The word "dialectic" comes from the Greek word *dialektikos*, which means "conversational."[2] Dialectic is "a discussion and reasoning by dialogue as a method of intellectual investigation . . . the techniques of exposing false beliefs and eliciting truth . . . investigation of eternal ideas."[3] You will notice that dialectic is closely related and connected to debate. In fact, debate always involves dialectic, for debate is nothing more than a formal, organized conversation that allows the intellectual exploration of a topic for the purpose of discovering truth and error in thinking. People have used dialectic and debate throughout history. That is, through discussion and debate, they have discovered new ideas and truths through exposing false beliefs and eliciting true ideas. It is important to note that historically, the practical and philosophical always intertwine. Both are necessary and often inform each other. We must have a reason and foundation for doing what we do—this is our philosophy; yet philosophy should always work practically in the world. On one hand, why think about some practical matter if it has no ultimate or eternal significance? On the other hand, if we have a philosophical theory but it doesn't appear to make sense in the world, how useful is it? A quick overview of history demonstrates how people have debated and discussed the practical and philosophical in order to figure out the best way to live.

---

1. Susan Ratcliffe, ed., *Oxford Dictionary of Quotations by Subject*, 2nd ed. (Oxford: Oxford University Press, 2010), 267.
2. J.T. Pring, *The Pocket Oxford Greek Dictionary* (New York: Oxford University Press, 2000), 49.
3. *Webster's Ninth New Collegiate Dictionary*, s.v. "dialectic."

The Ancient Greeks

Socrates once said, "This is an experience which is characteristic of a philosopher, this wondering: this is where philosophy begins and nowhere else."[4] Socrates argued that philosophy springs from wonder, and the same thing can also be said of debate. People have always wondered about the criterion for truth in all areas of life, such as science, philosophy, theology, and politics. This has led to significant debates that have profoundly affected the way we view our world and the decisions we make because of these views. The ancient Greeks were some of the people who first took debatable issues seriously. For instance, the Greeks were fascinated about how the world worked and debated the nature of it. One of the first questions the ancient Greeks debated was, which substance constitutes the world? One early Greek philosopher, Thales, posited that the basic substance of all matter was water, while another one, Empedocles, proposed that all matter was composed of four basic elements: earth, water, fire, or air.[5] Still another philosopher, Democritus, stated that all substance must be composed of small particles that we cannot see: atoms. In fact, the word "atom" comes from the Greek word meaning "too small to cut."[6] As you can see, this idea later influenced our scientific views about matter.

Of course, people have always wondered about the world around them, but they have also wondered about a world beyond the one they see. Throughout history, people have always asked questions such as: Is there anything beyond this life? Are there moral laws of the universe that tell us what to do? What is the good? Socrates, Plato, and Aristotle, very well-known Greek philosophers, often discussed or debated about ideas such as these. Plato (429–347 BC) was a student of Socrates and wrote down Socrates's theories—in fact, the only way we know any of Socrates's ideas is through Plato, because Socrates didn't record anything in writing.[7] Socrates loved to walk around Athens to discuss and debate ideas with people, including what morality is; what the good is; and whether it is better to stay in your country and protest injustice, though it may lead to your death, or to flee from your country to preserve your life (this was a choice Socrates actually had to make at the end of his life).

Socrates was devoted to finding the truth of these matters, and he often upset the people he was talking with by exposing the error of their views on these matters. He actually made some people so angry by his questions and teaching methods that he was eventually executed on the charge of corrupting the youth of Athens and teaching them to worship different gods than the established gods of Athens.[8] Socrates's student, Plato, carried on his teacher's pursuit of knowledge. One of Plato's most important philosophical ideas was something he called the forms. Plato was interested in how we can make sense out of a world that is constantly changing, and in many of his dialogues, Plato suggests that it is only through the forms that we are able to make sense out of a world that changes all the time. The forms are perfect and eternal, nontemporal, nonspatial, perfect patterns or essences that act like standards to help us make sense of the particular things in the world.[9] This is a philosophical idea Plato worked on a lot throughout his dialogues. He was also very interested in the nature of virtues such as justice and courage and piety.

4. Plato, *Theaetetus*, in *Plato: Complete Works*, ed. John M. Cooper (Indianapolis, IN: Hackett Publishing Co., 1997), 155d.
5. Bryan Magee, *The Story of Philosophy* (New York: Dorling Kindersley, 2001), 13, 17.
6. Ibid., 13–14.
7. Marcus G. Singer, "Philosophy," in *World Book Encyclopedia* (Chicago: World Book, 1992), 386.
8. Magee, *Story of Philosophy*, 24.
9. Allen Silverman, "Plato's Middle Period Metaphysics and Epistemology," in *Stanford Encyclopedia of Philosophy*, July 14, 2014, http://plato.stanford.edu/entries/plato-metaphysics/#3.

It is sometimes difficult to distinguish between what Socrates believed and what Plato believed. Socrates was Plato's teacher, but Socrates never actually wrote anything down, so a great deal of what we know about Socrates's philosophy comes from Plato's dialogues. In almost all of the dialogues Plato wrote, Socrates is the main character, and Socrates discusses a wide variety of ethical and moral issues with his interlocutors. It is important to note that Plato never appears in his own dialogues. The absence of Plato as the main character of the dialogues can sometimes make it difficult for us to determine which of the views Socrates seems to advocate in the dialogues are Socrates's views and which ones are Plato's views. One way that some philosophers have tried to solve this problem is by dividing Plato's dialogues into early, middle, and later dialogues and by arguing that while the views Socrates promotes in the early dialogues are actually his own views, Socrates increasingly becomes a mouthpiece for Plato's own views in many of the middle and later dialogues. So, some philosophers argue that early dialogues such as Plato's ***Crito***, ***Euthyphro***, and ***Gorgias*** are dialogues in which the views that Socrates proposes are actually his own views. These philosophers will also argue that in the middle dialogues such as Plato's ***Phaedo***, ***Republic***, and later dialogues such as ***Theaetetus*** and ***Parmenides***, Plato uses Socrates to express his own views. No matter what view people hold about the distinction between Plato and Socrates's views, it is certainly true that Plato cared a great deal about philosophical ideas such as the forms and nature of justice.[10]

10. Richard Kraut, "Plato," in *Stanford Encyclopedia of Philosophy*, September 11, 2013, http://plato.stanford.edu/entries/plato/.

Aristotle (384–322 BC),[11] a student of Plato, followed in their tradition and solidified the passion of Greek philosophy for seeking knowledge and truth and the meaning of existence. One of the things he was most interested in was the ultimate cause of things. He wrote about and discussed this idea a great deal in books such as *Metaphysics*.[12]

All this is pretty heady stuff, but people from this time period also wondered about what to do from a practical standpoint. For instance, one of their practical concerns pertained to the purpose of government. Aristotle wrote a book called *Nicomachean Ethics* in which he argued that the purpose of government is to help people find happiness by pursuing a life of virtue.[13] Another Greek statesman, Demosthenes, used his oratorical and debating skills to speak against King Philip of Macedonia, a nearby king whom Demosthenes believed was a threat to Athens. Although Demosthenes's *philipics* ("speeches against" Philip) are orations rather than debates with another person, there is no doubt that they grew out of discussions he had with others about whether Philip truly posed a threat to Athens. Unfortunately, Demosthenes was not as persuasive of the Athenians as he would have liked, and Athens was later conquered by Philip of Macedonia's son, Alexander the Great.[14]

The Ancient Romans

The Romans, whose empire was highly influenced by the Greeks and who became the most powerful people in the world, were a very practical people, intent on conquering Europe and establishing the Roman Empire. They were known for their vibrant political and oratorical life, and most of the famous debates during the Roman Empire were about political issues. For example, the famous orator Cicero delivered some of his most well-known speeches against Catiline, a fellow Roman, concerning whether Catiline had plotted to overthrown the Roman government.[15] Catiline was a Roman from a wealthy family, but by being greedy, ruthless, and corrupt, he ruined his reputation with many of the leaders and wealthy men of Rome. Catiline wanted to be a powerful ruler of Rome, but because of his bad reputation, many people were not willing to vote him into high government offices. Therefore, he hatched a

11. Christopher Shields, "Aristotle," in *Stanford Encyclopedia of Philosophy*, July 29, 2015, http://plato.stanford.edu/entries/aristotle/.
12. Singer, "Philosophy," 386.
13. Magee, *Story of Philosophy*, 38.
14. Donald Kagan, "Demosthenes," in *World Book Encyclopedia* (Chicago: World Book, 1992), 131.
15. Joseph R. Tebben, "Cicero," in *World Book Encyclopedia* (Chicago: World Book, 1992), 552.

plot with some other malcontent Romans to lead a revolt and seize control of the Roman government by force. Cicero, who rightfully held a Roman consulship, the highest office of Rome, discovered Catiline's conspiracy and exposed it to the senate. Given that it took four speeches for Cicero to convince the senate of Catiline's guilt, this was probably an issue of great debate in the senate.[16]

Later on, another famous Roman named Julius Caesar became a hero and lifelong emperor of Rome. Although there was no publicized debate, we can be sure that many men in the senate debated whether Caesar was a threat to Rome's liberty and tradition as a republic. We know this because, as history tells us, a group of men—including Caesar's best friend Brutus—conspired and successfully murdered Caesar. Following Caesar's death, the emperor's supporters were able to defeat his enemies and continue his legacy, building a successful career for themselves, ostensibly by quelling people's fears about Caesar's power.[17] In Shakespeare's famous play *Julius Caesar*, Mark Antony, Caesar's friend and heir, delivered a eulogy for Caesar right after Brutus gave a speech explaining why he had killed Caesar, though he loved him.[18] Although Shakespeare does not present Brutus and Antony's speeches as formal debates, Mark Antony's speech is a clear rebuttal (or refutation) of Brutus's purported reasons for killing Caesar. In a later chapter you will examine this debate. Throughout history, many debates occurred that either soothed angry crowds or whipped them into frenzied rage.

Debate over the Centuries

Some Greek and Roman philosophers, such as the Stoics and Epicureans, debated the best way to achieve a happy life. The Stoics argued that happiness came from accepting one's fate and maintaining tranquility of emotion. The Epicureans, however, argued that the best way to have a happy life was to pursue the pleasure that comes from simple, healthy food, and fellowship with good friends.[19] During the Middle Ages, after Rome fell, philosophers became increasingly concerned with theological debates. For example, when people began to discover ancient teaching and literature (e.g., works by Plato and Aristotle), people debated whether ancient Greek teachings and Christian teachings were compatible. Philosopher Saint Thomas Aquinas believed they were, and, in fact, he used ancient Greek philosophy to try to prove the existence of God.[20]

Often throughout history, major debates developed because of significant developments in knowledge and learning. For example, during the Renaissance (1400–1600), which was a transitional period between the Middle Ages and modern times, many people began developing ideas and theories that were hotly contested. For instance, as knowledge and learning began to flourish more in the Renaissance, people began to place more emphasis on human knowledge and theories, rather than church doctrine. Furthermore, during the Protestant Reformation (1517 is often considered the starting date of the Reformation),[21] people began to question the supremacy of the Catholic Church and started to debate ideas that would have been considered indisputable only a century before. As these conflicts continued, many people began to see religion and science as enemies, locked in an eternal struggle with one another. Some argued that religion should always be favored over scientific and human views. Others believed that science should always be favored over religious views. Still others believed that science and religion were compatible, and that supposed contradictions were due to people incorrectly interpreting either religion or science. For example, in 1542 Copernicus wrote a book claiming that the sun was the center of the universe, which contradicted the previously held geocentric (or earth-centered) theory of the universe.[22] For years, this was fiercely debated, and many scientists who held this view

16. Lilian Hines and Ruth B. Howard, *Our Latin Heritage*, Book III (New York: Harcourt, Brace, and World, 1967), 118–119.
17. Suetonius, "The Lives of the Twelve Caesars: Volume I: Julius Augustus. Tiberius. Gaius, Caligula," in *Loeb Classical Library*, ed. by Jeffrey Henderson (Cambridge, MA: Harvard University Press, 1913), 113; www.gutenberg.org/ebooks/6400. See also Plutarch, "The Parallel Lives," in *Loeb Classical Library*, ed. by Jeffrey Henderson (Cambridge, MA: Harvard University Press, 1913), 597–599.
18. William Shakespeare, *Julius Caesar* (New York: Dover Publications, 1991), act 3, scene 2.
19. Magee, *Story of Philosophy*, 44–46.
20. Ibid., 58–59.
21. Lewis W. Spitz, "Reformation," in *World Book Encyclopedia* (Chicago: World Book, 1992), 197.
22. Magee, *Story of Philosophy*, 64.

were persecuted and threatened with imprisonment, and even execution. However, the Church later decided that it was interpreting Scripture incorrectly on this issue, and the geocentric and heliocentric (or sun-centered theory of the universe) debate ended.

As the world moved into the 1600s, people attempted to apply scientific thinking and reason to all areas of life. At this time, one area of life people began to debate more frequently was the role of government in people's lives. That is, they began to ask, "What is the best way for the government to rule the country?" For many years, countries had been ruled by absolute monarchs who, supposedly, had inherited their right to rule from God and who ruled their respective countries with absolute power. However, people began to question whether this type of government was legitimate. For example, in 1690 in a book titled *Second Treatise of Government*, a man named John Locke challenged the notion of monarchical absolutism when he theorized that all people have inherent rights, and that they contract with the government to help protect these rights and provide social stability.[23] Furthermore, Locke posited that if a government becomes destructive of these rights, the people have a right to abolish their government and establish a new one.[24] These ideas, discussions, and debates were quite revolutionary. Suddenly, the reality of government in the world and the nature of authority were up for debate. Although many people were influenced by this thinking, others continued to hold to a much more traditional view of the government's power.

As you have probably figured out, one of the most profound results of this debate about government was the American Declaration of Independence (1776) that came out of the American Revolution and ultimately resulted in the formation of the United States. It is important to notice that, from its inception as a loose collection of colonies, debate has always been an important part of the United States because, since the colonies had to rule themselves given their great distance from Britain, they had to make many decisions about their own self-governance and about the way they wanted to run their towns. In fact, their survival depended upon their discussing and debating the most effective way of governing themselves and the people and resources of their colonies. As the colonies became more established, and as they began to question the benevolence of Mother England, debate took on an even more significant role. Many people believed that England was treating the colonists in an unfair, ill-informed, unlawful manner, and that this behavior might eventually jeopardize the well-being and survival of the colonies and their colonists. These people began to argue for independence from Britain. Others argued that Britain was their lawful ruler, and that to declare separation was foolhardy and, perhaps, even suicidal.

Because of the great emotion that went into the debate, and the significant consequences hanging on the outcome of it, this debate produced some of the finest thinking and oration in history. Because America has been such a grand experiment in democracy and participation of the people in government, our history is marked by numerous monumental debates. For instance, we have had significant public debates about

23. Stephen A. Erickson, "John Locke," in *World Book Encyclopedia* (Chicago: World Book, 1992), 417.
24. Magee, *Story of Philosophy*, 107.

the issues of slavery, the right of the South to secede from the North, civil rights, women's right to vote, and the rights of workers. Political debate still remains an important part of our country today. After all, if America is truly a democracy and our government leaders rule at our behest, then the people of the United States need to debate issues so that we can make informed choices about how our leaders should govern us. Unfortunately, many people believe that American political debate has become increasingly rancorous and illogical and that it does little good to the people involved with or listening to the debate. In addition, many other people feel that the American people as a whole have lost interest in debating these crucial issues that define who we are as a nation.

Debate has certainly played a critical role in the development of America as a great, innovative nation. However, as we look at how other countries have changed and developed through time, it is clear that debate over philosophical, political, and practical issues has only increased, rather than decreased, over the years. In the 1800s, the world saw the rise of such earth-shattering theories as Darwin's theory of evolution and Karl Marx's political theories.[25] As these new ideas became more mainstream, people debated them fiercely. For example, people debated whether new scientific theories contradicted religious teachings, and whether the theory of communism (which people attributed to Marx) addressed the problems of society more adequately than its rival economic system, capitalism. For years, communism and capitalism were locked in an intense, and sometimes violent, debate.

Debate Today

As world wars and rapidly changing technology have continued to revolutionize the world, philosophers and social theorists posit new ways of thinking about the world and new belief systems, many of which became significant topics of debate. These debates are still going on today. We still debate over religious and scientific issues. We debate over politics and the government's role in people's lives. We continue to debate life's purpose, and what the goals of our lives should be. We debate social issues, including whether capital punishment should be legal, whether interrogation techniques such as waterboarding are appropriate for Americans to use on suspected terrorists, and whether scientific endeavors such as human cloning and stem cell research is permissible.

Debate, in some ways, has become even more important today because, due to our advances in science and technology, the consequences of our actions can be so much more drastic. When we engage in debate effectively, it is a powerful tool because we can positively affect each other's actions. Because we are all limited by personal biases, prejudices, and blind spots, discussing things together helps us think more clearly.

And now we come to you. You must realize that you are becoming a part of, and helping with, the creation of history. Right now, your concerns probably revolve mainly around issues directly related to you, rather than some of the big topics we have mentioned in this chapter. However, realize that the discussions and debates you have today—whether they are about which movie you plan to see, how you should spend your money, or which topic to write about in your history report—can be significant, if you let them. Have you ever heard of the saying "Rome wasn't built in a day"? This saying means, in essence, that it takes time to build complex things. Excellent debating is a complex skill. When learning a complex skill, it is perfectly reasonable to start with simple practice activities before moving to more complicated ones. As you learn the skills in this book and begin applying them to simple debates such as the ones mentioned previously, you will find that not only do you approach these issues more thoughtfully, but also your improved thinking skills lead you to larger, more significant issues.

25. Singer, "Philosophy," 389.

Review Exercises

Explain

In this chapter, we have looked at how history has been marked by the way people have debated and discussed important ideas. In fact, much progress in philosophy, government, and science has occurred because of these debates. Below are some of the major time periods of history, as well as key figures who were involved with great debates or discussions during this time. For each period, name the major accomplishment of the figure (or group) listed and also briefly explain the major debate he (or it) was involved with.

1. Ancient Greece:

Thales: ______________________________

Empedocles: ______________________________

Democritus: ______________________________

Debate: ______________________________

Socrates: ______________________________

____

____

Plato: ______________________________

____

____

Aristotle: ______________________________

____

____

Debate: ______________________________

____

2. Ancient Rome:

Stoics: ____

____

Epicureans: ____

____

Debate: ____

____

3. Middle Ages:

Aquinas: ____

____

Debate: ____

____

4. Renaissance/Reformation/Scientific Revolution:

Copernicus: ____

____

John Locke: ____

____

Debate: ____

____

5. Colonial United States:

Debate: ____

____

6. Modern Times:

Karl Marx: ____

____

Charles Darwin: ____

____

Debate: ____

____

Everyday Debate

Develop

There is a lot of debate in our culture right now about the importance of saving energy. Consider this debate resolution: "Resolved: People should ride their bikes more than they drive cars." Take a few minutes to develop at least one argument for and against this resolution. Later, you will receive specific instruction to learn how to develop an argument. Right now, just do the best you can. To help yourself develop an argument, think about the answers to the following questions:

- **What** do you believe about this resolution?
- **Why** do you believe that? (This is your evidence for your belief.)
- **How** does your evidence support your belief?

Learning from the Masters

Read and Consider

As mentioned earlier in this chapter, one of the masters of debate and thoughtful dialogue was Socrates. To see how he cleverly used questions and dialogue to probe his opponents' ideas and undermine weaknesses in their reasoning, read the Socratic dialogue *Euthyphro* and answer the following questions.

To give you some background knowledge on this dialogue, you should know, as we implied in this chapter, that

Socrates was eventually put on trial, and later executed, for corrupting the youth of Athens. The dialogue *Euthyphro* actually takes place while Socrates is waiting to be called to trial. In this dialogue, he encounters a young man, Euthyphro, who is prosecuting his father for murder. Upon questioning Euthyphro, Socrates discovers that a slave belonging to Euthyphro's father cut another slave's throat. Euthyphro's father was so angry with the slave that he bound him hand and foot, and threw him into a ditch until he could discover what the law would do with him. While the father was seeking this out, however, the slave died from cold and hunger.

Therefore, Euthyphro decided that he would prosecute his own father for murder. Upon even further questioning, Socrates finds out that Euthyphro is overly confident in himself and his own judgment. Euthyphro believes his intelligence level is quite a cut above average, especially in matters pertaining to justice and the will of the gods. This was just the kind of person with whom Socrates enjoys discussing matters: someone who is not wise but believes he is. Through clever questioning, Socrates shows Euthyphro that he holds contradictory beliefs.

Read the full dialogue of *Euthyphro* (Link 2-1). Then answer the questions that follow.

1. What contradictory belief does Euthyphro hold concerning what piety is?

____

____

____

____

____

____

____

____

2. How does Socrates show Euthyphro that the belief he holds is contradictory?

____

____

____

____

____

____

____

Chapter 3

Debate: The Janus-Faced Discipline

> FOR WHAT SHOULD A MAN LIVE, IF NOT FOR THE PLEASURES OF DISCOURSE?
>
> —PLATO[1]

Debate: Logic or Rhetoric?

What skill or skills are crucial for someone who wants to be an effective debater? Is it logic? Is it fine speech? Is it the ability to make people laugh? Is it the ability to rattle off a litany of facts at the drop of a hat? No doubt, the ability to connect with and catch the attention of your audience is crucial. However, it is also crucial that people are logical and sensible when they speak; otherwise, they will have serious trouble convincing their audience. In other words, in order to be a good debater, you must speak well, but you must also certainly think before you speak. Those of you who have already studied logic or rhetoric may wonder how debate fits into these subjects. It is safe to say that debate is a very interesting hybrid of logic and rhetoric, and it takes both skills to be an effective debater. To make sure we are all on the same page about what we mean when we use the terms "logic" and "rhetoric," let's take a look at a brief definition of these words (a more detailed definition and explanation will be presented later).

"**Logic**" can be defined as the art and science of reasoning.[2] Logic helps us analyze our thoughts. In a sense, developing your logical skills allows you to dissect and operate on your thoughts; that is, it lets you identify both the good and bad and then get rid of what is unhelpful and illogical in your thinking.

Additionally, debate is more than logic. That is, it requires more than an ability to identify good arguments and bad arguments. It also requires skills in rhetoric. **Rhetoric** is the art and science of public speaking. In other words, there are rules and formulas you can follow to craft effective speeches and debates—this is the science of rhetoric. However, there is an artistic side to public speaking as well. This artistic side requires a speaker to read his audience, connect with the people, and word his speech in such a manner that it meets them where they are. Good **rhetoricians** often possess a collection of jokes, sayings, stories (these are called ***copia***), and speaking devices (or rhetorical devices). Later you will learn more about these rhetorical devices, which allow you to add personality, humor, and beauty to a speech in just the right way that resonates with the audience. In fact, in this chapter, you will start a new activity in the "Review Exercises" section called "Building Copiousness," which will teach you to do just this: It will help you cultivate a collection of sayings, jokes, and stories that you can use to connect with your audience and enliven your speech while expressing your unique personality.

---

1. Susan Ratcliffe, ed., *Oxford Dictionary of Quotations by Subject*, 2nd ed. (Oxford: Oxford University Press, 2010), 98.
2. Aaron Larsen, Joelle Hodge, and Christopher Perrin, *The Art of Argument* (Camp Hill, PA: Classical Academic Press, 2003–2007), 227.

An Illustration from Presidential Debates

The 2008–2009 presidential debates of John McCain and Barack Obama, and vice-presidential candidates Sarah Palin and Joe Biden, aptly illustrate the dual logical and rhetorical nature of debate. Both presidential and vice-presidential candidates had to know key facts and statistics. For instance, because the state of the economy was such a significant concern during this presidential election, news reporters, debate moderators, and even debate audience members (e.g., in the "town hall" debate between Obama and McCain) asked very specific questions and expected precise answers. The press generally panned Palin after several interviews she had with journalist Katie Couric because she could not give strong, definitive answers to questions Couric asked about important legal decisions, economic concerns, or recent books she had read.[3] And, in fact, on several occasions, Palin's thinking appeared very muddled on the issues. On the other hand, presidential candidate Obama was generally highly praised for his academic, knowledgeable presentation, and this seemed to demonstrate that although Americans certainly like to be entertained, they also place a high value on good logic and knowledge, especially when demonstrated by presidential candidates.[4]

Nevertheless, although logic and argument content was very important in this debate, it was not enough. For example, Obama was sometimes criticized for appearing too aloof with his audience and not showing his emotions.[5] In addition, he repeatedly smiled and shook his head, some thought with condescension, when McCain said something he found objectionable. These small actions offended and alienated some viewers. In addition, after the first debate, Senator McCain was heavily criticized for his facial expressions looking mean or angry.[6] Interestingly, he noticeably smiled more frequently in the ensuing debates, and both candidates went out of their way to show that they could relate to the common person. Obama talked about his humble upbringing as the son of a poor, single woman who had, at least at one time, subsisted on food stamps. McCain used the phrase "my friends" to connect with the audience and frequently evoked folksy images of "Joe the Plumber," a common working man who became a symbol of the American people.[7]

These actions demonstrated that both candidates were aware that facts, statistics, and logic were not enough. Though these emotional elements of both candidates' speeches were effective at times, at other times they appeared to be contrived, and sometimes they actually backfired. For instance, after a while, many people felt that the "Joe the Plumber" card had been played too heavily, and some comedians, for example those on the television show *Saturday Night Live*, satirized "Joe the Plumber" as being McCain's imaginary friend who lived under his bed with Simon the unicorn.[8] This shows that while emotional connection can be very important, it can also fail if viewers perceive it as being overdone or insincere.

Putting Your Best Face Forward

A look at another historical presidential debate will demonstrate that appearance and connecting with the audience can be just as important as logic in debates.

3. See, for example, Katharine Q. Seelye, "McCain and Palin's Interview with Couric" (blog), *New York Times*, September 28, 2008, http://thecaucus.blogs.nytimes.com/2008/09/29/mccain-and-palins-interview-with-couric/comment-page-28/?_r=2.
4. See, for example, "Obama-McCain Presidential Debate Reaction: HuffPost Bloggers Weigh In" (blog), *Huffington Post*, originally posted October 27, 2008, http://www.huffingtonpost.com/huffingtonpost/presidential-debate-react_b_129793.html; Madeleine Albright, "A Breakthrough Night for Obama" (blog) *Huffington Post*, originally posted October 27, 2008, http://www.huffingtonpost.com/madeleine-albright/a-breakthrough-night-for_b_129786.html.
5. See, for example, Paul Reiser, "Obama Underwhelms, McCain Patronizes" (blog), *Huffington Post*, originally posted October 27, 2008, http://www.huffingtonpost.com/paul-reiser/obama-underwhelms-mccain_b_129818.html.
6. See, for example, Chris Durang, "Barak Did Great, McCain Okay But Angry" (blog), *Huffington Post*, originally posted October 27, 2008, http://www.huffingtonpost.com/chris-durang/barack-did-great-mccain-o_b_129802.html.
7. See, for example, Jackson Williams, "Joe the Plumber Meets Sarah the Energy Expert" (blog), *Huffington Post*, originally posted February 28, 2009, http://www.huffingtonpost.com/jackson-williams/joe-the-plumber-meets-sar_b_135312.html.
8. Lynn Sweet, "'Saturday Night Live' Third Debate Special" (blog) *Chicago Sun-Times*, October 17, 2008, http://blogs.suntimes.com/sweet/2008/10/saturday_night_live_third_deba.html.

The problem of an emphasis on content over appearance or style is aptly illustrated by the 1960 debate between Richard Nixon and John F. Kennedy, which was the first televised debate ever in the history of America. Historians generally agree that Nixon had the stronger arguments, and that, had the debate been broadcast by radio, Nixon would have won the debate.[9] However, several aspects of Nixon's presentation, appearance, and style (or lack thereof) did not sit favorably with his audience. Nixon had been ill and was exhausted on the night of the debate. As a result, his face had a haggard, gray pallor. In addition, he refused any makeup for the camera, believing it was unnecessary and showy. Kennedy, on the other hand, had a fresh, tan appearance, and—possibly because he was more aware of the importance of TV aesthetics—he accepted the makeup, which, on TV, increased his healthful, vigorous appearance. Needless to say, after watching the televised debates, people who had formerly been strong supporters of Nixon wondered if he was physically capable of handling the job, while Kennedy, who previously had been considered too young and inexperienced for the job, rose significantly in people's estimation.[10] While it is true that most of us will never run for political office or participate in a televised debate, we should realize that everyone who hopes to persuade someone else (and we all do at one time or another)—whether in an informal discussion or a formal debate—must learn the art of tailoring speeches, words, and ideas to an audience. You may be among those who feel that this is disingenuous (not completely honest or sincere), and perhaps even pride yourself on "telling it like it is." Although honesty, accuracy, and sincerity are of the utmost importance in any debate, it is important to realize that there are many different ways of saying the same truth. The wise debater considers how she can best arrange and communicate the facts and the truth so that her opponent and audience will best comprehend and be most receptive to them. After all, debate and discussion are not about winning, proving intelligence, or crushing the opponent. The true purpose of debate and discussion is the pursuit of truth and understanding. If you keep this core function of debate in mind, it will help you realize that while strong logic and a good grasp of the facts are essential to effective debate, you must also consider how to build bridges to your audience and, yes, even your opponent so that you can best understand and communicate to one another.

It is important to note that while logic, rhetoric, and debate can all be done with sincerity, integrity, skill, and concern for audience members, they also can be done in a deceitful or manipulative manner, or with a complete disregard for audience members or opponents. Unfortunately, people engaging in logic, rhetoric, and debate with this approach have given debate a bad name. For instance, in the 2008 election, both McCain and Obama promised to run a different kind of presidential election—one in which they refused to stoop to name-calling and backstabbing. Unfortunately, the camps of both of these candidates eventually used dirty tactics and, at times, it appeared both candidates were dragged into these dirty battles. In addition, one has to watch only a few political commercials during any senatorial

9. Erika Tyner Allen, "The Kennedy-Nixon Presidential Debates, 1960," *Museum of Broadcast Communication*, http://www.museum.tv/eotvsection.php?entrycode=kennedy-nixon.
10. Ibid.

or legislative campaign to see that, sadly, much political public rhetoric and debate consists of name-calling and mudslinging.

Another less than ideal approach is when people engage in debates that, while free from mudslinging, are filled with academic minutia and language that is incomprehensible to the common person. Sometimes academic debates can seem to be a contest in out-footnoting the opponent or using the biggest, most incomprehensible and obscure vocabulary words. Neither of these approaches to debate is helpful. The former makes cynics out of its audience; the latter bores, frustrates, and belittles the audience. It is important to note that debate (and, therefore, logic and rhetoric) can and should be an honest, intelligible, and interesting activity. In conclusion, let's refer to the title of this chapter—it is called "Debate: The Janus-Faced Discipline." Janus was the Roman god of doors and gates. He is typically represented as having two faces[11] looking in opposite directions. Debate has been referred to as "the Janus-faced discipline" here because it is an activity that requires you to look both inward and outward simultaneously. You must first look inward to make sure your thoughts and reasoning are correct. However, you must also look outward—that is, to your opponent and your audience. Certainly, both of these activities should be done with honesty, integrity, and care for your opponent and audience. As you read this book, you will learn skills that will help you debate effectively with yourself, with another person, or with a group of people. First, you'll learn how to think like a debater, which is a skill that is beneficial to everyone. Next, you'll learn how to research and develop arguments so you can support your views and critique your opponent's views. Lastly, you will learn the format of a formal debate—this way, if you choose to participate in such an activity, you will understand and be prepared for each step of the process. As you learn these steps, you will become well prepared to engage in everyday debate!

11. Micha F. Lindemans, "Janus," in *Encyclopedia Mythica*, modified August 28, 1999, www.pantheon.org/articles/j/janus.html.

Review Exercises

Define

Give an appropriate definition for each of the following words:

Logic: ______________________________

Rhetoric: ______________________________

Explain

Explain why debate could be called the Janus-faced discipline.

____

____

Building Copiousness

Consider

From now on, you will see this new section in the review exercises of each chapter: "Building Copiousness." The technique of building copiousness dates back to ancient rhetoric. The word *copious* means "many." Ancient rhetoricians memorized *many* quotes and stories on general themes such as love and hate, justice and injustice, bravery and cowardice, freedom and slavery. This was called copiousness because it helped them build mental storehouses of many quotes and stories they could use on the spot to elaborate, enrich, and beautify any speech they gave. You might actually remember an example of this from the movie *The Great Debaters* (see chapter 1). In one of the beginning scenes of the movie, the debate coach Melvin Tolson holds debate tryouts. In this scene, he calls Henry Lowe to step into what he calls "the hot spot." Then, Professor Tolson gives Henry a topic, and Henry has to come up with a quote from literature on this topic. When he does this, Henry calls on the copiousness he had built up from reading and absorbing so much great literature.

Now, you may be a person who just readily absorbs everything you read and can often call a quote or story to memory on the spot. You might even have a photographic memory. However, it is not necessary to remember everything you read to build copiousness. Instead, one method of accomplishing this is to memorize fifteen to twenty quotes or stories on common topics such as those the ancient rhetoricians memorized—love, hate, freedom, slavery, goodness, or evil. It is wise to memorize these quotes or stories on general topics, rather than narrow ones such as baseball or monarchs of England. You can probably see why. The more general your quote is, the more likely you will be able to easily apply it to a variety of speeches in a variety of settings.

In each chapter's "Building Copiousness" section, you will be provided with a quote or story on a general topic. In order to help yourself memorize the quote, read it several times. Make sure you understand what it is saying, and make sure you ask someone for clarification if you don't understand it. Think about the logical parts of the quote or story. When you believe you have the basic quote or story memorized, practice reciting it out loud with a friend or family member. Don't worry if you don't get it completely right the first time. Try to quote it as accurately as you can. Then study it a bit more. Practice writing it a few times and saying it to someone again. Remember the author's name (if there is one). Eventually, you will be able to say the quote almost perfectly, especially if you keep reviewing it each chapter, which you will be asked to do. Here is your first quote for building copiousness:

> "Love is free; it is not practiced as a way of achieving other ends." —Pope Benedict XVI[12]

12. Ratcliffe, *Oxford Dictionary of Quotations*, 292.

Everyday Debate

Consider

Consider the quote that you are memorizing in the "Building Copiousness" section of this chapter:

"Love is free; it is not practiced as a way of achieving other ends." —Pope Benedict XVI

On the one hand, this seems true. Love is a beautiful thing and one of the most prized possessions in our world. Think of the stories, movies, and songs written in the name of love. On the other hand, people have done some pretty horrible things in the name of love. You can probably think of some examples. In some terrible cases, it seems that people use love just to achieve their goals. Some people argue, in fact, that this is all love ever is—just cleverly disguised selfishness. Therefore, this quote certainly seems debatable.

Take a few minutes to develop at least one argument for this quote and at least one argument against it. To develop an argument, first decide what *you* believe about this quote. Do you believe it is true? Do you believe it is false? Now ask yourself, *Why do I believe what I do?* You must have some reason for believing what you do—based on your personal experiences, others' experiences, information you have read, movies you've watched, and so forth. Figure out the reason why you believe what you do. Once you figure that out, ask yourself how this experience proves your point. For example, if your experiences have taught you that this quote is indeed true, then explain what those experiences were and how they prove this quote.

Once you have figured out why you believe what you believe, your next job is to figure out why the opposition believes what it believes. Go through the same process. Ask yourself, *Why might somebody believe the opposite position to what I believe?* Once you figure out what in the world (literally) might make them think that, ask yourself what it is about those experiences that could make people with an opposing view believe as they do.

Listen

Now that you have developed your arguments, share them with three other people in your class and then listen to their arguments. When you are finished, choose which of your classmates' arguments was the strongest, in your opinion, and summarize it on a piece of paper. In addition, explain why you believe it was the strongest.

Learning from the Masters

Observe

Watch a clip of the 1960 debate between John F. Kennedy and Richard Nixon (Link 3-1). On a piece of paper, list what you believe are the strengths and weaknesses of each speaker. Which speaker do you believe is more effective overall? Why?

Chapter 4

Thinking Like a Debater

> *ACTIO SEQUITUR ESSE.*
> (TRANSLATION: ACTION FOLLOWS ESSENCE.)[1]
>
> AN UNEXAMINED LIFE IS NOT WORTH LIVING.
> —SOCRATES[2]

In 1984 a popular film called *The Karate Kid* came out in theaters.[3] In this movie, the main character, high school student Daniel, decides he wants to study karate seriously. Enter Mr. Miyagi, the local karate expert. Miyagi tells Daniel that he will teach him karate, and Daniel visits his house soon after, eager to begin lessons. Much to Daniel's chagrin, instead of teaching him karate, Miyagi sets him to work. He tells Daniel to wax his cars, using very particular hand patterns Miyagi shows Daniel by moving his hand in a circular pattern one way. "Wax on," he would say. Then he would move his hand in a circular pattern the other way: "Wax off." Next, Miyagi tells Daniel to paint the fence. Once again, Miyagi makes him paint it with very specific hand motions—all the way up, flicking his wrist, and then all the way down, flicking his wrist. While Daniel does all this work, Miyagi sits around trimming his Bonsai trees and catching flies with chopsticks! As you can imagine, Daniel ultimately becomes so disgusted that he almost quits, but just as he is about to walk away, Miyagi tells Daniel to "wax on" (i.e., make the particular repetitive movement Daniel had been using to wash the car). When Daniel does this, Mr. Miyagi throws a punch, and Daniel is able to block it. Then, Miyagi tells Daniel to "paint the fence." When Daniel does this motion, Miyagi throws another punch and, again, Daniel is able to block it. Daniel suddenly realizes that, through doing his chores as he had been instructed, martial arts have been ingrained into his mind and muscles so effectively that he can now perform these skills automatically and effortlessly.[4]

The Karate Kid is certainly not a movie about debate, but it makes a good point in these scenes that we can apply to debate. Whenever you are learning a new skill, you must first build a strong foundation by understanding, practicing, and assimilating the basic components of that skill. If you don't master the basic components, you may learn some fancy tricks, but you won't be able to progress to any level of proficiency. In other words, as the Latin quote states at the beginning of the chapter, "action follows essence," or, put another way: What you do flows out of who you are. Let's relate this to debate. It may seem obvious, but it needs to be stated anyhow: The first step to being a good debater is learning to think like a debater. For instance, it would be easy to learn some famous philosophic quotes

1. Richard Foster, "Spiritual Formation Agenda," *Christianity Today* 53, no. 1 (2009): 29.
2. Louis P. Pojman, *Classics of Philosophy: Volume I: Ancient and Medieval* (New York: Oxford University Press, 1998), 39.
3. You might be familiar with the latest version of *The Karate Kid*, which came out in 2010. This movie was based on the original film by the same name, which was released in 1984. In the original, the teacher is Mr. Miyagi (rather than Mr. Han), and the student is Daniel (rather than Dre).
4. See John G. Avildsen, et al., *The Karate Kid*, directed by John G. Avildsen (1984; Culver City, CA: Columbia Pictures, 2005), DVD.

Any athletic endeavor—basketball, dancing, acting—involves the constant use of muscle memory. When the right action or motion becomes so deep-rooted, so practiced, and so habitual that the body acts without conscious intentionality, we call this the use of muscle memory. What's in your debating muscle memory? We all have habits—ways of thinking, ways of speaking—that we've developed in our lives, consciously or unconsciously. Think back on the most recent debates, discussions, or arguments you've had. What patterns do you fall into? Are these helpful, or even good? Many people say "like" or "um" when they don't know what to say, using these words like a pause for breath but making the impression that they're not sure what they're about to say. Making a conscious effort to take a breath, instead of filling the void with sound unnecessarily, can help counteract these habits. Spend some time reflecting, and then make an inventory, or list: What are your habits? Are they useful or counterproductive? What can you do to sharpen or stop them?

and stock logical arguments that could impress your audience, much like clever magic tricks. Of course, these tricks can be helpful, and we will certainly learn some of these later. However, it is important that you first learn how a good debater thinks, as well as the skills that allow her to construct good arguments and refute poor ones. In other words, you should strive to become a debater internally so that proper debating actions will flow out of you naturally. In the next couple of chapters, you will be introduced to these important skills—don't worry, you won't have to wax any cars or paint any fences!

The Marks of Good Thinking

The foundational skill for successful debate is effective, clear thinking. But even though humans are constantly thinking, not all of it is clear and effective. Countless lists of successful thinkers' characteristics have been made, most of which disagree with each other. But nearly all agree that skilled thinkers (a) are critical, (b) are logical, (c) are careful and accurate, (d) are civil without selling out (i.e., are open-minded), and (e) listen carefully and ask great questions.

Effective Thinkers Are Critical

The first characteristic of effective thinkers is that they are critical. At first, this may sound like a bad thing. After all, aren't critical people really negative? It is true that a critical person can be negative. However, critical thinking does not necessarily entail negativity. A closer look at the definition of the word "critical" will help to illustrate this point.

The entry for the word "**critical**" in *Webster's Ninth New Collegiate Dictionary* states that the word comes from the Latin word *criticus*, which means "able to make judgments," or "to separate or decide." Notice that nothing in these definitions indicates that a critical person must be negative. The definitions do require, however, that a critical person must carefully consider, judge, and weigh evidence and arguments. In fact, Lewis Vaughn, author of the book *The Power of Critical Thinking*, defined the term "**critical thinking**" as "the systematic evaluation or formulation of beliefs, or statements, by rational standards."[5] So what do these definitions tell you about what you must be like in order to become a good debater? The best thing for you to do is to be an *active*, rather than a passive, thinker. This means that when you hear a claim of evidence or an argument, you need to actively evaluate whether it is a strong argument, rather than just accepting it as true, even if it sounds good or persuasive.

As odd as it may seem, many people go through their lives without doing this at all. That is, many people live day to day just accepting claims and believing arguments handed to them by their friends, by advertising, by themselves, and by authority figures. It is fair to admit that sometimes it is necessary to simply accept certain things. After all, if your mother says, "Please go get the groceries—they're in the backseat of the car," it is neither necessary nor wise, for that matter, to stop and deliberate over whether the groceries are, in fact, metaphysically and truly in the backseat of the car, or whether your mother has the fundamental authority to tell you to get the groceries. You must accept some things as true, or you will be perpetually paralyzed by indecision and inaction (or you will get grounded).

5. Lewis Vaughn, *The Power of Critical Thinking: Effective Reasoning about Ordinary and Extraordinary Claims*, 2nd ed. (New York: Oxford University Press, 2008), 4.

Furthermore, a wise person understands that, in many cases, authority figures are in their respective positions because they possess wisdom, insight, and knowledge that we do not have, often gained through sensible living or years of experience. It would be silly to ignore the advice of our betters. Although accepting some things without questioning them is necessary for living, uncritical acceptance can become a problem when we do not consider the source of the argument, and when we fail to recognize the difference between reliable and unreliable sources. It also becomes a problem when we cannot tell the difference between arguments that bear the ring of truth and those that are patently manipulative, factually confused, shallow, or nonsensical. Therefore, the first characteristic of an effective thinker is that she listens to arguments and weighs their effectiveness and legitimacy.

Effective Thinkers Are Logical

After reading about this first characteristic of effective thinking, you may be wondering, *Well, how do I tell if an argument is effective or not?* That is a great question, and it leads us to our second characteristic. Effective thinkers are critical, but they are also logical. When skilled thinkers use logic well, it means that they have logical and sound thinking patterns. That is, whenever a skilled thinker makes an argument, he supports his conclusion (what he believes) with sufficient and convincing **premises** (his evidence). At a basic level, effective thinking is simple: Make sure that your premises support your conclusions. However, learning to do this well is a little more complicated, so there are several chapters in this book dedicated to teaching you how to support your conclusion with effective premises. This chapter provides an overview of the two basic types of logic you will use or encounter in everyday debate: inductive and deductive logic.

The first type of logic, **inductive logic**, is the most common type of logic you will experience in everyday discussions with people, and even in most formal debates. Simply put, when a person argues inductively, he makes reasonable generalizations based on a pattern of examples. For example, if someone wants to argue that crime will decrease if handguns are outlawed in the United States, an argument he will likely use is one based on examples of countries that have outlawed handguns and have experienced a decrease in crime. That is, he may find examples of a dozen or so countries in which crime decreased once handguns were outlawed. Furthermore, from his research he may discover a handful of countries in which handguns are legal and crime is high. Based on the pattern of these examples, he could generalize that making handguns illegal decreases crime, and therefore handguns should be made illegal in the United States in order to decrease crime. As another example,

What makes a source reliable or unreliable? Basic factors to consider are **authority**, **bias**, and **corroboration**. Does the source have established authority? An **authoritative source** will have experience, knowledge, or credentials relevant to the issue at hand. Reading scholarly books about bear attacks (knowledge), serving a summer internship with the US Forest Service in Yosemite National Park (experience), and receiving a master's or doctorate degree with a concentration in forestry or ursine biology (credentials) would give a source authority to speak reliably about bears. Sources who lack one or more of those qualities become more suspect. Also be wary of sources whose authority is not relevant to the issue at hand—a star quarterback is probably not a reliable spokesman for the quality of a car dealership, for instance. (In logic, we call this error of appealing to an illegitimate authority the ***ipse dixit* fallacy**. The phrase *ipse dixit* is a Latin phrase which means "he said it himself.") Does the source have bias—that is, prejudice or self-interest—that makes her potentially unreliable? A politician who accepts money from an organic farming lobbying group might not be the most trustworthy voice on certain farming issues. By the same token, a politician who accepts money from an oil lobbying group might not be the most trustworthy voice on certain issues regarding the impact of oil drilling on the environment. Corroboration is also a critical factor. Can you find only one source that suggests a certain conclusion, for instance, that certain farming or drilling practices are bad or good? Has a source been consistently right, or wrong, about similar issues in the past? Taking into account both possible bias and whether corroborating evidence exists can help determine whether an authority is a good authority or not.

someone might want to argue that talking or texting on the phone while driving should be made illegal in the United States. In her research, someone could come across studies that suggest that phones are involved in a large percentage of car crashes. She might also come across research and testimonials suggesting that texting while driving inevitably distracts drivers and weakens driver response time. The person researching this may generalize, from dozens of testimonials and research studies, that talking on the phone or texting while driving is too dangerous and should be made illegal.

Whenever you hear people presenting a variety of statistics or examples, or quotes from authority figures, or testimonies from people in order to support a conclusion, that person is using inductive logic because he is making a generalization from various examples in order to support his conclusion. It is important to note that inductive arguments can never be 100 percent accurate because they are based on generalizations. Even one set of a thousand examples proving one point can be countered by another set of a thousand examples proving the opposite. However, even though you cannot construct an inductive argument that is 100 percent guaranteed, you *can* construct one that is very strong and reasonable.

Deductive logic is the second type of logic. When a person uses deductive logic, she begins with statements that are already generally accepted as true.[6] Then, she uses these statements to proceed to new truths. That is, she uncovers what can be learned, or inferred, from previously existing truths. In some ways, deductive logic is mathematical because it is extremely straightforward and black-and-white in nature. For example, let's say someone was contemplating democracies and the duties of citizens in a democracy. She might make the following argument:

A democracy is an entity that thrives only through an informed citizenry.

America is a democracy.

Therefore, America is an entity that thrives only through an informed citizenry.

As you can see, the first two statements (these are the premises) are truths—foundational beliefs that are accepted as given. That is, everyone (or almost everyone) would have no difficulty accepting these statements as true. Furthermore, these premises imply the conclusion. In other words, if these premises are true (which these happen to be), the argument is structured in such a way that the conclusion naturally follows, and it cannot be denied. It is important to note that sometimes when a person

6. When you make a deductive argument, the more widely accepted your premises are, the more convincing your argument will be.

confirmation bias – look only for the evidence we want – opposite is careful examination of all facts

uses deductive logic, he builds a deductive argument on statements that are not *a priori* statements—he could build an argument in which the conclusion follows the premises; however, the arguer may need to demonstrate that his premises are true. For example, consider the following deductive argument:

> All actions that deprive humans of dignity are morally wrong.
>
> Capital punishment deprives humans of dignity.
>
> Therefore, capital punishment is morally wrong.

Note that this is a deductive argument because the conclusion is implied by the premises. However, the premises are not necessarily ***a priori*** truths. That is, these premises are not ones that everyone automatically accepts as true. Some might argue that the first premise is false. For example, they could argue that a murderer has forfeited his right to be treated with dignity. Some people might argue that the second premise is false. They could argue that some forms of capital punishment (e.g., lethal injection) treat convicted criminals with dignity while restoring justice. Therefore, sometimes when a person makes a deductive argument, it is necessary for him to prove that his premises are strong claims.

It is important to observe that deductive logic is often used with inductive logic. Furthermore, deductive arguments are often linked together to form a more complex argument. For example, let's go back to the deductive argument about democracy.

> A democracy is an entity that thrives only through an informed citizenry.
>
> America is a democracy.
>
> Therefore, America is an entity that thrives only through an informed citizenry.

Let's say that someone used this argument as a part of a debate discussing the importance of education and the best type of educational system. She might begin her whole argument with this deductive argument, and then she might present statistics or quotes from authorities to argue for the best type of education. In order for a deductive argument to be correct (valid), it must be structured correctly, the premises must be accepted *a priori* or proven true, and all of the terms in the premises and conclusion must be clear and unambiguous. Just as you will learn how to construct a strong inductive argument in coming chapters, you will also learn how to construct valid deductive arguments.

Effective Thinkers Are Careful and Accurate

painstaking

As you read about logical thinking in the previous paragraphs, you probably realized that arguments are only as good as the grounds upon which they are based. For example, someone could structure a very thorough, fact-filled argument; however, if his facts are wrong, the argument will, ultimately, be ineffective. Therefore, the third characteristic of effective thinking is careful research and accuracy. When you research for a debate, either by constructing arguments from your own understanding or by researching other information, you must carefully check sources and examples, as well as examine a wide variety of sources, examples, and views pertaining to an issue. Furthermore, you must make sure that your report of the facts is clear and accurate. Many a debater has weakened his argument by reporting inaccurate information or failing to consider another important and obvious aspect of the debate. Why would someone be so careless? It is likely because careful research takes time and is not as glamorous as some of the other parts of the debate process.

Many people are drawn initially to debate because verbally sparring with people can be perceived as fun and can evoke an adrenaline rush, especially if you win. However, to be truly effective in debate, you must read a lot of information and carefully analyze numerous arguments. This requires a great deal of thinking, which, to be honest, can be mentally exhausting. Although debating can be enjoyable, there are parts of preparing for debate that are just plain hard work. However, compare it to any other skill. If you want to be an excellent basketball player or swimmer, you must constantly do drills in which you run or swim far beyond the point of enjoyment to increase your endurance. If you want to be a good pianist, you must spend endless hours doing scales to increase the agility of your fingers. If you want to be a confident speaker of

Spanish or Latin, you must devote hours to memorizing and absorbing grammar and vocabulary. Anyone who has practiced these skills or others like them knows that while these activities may not be enjoyable in themselves, they certainly increase the ease and enjoyment with which someone can play a sport or an instrument, or speak fluently in a foreign language. Therefore, as you practice debate and spend hours researching and thinking, know that this is a drill that will increase your confidence and satisfaction in debating itself.

Is the truth, which can so often trouble us, jeopardize our happiness, or strip away what makes the world familiar, worth knowing? Many stories and accounts have explored this question. Consider Sophocles's famous tragedies about Oedipus, who persistently ignored truths he didn't like, until he came face to face with a horrible truth about who his parents were, and who he really was, that nearly crushed him. Socrates, the famous Greek philosopher, pursued the truth so relentlessly that it eventually led to his being sentenced to death by his fellow Athenians. Sometime pursuing the truth is painful. Most people would rather pursue the truth, although it brings pain, rather than live a life of comfortable deception.

In addition, it is important to realize that we often like to think we are right, and we naturally gravitate toward evidence that supports our current beliefs. This is because discovering our beliefs and changing them can be uncomfortable and inconvenient. For example, let's say that Nadine, a college freshman, likes to skip class a lot and goof off with her friends, who skip class a lot, too. One night, Nadine gets in a discussion with her roommate, Caris, about skipping class. Caris makes some strong arguments against this habit. However, as Nadine listens, she starts to feel ashamed about all of the time she has wasted skipping class and goofing off. Furthermore, she doesn't really know what she'll do if she starts attending class regularly. It sounds pretty boring to her. After all, it appears that everyone who attends class regularly, such as Caris, are constantly studying, and that sounds like a drag to Nadine. Furthermore, Nadine thinks all of her friends who skip class with her are fun. She truly likes them and would miss them if she didn't skip class and hang out with them. She worries about what they would think of her if she started attending class all the time.

As you can see, if Nadine isn't careful, it's going to be pretty easy for her to talk herself out of believing Caris's arguments; after all, changing her habits would be difficult and even uncomfortable. The point is that all of us have some bad habits and inaccurate, or blatantly wrong, beliefs, just as Nadine is struggling with in this example. Some of our habits and beliefs are easy to change, but others are truly difficult, and changing them would force us to give up long-cherished convictions or activities. Too often, we ignore arguments that require us to alter our ideas or habits. It is incredibly important for you to realize and fully comprehend this tendency if you plan on becoming a good thinker. You will need to be willing to seek and accept the truth, even if it is uncomfortable for you to do so.

Effective Thinkers Are Civil without Selling Out

The fourth characteristic of an effective thinker is that he is civil without selling out. Another way of saying this is that effective thinkers are open-minded. Sometimes people speak disparagingly of being open-minded, saying warnings such as, "Don't be so open-minded that your brain falls out!" Please understand that when this text uses the term "open-minded," it does not mean that you are willing to agree equally with all viewpoints. This would be silly to recommend, especially if the viewpoints are mutually exclusive. For example, the statements "Extraterrestrial intelligence exists" and "Extraterrestrial intelligence does not exist" cannot both be true, and it would be ridiculous to say that someone is open-minded about this matter only if he agrees with both positions. No, this is not the meaning of open-mindedness. Pliny the Elder once said, "No man is wise at all times."[7] This quote might help us understand why it is important to be open-minded. When we are open-minded, we realize that because we are finite humans, we are necessarily limited in our understanding and knowledge. This means

7. Susan Ratcliffe, ed., *Oxford Dictionary of Quotations by Subject*, 2nd ed. (Oxford: Oxford University Press, 2010), 510.

seek to understand as much as to be understood (Harry Stephenson)

that sometimes when we are convinced we are right, we are actually wrong, or we are missing important information on a subject. An open-minded person realizes that she could always be wrong about a subject. Therefore, she listens to opposing opinions, considers the evidence presented, and then decides whether to accept or reject part or all of the opinion being presented. Often by listening to others' ideas and opinions, we come to see how our ideas are limited, simplistic, or one-sided. Someone who can listen to an opposing argument, weighing his strongly held opinions in light of new evidence, is an open-minded person.

Socrates may serve as a model as to how we can be open-minded without accepting every notion as equally true. As we have already discussed, Socrates was known for his relentless pursuit of truth. Early in his life, he visited the Oracle of Delphi with a friend, and the Oracle told him that there was no one wiser than he was. Socrates did not believe this was true. Therefore, he went around to all of the people who considered themselves wise, or who other people considered to be wise, to discover if they truly were. Through a series of questions, Socrates often discovered that they weren't wise, and he felt obliged to tell them—which, as you can imagine, they did not appreciate!

At this point, you may be thinking that, on second thought, maybe Socrates isn't the best model to follow. After all, habitually pointing out people's stupidity is not the way to win friends or influence people. Certainly, Socrates was mischievous, and when a person with whom he was discussing a matter was obviously ignorant, Socrates loved to point out his absurdity (as you have already seen from *Euthyphro*, which was discussed in chapter 2). However, reviewing Socrates's mode of discussion can be very enlightening. In a famous dialogue (which was recorded by Plato), he said, "I tell you that no greater good can happen to a man than to discuss human excellence every day and the other matters about which you have heard me arguing and examining myself and others . . . an unexamined life is not worth living."[8]

In his dialogues with people, Socrates would regularly pose questions such as the following: What is pious (good)? Can virtue be taught? What is justice? Whoever he was discussing the matter with would present his opinion. Then Socrates would ask him a series of questions to demonstrate the contradictory nature of his beliefs. However, all the while, Socrates modeled the search for truth in his discussion with people. He often claimed that he did not know the answer to his questions and that he was looking for the answer just as much as the other person or people in the discussion were. Furthermore, at times people would question his hypotheses and, rather than getting defensive or angry at their questioning, he would patiently work through the inferences and conclusion of his own hypotheses in order to see if they were truly logical. Socrates is a model of how we can be open-minded without accepting every claim as equally valid. We need to place the pursuit of truth as our utmost aim in every discussion. Then, if we believe our opponent's claim is invalid or incorrect, we need to kindly challenge him through self-revealing questions or through the careful construction of correct arguments and facts. Furthermore, we must be open to the notion that we, ourselves, could be wrong. And we must be willing to examine the logic and validity of our own beliefs, and be willing to correct them if they are incorrect or illogical.

Who are the people with whom your debates quickly turn into arguments or insults? Is it with your parents, siblings, or certain friends? It may be helpful to make a list of the people with whom, or the topics about which, discussions tend to deteriorate. Not every debate will, or should, end with hugs and happiness. But a thoughtful and respected debater will always have a worthy end goal in mind. Often, debates sour when the end goal is inappropriate (e.g., "Win at all costs!" "Make this person believe I'm right!" "Impress the cute bystander who is listening!"), or inappropriate to that particular conversation. As you begin to debate, develop the habit of reflecting: *What is my goal?* Even in formal debates, in which winning is an expected and stated goal, extra motivations might creep in to poison the debate, or even limit your own effectiveness as a debater.

There is another important thing you should consider about the pursuit of truth. Debate works best when the pursuit of truth is not only your goal but also is the goal

8. Pojman, *Classics of Philosophy*, 39.

Consider this infamous anonymous quote: "Never argue with an idiot. He will drag you down to his level and beat you with experience." As the word "idiot" may be too harsh and inaccurate a term for most people with whom you'll discuss issues, simply remember this: Some debates aren't worth having.

of your opponent. You can probably imagine why. If you are debating and discussing in order to pursue truth, but your opponent only desires to win, you will likely become frustrated because your opponent may be a poor listener, and she may engage in insults and attacks (i.e., attacking you rather than the argument) rather than analyzing the merits of your argument. Sometimes, when your opponent is in this frame of mind, the best thing you can do is avoid debate altogether (of course, you would only do this in an informal debate setting). However, if you feel as though you can participate in the argument without being insulted, you might be able to use Socratic questioning to help your opponent recognize her faulty thinking. In fact, careful, pointed questioning is one of the most effective argument techniques you can use with bombastic (i.e., highly opinionated and argumentative) people, for they often love to air their opinions—even ones that aren't supported well—and they often eventually talk themselves into a corner. Perhaps this is the motivation behind the famous biblical proverb, "Even fools are thought wise if they keep silent, and discerning if they hold their tongues."[9] Of course, if you are in a formal debate, the debate must continue regardless of your opponent's motivations. However, the ability to recognize your opponent's motives in a formal debate setting will help you better strategize your responses.

Effective Thinkers Listen Carefully and Ask Great Questions

All of this talk of pursuing the truth and being civil to your opponent leads us to the final quality of effective thinkers: They listen well and ask great questions. It is true that, technically, these are really two qualities, not just one—but these principles go hand in hand. Let's examine the skills of listening first. It may seem obvious that a good thinker would need to listen carefully. After all, how can you debate if you are not listening to your opponent? However, consider this question: How many times have you been in a conversation in which you felt that the other person was only thinking about what she would say next, rather than actually listening to what you were saying? How many times have you failed to listen to a person in a conversation and instead focused on what you were going to say next? If you are like most people, you will realize that people have done this to you a lot in conversations—but you have done it to them, too. It is one of the most common pitfalls that trap people when they debate and discuss issues with which they disagree.

Why do we have such a problem listening to others? Listening can be difficult because it requires focus, patience, and humility. When you sincerely listen to another person, you must block out all of the other activities and stimuli going on around you, even if they seem more interesting than the person you are listening to. This takes practice. Buddhist monks used to practice this skill by sitting and staring at an orange for hours. The goal was for them to notice everything about that orange, as well as all the things about oranges they had never noticed before. As you can imagine, such activities certainly helped to improve the monks' focus. It is safe to say that with television, video games, millions of radio channels, and constant traffic noise in today's culture, we don't get a lot of practice in focus and concentration. It isn't being suggested that you go and meditate on an orange for several hours this weekend (although you might learn a few things from such an activity). Merely noting your tendency to wander mentally—acknowledging your distractions—can help you focus more. It is also important to realize that listening requires

An easy tip for breaking this self-focused habit, as well as demonstrating your sincerity as a listener, is to simply wait two seconds (the time of a breath) after someone has finished talking before speaking up yourself. Though it might seem artificial or disingenuous at first to be counting out in your head the time until you get to talk, you may be surprised at how quickly this becomes a habit. This process allows you to listen first and not rush to speak your point without first processing and considering what the other person just said.

9. Proverbs 17:28 (NIV).

patience. To be honest, sometimes the person we are listening to is, frankly, downright boring—but keep in mind that you can be boring, too. It takes patience and humility to realize that you can learn something from even the most seemingly uninteresting person.

The more you listen, the better you can ask questions. During a discussion, it is sometimes tempting to do all the talking. We love to hear our own opinions, after all. However, it can be more effective to ask people questions rather than to make constant statements during a debate. This is because when you ask people questions about their arguments, you make them do most of the work. They then have to explain *why* they believe what they do, and in this process they often expose the faults in their own arguments. In addition, many times when people go through this process, they ultimately realize their mistakes and decide to change their minds. This process gives them the opportunity to catch their own errors and possibly save face. So how do *you* question people in a debate? Here are some of the most common ways you can question a person's argument:

1. Ask them to clarify definitions.[10]
2. Ask them to state the origin of info or source.[11] In this way, you probe the rationale, reasons, and evidence behind a person's arguments.[12]
3. Ask them about the implications and consequences of their arguments.[13]
4. Ask them about opposing thoughts and objections.[14] When you do this, you are probing how they reconcile their viewpoints and perspectives with opposing viewpoints and perspectives—or if they've considered alternatives at all.

In conclusion, if you want to be a good debater, you must begin to think like a debater. To do this, you need to (a) be critical, (b) be logical, (c) be careful and accurate, (d) be civil without selling out (i.e., be open-minded), and (e) listen carefully and ask great questions. Furthermore, like Socrates, you must be civil, and you must place the discovery of truth over the desire to trump your opponent. Be aware of your opponent's motivations as well. In an informal discussion (e.g., in a coffee shop), you may decide to disengage with a person who has the wrong motives for debate, or you may decide to use Socratic discussion. In a formal debate, you will need to continue the debate regardless of your opponent's demeanor. However, detecting your opponent's attitude can help you better strategize your responses. If you cultivate these mental habits and approach debates with appropriate Socratic civility, you will be well on your way to becoming an effective debater.

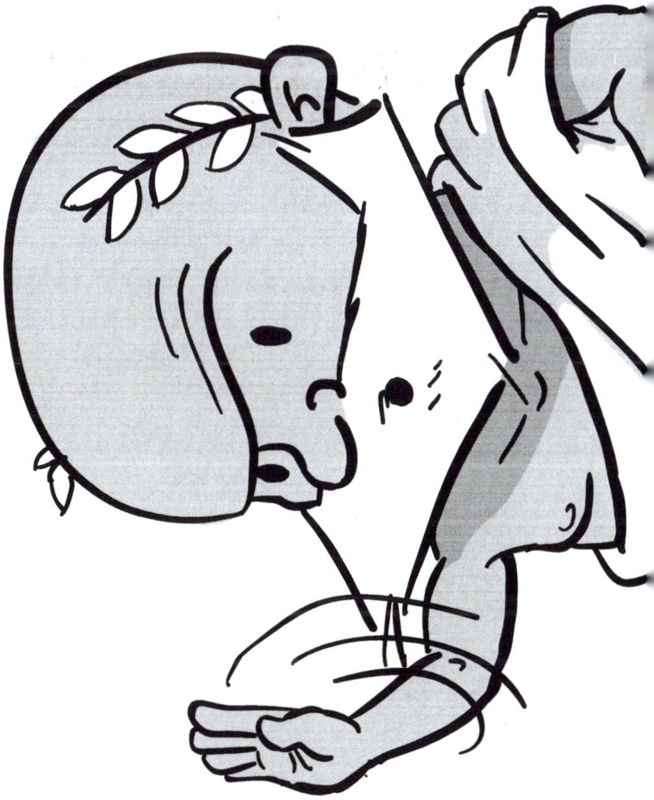

10. David Straker, "Refuting Arguments," Changingminds.org, May 21, 2005, http: changingminds.org/disciplines/argument/making argument/refuting_argument.htm.
11. Richard Paul and Linda Elder, *The Thinker's Guide to the Art of Socratic Reasoning* (Dillon Beach, CA: Foundation for Critical Thinking, 2006), 13.
12. Straker, "Refuting Arguments," Changingminds.org.
13. Paul and Elder, *Thinker's Guide*, 13.
14. Ibid.

Review Exercises

List

List five characteristics of effective thinkers.

a. critical
2. logical
3. careful and accurate
4. Openminded (civil w/o yelling out)
5. listen carefully and ask good questions

Explain

Explain who Socrates was and what it means to approach a debate with Socratic openness.

Socrates was a Greek philosopher known for using questions must defend what you say forces opponent to argue against themself this goal is truth

Building Copiousness

Review

Review the quote about love from last week and then memorize the quote below. (Eventually you will incorporate these quotes into your debates.)

Practice

Practice saying the quote to someone in your class, or practice writing it down on paper.

Memorize

Memorize your new quote:

> A truth that's told with bad intent
> Beats all the lies you can invent.
>
> —William Blake[15]

Everyday Debate

Debate

In the past decade, cell phones have become a fixture of everyday life. Everywhere you go, you see and hear people talking on cell phones, whether they are walking down the street, riding in an elevator, visiting the restroom (good grief!), or watching a movie. One everyday debate you might frequently hear is about whether people should talk on their cell phone while they are driving a car. This is the topic we will examine in this chapter's "Everyday Debate" exercise.

In the last chapter you practiced constructing an argument on each side of an issue, and you practiced developing this argument by asking yourself why you believed what you did about that issue, and why other people might take an opposing stance to the issue. Here is a technique that will give you a bit of a formula to use to develop arguments: the **Toulmin model**. Debaters frequently use this model when they develop their arguments. It was developed by philosopher Stephen Toulmin in 1958, and it provides a layout of the basic components of an argument.[16] When Toulmin first developed this argument technique, he looked at four parts of an argument: claim, evidence, warrant, and reservations. It's important to note that this is a *general* look at how a basic argument might work. There are other elements of argumentation not included in this model that we will discuss later, and a more complex argument will include other elements, but this is a good tool to use to get started.

Let's look at each of the four parts of an argument in reference to the cell phone topic: whether talking on cell phones while driving a car is a good idea. Your claim is what you believe about this issue, that is, whether you believe it is a good or bad idea. Your evidence is the reason why you believe what you do. Your warrant is how this piece of evidence gets you to your conclusion. In other words, why has that piece of evidence led you to this conclusion? Your reservation would be any concerns you have or possible instances in which your evidence might not hold up. Try developing an argument about talking on cell phones while driving by answering the following questions:

a. Claim: Do you believe that it is acceptable to talk on a cell phone while driving a car? Yes or no?
b. Evidence: What is one specific reason that you believe this?
c. Warrant: How did this evidence lead you to believe your conclusion?
d. Reservations: Can you think of any weaknesses to this evidence or any times when your chain of reasoning might not apply? (There is almost always at least one potential weakness to a piece of evidence or at least one time it might not apply. The better you get at spotting this, the better debater you will become.)

---

15. Ratcliffe, *Oxford Dictionary of Quotations*, 486.
16. Robert Trapp, *The Database Book: A Must-Have Guide for Successful Debate*, 3rd ed. (New York: International Debate Education Association, 2004), 10–11.

Consider

Now that you have used the Toulmin model to develop an argument for what you believe, pretend that you believe the opposite side and answer the same questions, pretending that you completely believe the opposite point of view. Now, if you utterly and completely reject the opposing viewpoint, you may be tempted to provide illogical, patently ridiculous answers to the questions. However, you need to realize that any major controversial issues in society will have two legitimate viewpoints, and that logical, intelligent people will be found as supporters on either side of a given issue. That is why it is an actual controversy. If one side was totally stupid, there would be no controversy. Therefore, you need to train yourself to see the logic and intelligence of the opposing arguments even if, ultimately, you disagree with the arguments. In this way you are entertaining an idea without accepting it. So, just for a minute, pretend that you believe the opposing arguments and go back and answer the preceding questions from this viewpoint.

Provide an Argument *Against* Talking on Cell Phones While Driving:

1. **Claim:** Do you believe that it is acceptable to talk on a cell phone while driving a vehicle? Yes or no?

____

2. **Evidence:** What is one specific reason that you believe this?

____

____

3. **Warrant:** How did this evidence lead you to believe your conclusion?

____

____

____

____

____

4. **Reservations:** Can you think of any weaknesses to this evidence or any times when your chain of reasoning might not apply?

____

____

____

____

Provide an argument *for* talking on cell phones while driving:

1. **Claim:** Do you believe that it is acceptable to talk on a cell phone while driving a vehicle? Yes or no?

   ____

2. **Evidence:** What is one specific reason that you believe this?

   ____

   ____

3. **Warrant:** How did this evidence lead you to believe your conclusion?

   ____

   ____

   ____

   ____

4. **Reservations:** Can you think of any weaknesses to this evidence or any times when your chain of reasoning might not apply?

   ____

   ____

   ____

Just as you did in the last chapter, share your best arguments with three people in your class and then listen to their arguments. Choose the argument that you believe is the strongest. Write a summary of the chosen argument and explain why you think it is the strongest.

Learning from the Masters

Read and Consider

Read the *Apology*, Plato's account of the speech given by Socrates.[17] In one of the previous chapters, you read *Euthyphro* to learn about questioning from Socrates, the master of questions. Learning the art of questioning is especially important because, in many cases, the mark of a good debater is that he can ask pointed questions that expose the weakness in other people's arguments.

17. Plato, *Euthyphro, Apology, Crito, Phaedo: the Death Scene*, trans. F. J. Church (Upper Saddle River, NJ: Prentice Hall, 1948); see also Plato, *Apology*, trans. Benjamin Jowett, http://classics.mit.edu/Plato/apology.html for the text online.

Read the *Apology* and then answer the following questions:

1. What did the Oracle at Delphi reveal to Socrates?

____

____

2. How did Socrates go about trying to prove the Delphic Oracle wrong?

____

____

____

3. Why did Socrates's attempts to prove the oracle wrong anger some of his fellow citizens?

____

____

____

4. What were the two charges brought against Socrates?

____

____

____

5. When Socrates was found guilty, he made a joke about what his sentence should be. What did he say his sentence should be, and why did he say it should be that?

____

____

____

6. Why, according to Socrates, could he not stop himself from doing what he was doing?

____

____

____

Chapter 5

Deciding to Debate

> IT BELONGS TO ALL PEOPLE TO KNOW THEMSELVES AND TO THINK RIGHTLY.
>
> —HERACLITUS[1]

Informal Debate in Day-to-Day Life

Isabel and Andrew are twins. Their parents have gone to a sociology presentation at the local university, and they have given Andrew and Isabel money to rent a movie and order pizza. As the siblings are attempting to figure out what movie to watch, the following conversation ensues:

Andrew: I really want to see that new *Rambo* movie. Stallone is amazing. He's way older than Dad, and he can still kick some major . . .

Isabel: Oh, for Pete's sake! I am not watching a *Rambo* movie! It's nothing but plotless violence and ridiculous fight scenes. Why do boys watch such stupid movies?

Andrew: Don't be such a girl! You probably want to watch some incomprehensible foreign film in which mysterious strangers fall in love but are too stupid to actually talk to each other, so they spend the whole movie crying, writing in their journals, and sending lawn ornaments on imaginary adventures around the world. I'd rather watch paint dry!

Isabel: Why do you have to be so melodramatic and ridiculous all the time?

As you can see, Andrew and Isabel's "debate" is rather aimless and ineffective right now because it is too full of emotion and stereotypes, and while they are supposed to be discussing what movie they should get, they instead are arguing about everything else under the sun, such as whether boys watch stupid movies, or whether movies involving crying and traveling lawn ornaments are worthwhile, or whether Andrew is melodramatic and ridiculous all the time. As you can imagine, this will not be a very productive conversation because none of these issues really pertains to the heart of the matter: what movie should the siblings watch together. What Andrew and Isabel need is a good, clear topic or idea that focuses their attention on something they can actually debate. For instance, imagine if they approached the movie debate this way:

Andrew: Isabel, we're not going to get anywhere if we keep arguing about stupid things.

Isabel: I agree. OK, let's figure out a fair system for selecting a movie.

Andrew: That sounds like a good idea. What kind of system did you have in mind?

---

1. Patricia Curd, ed., Richard D. McKirahan, trans., *A Presocratics Reader: Selected Fragments and Testimonia* (Indianapolis, IN: Hackett Publishing, 1995), 33.

Isabel: I propose we take turns choosing movies. So, one of us chooses the movie this time, then the other person gets to choose the movie next time.

Andrew: That sounds pretty fair, but I have one counterproposal. Could we both agree, when it's our turn to pick, to avoid choosing a kind of movie that the other person hates? To make this easier, how about we each get to veto one type of movie from the get-go.

Isabel: That makes sense. Let me guess . . . no crying, journal-writing foreign films for you, right?

Andrew: And no brainless, fight-filled flicks for you.

Isabel: All right. Should we flip a coin to see who picks first?

Andrew: Nope, you can pick first, since you're being such a good sport.

Isabel: Aww . . . what a pal! OK, let's watch . . . a somewhat *thoughtful* fight flick.

Andrew: Now you're talking!

This debate or discussion is certainly informal. Andrew and Isabel are not presenting their arguments before any type of judge or deliberative body. They are simply debating and discussing between the two of them the best way to choose a movie that they will both enjoy watching. Nevertheless, even though this is an informal debate, it is still crucial for them to pick a tangible, specific topic they can discuss. As you can see from the argument, Isabel provided this focus by suggesting they discuss a system that would allow them to select a movie fairly. Once they agreed upon this as the focus of their conversation, their discussion was much more effective and profitable. In an informal debate, people rarely say, "The topic we will be discussing is . . ." Instead, people will often clarify the topic at hand by prefacing with a statement such as, "The main point is," "What we're really trying to decide is," or "The important thing here is . . ." Because an informal debate is loose and organic by nature, people involved in this kind of debate may spend more time talking about other issues that are unrelated to the main topic. However, at some point they must clarify what it is they are really talking about, or they will make little progress in discovering truth.

Establishing a Proposition

Establishing a clear proposition in a formal debate is much easier because the proposition is usually established by an outside party such as a teacher, a judge, or a debate committee. If you'll recall, the concept of a proposition was introduced in chapter 1. A proposition is a factual statement that can be proven true or false. It is a carefully worded statement that makes clear the positions of both the affirmative and negative sides. In formal debates, people often express the proposition in a manner such as the following: "Resolved: Global warming is correlated to human activity and is a threat to humanity," or "Resolved: Growing a garden is essential for optimal health." The word "resolved" indicates what the people involved in the debate have decided to argue for or against. It does not mean that both people agree with the proposition. It simply means that this proposition is the focus of the debate. The **resolution** is the proposition that two people or teams will argue in a debate. Once people have established the proposition for a debate, one side develops arguments in support of the proposition—this is the **affirmative side**. The other side develops arguments against this proposition—this is the **negative side**.

Now that you understand the importance of establishing a proposition as the focus of a debate, let me introduce you to two other teenagers, Christy and Josh, who are involved in a formal debate. Christy and Josh live in Lexington, Kentucky, and attend Xavier Academy.[2] They have joined an after-school extracurricular debate team, and their teacher, Mr. Bennet, wants the team members to do several in-class debates with classmates in preparation for the actual debate. Christy and Josh are scheduled to debate each other, and their topic is capital punishment, or the death penalty. Mr. Bennet has informed Christy and Josh that they must decide from which angle they wish to approach their topic, and he also wants them to present a clear proposition by the end of the next class period. In addition, he wants Christy and Josh to decide who will take the affirmative side and who will take the negative side. The following is a discussion Christy and Josh have as they were trying to focus their capital punishment debate and establish a proposition:

2. Xavier Academy is the name of a fictitious school that I have created for the purposes of this book.

The philosopher Aristotle addressed this issue in his idea of **stasis theory**. This is an ancient rhetoric strategy that uses four questions to help a speaker develop a clear understanding of his or her topic. The questions pertain to conjecture, definition, quality, and policy. The questions are "Did he do it?" (conjecture); "What did he do?" (definition); "Was it just/expedient?" (quality); and "Is this the right venue for this issue?" (policy).[3]

Debates can fail to go anywhere not just because debaters disagree, but because they don't even agree about the thing they're disagreeing over! The purpose of stasis theory is to identify the point about which two parties can agree to disagree. In order to discern the real issue at hand, Aristotle introduced four questions. The question of **conjecture** deals with a thing's existence. The question of **definition** deals with what the thing is that exists. The question of **quality** deals with what kind of a thing it is. And the question of **policy** deals with what should be done. On a basic level, we can use stasis theory to zero in on the disagreement.

As an example, using the four questions in order to process and approach a topic, let's see how Andrew and Isabel may tackle a debate of capital punishment: Would they agree that capital punishment exists (conjecture)? (Yes.) Would they agree on how to define it? (Most likely, though this may take some thought and effort.) Would they agree on the quality of capital punishment? (Probably not—and now they can start examining which specific qualities they would disagree). Lastly, would they agree that the issue of capital punishment is a matter of policy and that certain actions concerning it should be taken by lawmakers? (Yes, but they would think that different actions should be taken by lawmakers regarding capital punishment).

Stasis theory can also be used to think through an issue on a deeper level to see more sides and come up with more arguments about the topic. Conjecture prompts asking the following: Is capital punishment a new or an old practice? Do more communities today practice capital punishment than in centuries before? In what communities—countries, states, cities—is it currently practiced? Definition helps a debater explore what is defined as capital punishment: Is it different from the killing of a criminal or political enemy in a time of conflict? Are there forms of punishment that are too brutal, or too gentle, to qualify as capital punishment? Quality encourages the following inquiries: Is it expedient in deterring crime? Is it just in satisfying the victims, or society? Is it a civilized practice? Lastly, policy pushes the debater to ask the practical questions about what should be done: Should capital punishment be outlawed or allowed? Should it be regulated by the federal government or by individual states?

3. Gideon O. Burton, *Silva Rhetoricae*, s.v. "stasis," Brigham Young University, page last updated February 26, 2007, http://rhetoric.byu.edu/.

Josh: Well, Christy, what do you think we should debate about capital punishment?

Christy: That's a good question. I've heard people pose the question about whether capital punishment is ethical—you know, it kind of seems like repaying evil with evil.

Josh: Yeah, I've heard that idea before, too. I've also heard people argue about whether it's actually effective—for example, if it has any effect on crime at all. Some people say it reduces crime, and others say it actually increases the crime rate.

Christy: Hmmm. That might be interesting to study. Couldn't we focus on both?

Josh: Well, this first debate can only last fifteen minutes. It seems as though it might be hard to address both issues sufficiently in that time.

Christy: That's true. Boy, I'm not sure which one to debate.

As you can see, Josh and Christy are less emotional and more logical than Andrew and Isabel were during their first discussion, but they have an added element of a time restriction that Andrew and Isabel did not have with their debate. That is, Josh and Christy must defend their respective sides and rebut the opponent's views in only fifteen minutes, whereas Andrew and Isabel could discuss what movie they were going to rent as long as they wanted to discuss it. It is especially important for Josh and Christy to zero in on the exact topic they want to debate so that they don't waste time exploring a number of different tangentially related subjects instead of fully exploring and supporting one main issue related to the topic of capital punishment. Christy and Josh have already hinted at several ideas that could be formed into propositions, but in their discussion they were asking questions and considering different options, rather than wording things strictly in propositional format. Here are a few potential options for different propositions they could debate in relation to capital punishment:

> **Resolved:** Capital punishment should be abolished.
>
> **Resolved:** Capital punishment is a just and ethical response to murder.
>
> **Resolved:** Capital punishment deters (discourages) crime.

Note that all of these propositions are statements that can be proven true or false, and they serve the purpose of focusing the discussion.

We have stated that a proposition is a declarative statement that can be proven true or false. While this definition is fairly clear, it can be helpful to understand what something is by looking at some things that it is *not*. Therefore, it may be helpful to know what kinds of statements are not propositions. We have already examined a few of them. For instance, in Andrew and Isabel's debate, the question "Why do boys watch such stupid movies?" is not a proposition. Statements of preferences (either explicit or implicit), such as Andrew's "I really want to see that new *Rambo* movie" statement, are not propositions. Also, commands, such as Andrew's demand of "Don't be such a girl!" to Isabel, are not propositions. Of course, as you may have already surmised, such statements can eventually lead people to a good proposition or may contain an implied proposition—but these statements, in and of themselves, are not adequate focuses for debates. The only legitimate proposition is a statement that can be proven true or false. This proposition will be directly stated in a formal debate; it may only be implied in an informal debate.

Clarifying the Terms

Not only is it crucial to distill your topic into a proposition and to establish the affirmative and negative sides, it is also important for you to make sure that the terms in the proposition that you are debating are clear and common to all involved in the discussion. We have a tendency to assume that everyone understands words in the same way that we do. For example, when I was growing up, my family regularly used the word *skeejogged* to describe an object that was crooked. Later as an adult, after I was married, I referred to a picture hanging crookedly on the wall as *skeejogged*. My husband looked at me in total confusion, and I soon learned that *skeejogged* was not a part of everyone's vocabulary. Unless you are debating someone from a different country, it isn't likely that you will be using terms that are totally unfamiliar to the both of you. However, in debate, it can be common for people to use vague or unclear words, or terms that might be defined in more than one (different) way by different people. For example, Isabel and Andrew eventually decided to rent "a somewhat thoughtful fight flick." As you can imagine, it will be important for both Isabel and Andrew to define exactly what they mean by this to prevent further misunderstanding and conflict. The phrase "somewhat thoughtful" is vague and leaves a lot of room for interpretation. This means that Andrew could interpret this phrase very differently from Isabel.

By the same token, consider Josh and Christy's debate over capital punishment. For example, Josh decides he wants to argue that, in his words, "capital punishment is a horrible action." As you can probably imagine, the term "horrible action" is unhelpful for debate. After all, what does Josh mean by the word "horrible"—that it is violent, cruel, unethical, and/or frightening? Unless he clarifies exactly what he means by this, he will not be able to have a successful debate. As you can see, the best way to make sure that your debate statement is clear is to use specific words and to avoid vague terms (e.g., bad, good, horrible, nice, helpful).

Eventually, Andrew and Isabel clarified what they both meant by "a somewhat thoughtful fight flick." They decided to rent an action movie that not only had a strong plot and strong character development, but also contained some fighting and martial art scenes that were necessary for the development of the story. Christy and Josh also finalized their decision: They chose to debate about capital punishment and settled on this resolution: "Resolved: Capital punishment is ethical, and it deters crime." Christy decided to argue for the affirmative side of this statement, and Josh decided to argue for the negative side.

Once people in an informal or formal debate have established precisely what they are debating, they are in a much better position to gather arguments to support their position and to critique the other position. To do this, it is helpful for people to know that there are three main types of arguments, all of which are very helpful in a debate or discussion: arguments from logos (reason), arguments from pathos (emotion or passion), and arguments from ethos (character). In the upcoming chapters, you will examine the basic structure of a debate, as well as the places a person can look to gather information. In addition, you will examine how to use logos, ethos, and pathos to support an argument.

Such terms as "bad," "good," "horrible," "nice," and "helpful" express a moral or a value judgment that might be thought of as opinion, but that's not what makes them poor word choices in propositions. Rather, it's that each of these words is the conclusion of an unspoken argument. A thing is only "bad" if it has some characteristic of "badness," such as "unjust" in reference to a moral statement, or "bitterness" in a value statement about taste. Rushing to call something bad skips past important steps—agreeing whether the thing in question really is unjust or bitter (i.e., Toulmin model's evidence), and whether that characteristic or evidence qualifies (i.e., Toulmin model's warrant) the thing as bad.

Review Exercises

Define

Define each of the following words.

1. Proposition:

___

2. Resolution:

___

3. Affirmative Side:

___

4. Negative Side:

___

List

List three types of statements that are not propositions:

1. ______________________________

2. ______________________________

3. ______________________________

Explain

Explain why it is so important to carefully define the terms in an argument.

____

____

____

____

Practicing Clarifying Propositions

Clarify

Now you will learn a little more about Isabel and Andrew. Isabel and Andrew are fifteen-year-old twins. For most of their lives, they have lived in various Central and South American countries, most recently Bolivia, because their parents were English teachers abroad. Recently, their family has settled in Lexington, Kentucky, and they now attend Xavier Academy, the same school that Josh and Christy attend. Andrew and Isabel's parents have just informed them that the family will be settling down in one place, and so they can now get a pet, which they have desired to do for years. There is one catch, however: Isabel desperately wants a cat, and Andrew really wants a dog. Their parents have told them that, since they will be the primary caretakers of their pet, they must discuss and debate the matter themselves and present a joint proposal together on their desired type of pet. Furthermore, at this time, their parents have said that they only can have one pet; it is not an option to get both a cat and a dog—they must choose one or the other. Isabel and Andrew have been thinking hard about how they can persuade each other to adopt their preferred pet but, as you will read in the following conversation, they let their emotions interfere with the discussion. Read their conversation and then answer the following questions:

Isabel: I don't like dogs. They're too rambunctious and destructive.

Andrew: Don't be ridiculous, Isabel. Dogs are awesome! You can take them hunting and fishing. They can guard your house. Cats are stupid and boring.

Isabel: Cats are not stupid! You don't really think that! When we lived in Bolivia, you loved Mr. and Mrs. Portales's cat! You petted it all the time! Why are you so against cats all of a sudden?

Andrew: I'm not against cats. I just love dogs more. Wait . . . we're doing it again, aren't we? We're arguing in a circle.

Isabel: Good point. We need to figure out a clear point to discuss.

Discuss

What statements in this argument are not propositions?

Discuss

Which statements are propositions but are probably too broad, narrow, or irrelevant to serve as the focus of the debate?

Change

Andrew and Isabel are trying to decide which pet they should get. Turn this topic into a proposition that they can actually argue or discuss.

Consider

What term might be unclear in the proposition you just proposed? What word(s) could you substitute for this term to improve your proposition and make it less vague?

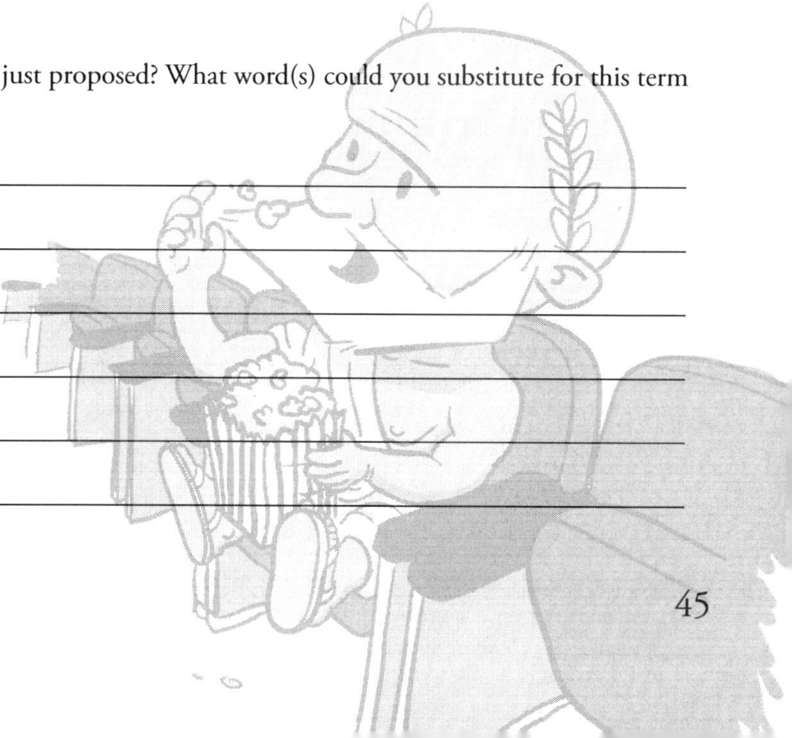

Building Copiousness

Review

Review your old quotes.

Practice

Practice saying the quotes to someone in your class, or practice writing them down on paper.

Memorize

Memorize your new quote:

> Injustice anywhere is a threat to justice everywhere.
>
> —Martin Luther King Jr.[4]

Everyday Debate

Develop

In the "Building Copiousness" section, you memorized the quote from Martin Luther King Jr., "Injustice anywhere is a threat to justice everywhere." In addition, in the last chapter, you practiced developing arguments using the Toulmin model. Use this model to develop arguments for and against this statement. Then, once again, share your arguments with three of your classmates.

Possible arguments *for* this statement:

When we allow injustice to occur in other places and to other people, we set a precedent that could allow this injustice to return to us.

If we don't help others who suffer injustice, they won't help us.

Injustice, like disease, feeds off of itself and grows stronger the longer it is allowed to flourish.

Possible arguments *against* this statement:

There are many injustices that never spread to other people.

Some people bring injustice upon themselves and it stops with them.

Some injustice is a part of life and does not necessarily spread to other places.

---

4. Susan Ratcliffe, ed., *Oxford Dictionary of Quotations by Subject*, 2nd ed. (Oxford: Oxford University Press, 2010), 265.

Learning from the Masters

Observe

Because the 2008 presidential race was such a historic race, political debates that went on during this time are great examples to watch and discuss. Watch a presidential debate between Senator McCain and the then-Senator Obama (Link 5-1).

Evaluate

Jot down the strengths and weaknesses of each speaker. Be ready to explain what you perceive to be strengths and weaknesses.

The Big Debate: Gun Control

Develop

Throughout this book, you will continue to explore two ongoing debates: Andrew and Isabel's pet debate, and Josh and Christy's capital punishment debate. As you watch how they develop arguments for their respective sides, you will have a chance to go through the same processes to develop arguments for a big debate that you will have at the end of this book: gun control. This is an extremely contentious issue in our culture today.

Take a few minutes to list several different resolutions people could debate related to gun control:

Chapter 6

Overview of a Debate

> IF WE CANNOT END NOW OUR DIFFERENCES, AT LEAST WE CAN HELP MAKE THE WORLD SAFE FOR DIVERSITY.
> —JOHN F. KENNEDY[1]

Structure of a Debate

By now you are probably gaining a strong sense of the difference between formal and informal debate. Before diving into your next lesson, review the main differences between the two types of debate: Informal debate is a debate that can take place anywhere—in your home, at work, in the car, in a coffee shop, or while eating lunch with your friends. It is usually free-flowing. That is, with informal debate, people take turns talking about their opinions. They might all talk a fairly equal amount, or one person could dominate the conversation more than the other person, or people, in the conversation. There is no time limit on an informal debate, and in most cases no judge is involved. Alternatively, formal debate is a structured event that could take place on the news, in a classroom, at a public event (e.g., college colloquium, church gathering), or at a national debate tournament. A formal debate can follow many different formats, but it typically has a specific order in which speakers talk, and speakers customarily have a time limit. Because formal debates are more structured than informal debates, it may be helpful for you to learn about the structure of formal debates first and then examine how you can apply this knowledge to informal debates.

There are many different formal debate structures that people have developed throughout history and in different countries. Furthermore, there are various common debate structures depending on whether you are in middle school, high school, or college. However, regardless of which structure you use, there are some universal elements to almost every debate—specifically, the affirmative and negative presentations, and the affirmative and negative rebuttals. (The **affirmative presentation** is the time in a debate when the affirmative side presents the arguments in favor of the resolution; the **negative presentation** is when the negative side presents the arguments against the resolution. The rebuttal is when both the affirmative and negative sides critique each other's arguments.) For instance, a conventional order for a basic debate might be formatted as follows:

Affirmative arguments

Negative arguments

Affirmative rebuttals

Negative rebuttals[2]

---

1. Susan Ratcliffe, *Oxford Dictionary of Quotations by Subject*, 2nd ed. (Oxford: Oxford University Press, 2010), 436.
2. Kate Shuster and John Meany, *Speak Out! Debate and Public Speaking in the Middle Grades* (New York: International Debate Education Association, 2005), 48.

A critical aspect of arguing your point well is the issue of the **burden of proof**. A burden of proof means that one particular side in a debate has the responsibility to prove something in order to succeed. The other side in such a debate has the advantage of representing the **status quo**, or the way things are. For example, in the American legal system, defendants accused of crimes are presumed innocent until proven guilty. Therefore, the prosecution bears the burden of proving the defendant's guilt—which, if not done, results in a decision for the defendant. In everyday informal debates, arguing for a position not commonly held typically bears the burden of proof. If Josh argues that the Tooth Fairy exists and is especially fond of front teeth, it is on him to prove this uncommon claim. (It is important to recognize that, informally, the person who is responsible for assuming the burden of proof depends on the community in which the argument takes place. If Christy argues that the Tooth Fairy does not exist with a group of five-year-olds at a typical American preschool, then she might bear the burden of proof.) Beyond the ever-present need to offer proof for the claims you make, in competitive debates—regardless of the side you take—any special burden of proof given to one side or the other will be specified by its particular rules.

One thing that you should know is that while some debate structures follow this basic pattern, other debate formats add a second round of affirmative and negative arguments, and a second round of affirmative and negative rebuttals. (The rebuttal is the time when you refute your opponent's argument by showing flaws in his research or reasoning.) In addition, some debate structures add another segment to the debate: **cross-examination**, which is when both the affirmative and negative sides ask each other questions to clarify points and expose weaknesses in the opposition's arguments. Mr. Bennet, coach of our debaters Christy and Josh, decides that they should have a cross-examination round in their debate. Therefore, Christy and Josh need to prepare for an argument session, a cross-examination session, and a rebuttal session. These are the most common elements of any debate format. Occasionally, a particular debate organization may change the names of these elements or combine elements; however, during any debate, speakers usually present their views and then have some time when the other side (or audience members) can challenge those views.

Different debate structures allot different time lengths to each of these segments. It's fairly common for the affirmative and negative argument section to run approximately six to eight minutes, and for the rebuttal session to last from three to five minutes. If the debate format contains a cross-examination time, it is common for this to last about two to four minutes. However, note that there are no set, written-in-stone rules for debate. It is the people who organize the specific debate who set the rules for the format and the time length of the segments. Therefore, if you are engaged in a formal debate, you should find out the particular format and time length in advance.

Checking In on Christy and Josh

Let's take a look at what debaters Christy and Josh will do in each part of their debate to help you better understand what takes place at each stage. They begin with the affirmative and negative presentation. Since Christy is the affirmative side, she goes first. That is, in the first segment of the debate, she will present her arguments that affirm the debate resolution: Capital punishment is ethical, and it deters crime. All of her arguments, therefore, should either prove why capital punishment is ethical, or they should show that it does deter crime. Josh is the negative side, which means he denies the resolution. He will be arguing that capital punishment is not ethical, and it does not deter crime.

As Christy and Josh investigate this topic, they will likely learn a lot about each other's positions, and if they do their research well, they will not only gain knowledge of each other's main arguments, but also glean information that critiques or disproves those arguments. Critiquing the arguments of the opposition is certainly a very important side of debate; however, it is often better to save this critique for the rebuttal rather than for the segment in which a person argues for his side. This is because your case will be stronger if you spend your argument time explaining why your position is true than it would be if you spend your time arguing why your opponent's position is false. For example, if two people were arguing about the existence of God, it would be odd if the person arguing for God's existence failed to explain why she believed God exists and, instead, spent all of her time showing why arguments against God's existence are poor arguments. This would make it appear that she actually didn't have any good arguments to support her case and was, therefore, arguing by tearing down the opposition.

Checking In on Isabel and Andrew

As another example, consider Isabel and Andrew's family pet debate. Andrew and Isabel ultimately decide to argue the following proposition: Cats are a more practical pet for our family than dogs. Isabel will argue the affirmative side, and Andrew will argue the negative side. It would be counterproductive if Isabel decides to spend most of her time arguing why dogs *are not* the most practical pet, rather than proving why cats *are* the most practical pet. By the same token, Andrew should spend most of his time developing arguments that show dogs *are* practical pets, rather than why cats *aren't* practical pets. Whether you are arguing for the affirmative or negative side, spend your presentation time arguing why your case is true, rather than arguing why the opponent's case is false.

Cross-Examination

Now that we have seen how Andrew and Isabel are doing on their debate, let's check on Josh and Christy's progress. After Josh and Christy present their main arguments, they will have a cross-examination round. The purpose of a cross-examination round is twofold. First, you want to ask about any arguments or parts of the speech that you didn't hear (or understand) clearly. After all, your rebuttal will be based on the opposition's arguments. Therefore, it is crucial that you know exactly what those arguments are, or you will not be able to rebut them. Clarification is one purpose of the cross-examination segment of the debate. The second purpose is exposure of weaknesses in the opposition's arguments. You can use questions skillfully to point out unsupported claims, weak evidence, or errors in reasoning. You will learn how to do this later. Right now, just keep in mind that the purpose of cross-examination is to clarify the opponent's arguments in your mind and then undermine them by exposing weaknesses through questions.

You can probably imagine that in order to cross-examine your opponent well, you need to be able to remember what they said. In order to do this, it is wise for you to take notes on your opponent's arguments during their presentation. Many people who participate in formal debates call this **flowing an argument**. When you flow an opponent's argument, you create a brief outline of his key claims and the evidence he uses to support these claims.[3] As you can imagine, flowing a person's arguments can highlight weaknesses in evidence or reasoning (you will learn how to spot these weaknesses later). It is interesting to note that sometimes a person's argument can sound great on the surface, but when you flow it, you find that the actual evidence supporting the claim is weak and insubstantial. Therefore, whenever you are listening to an opponent's arguments in a formal debate, always flow the argument, for this will help you cross-examine or rebut the argument more effectively. It is unlikely that you would flow an informal debate (such as one that occurs in a coffee shop or at a dinner table) by writing down the arguments, but it is certainly good to keep track of them mentally by listening for the claim your opponent is making and remembering the points of evidence she uses to support the claim.

A common mistake in these debates is to assume that a flaw in your opponent's argument (or lack of presented evidence that is contrary to yours) proves that your own argument is inherently correct. This is a fallacy called ***argumentum ad ignorantiam***, or "appeal to ignorance." For instance, if Isabel claims that cats are superior pets to dogs because Andrew (or anyone else) has failed to present satisfactory evidence otherwise, she relies on ignorance, or lack of knowledge, as her argument rather than positively presenting satisfactory arguments or evidence of her own for the proposition.

3. Ralph Janikowsky (upper school principal, teacher, and debate coach at Rockbridge Academy, Millersville, MD), in discussion with the author, summer 2009; Clint Jones, PhD (director of debate at Transylvania University, Lexington, KY), in discussion with the author, fall 2013.

Rebuttal

The last segment of the debate is the rebuttal. The word ***rebuttal*** means "to drive or beat back."[4] This presents a pretty accurate picture of the purpose of rebuttals. In the rebuttal segment of a debate, your goal is to beat back the opponent's arguments by showing flaws in his research or reasoning, or by presenting counterevidence that trumps (i.e., is stronger than) his evidence. As you can already see, there is certainly an element of **impromptu**—that is, on-the-spot, off-the-top-of-your-head—thinking and speaking in debate. The rebuttal sessions are always impromptu; after all, you don't always know what arguments your opposition will bring against you and therefore you cannot prepare your exact response in advance. You must be ready to respond to a range of different arguments.

4. *Webster's Ninth New Collegiate Dictionary*, s.v. "rebuttal."

Although the rebuttal session always has an element of surprise, it is not as wide-open as it may seem, and there are several ways that you can prepare for it. First, the most important thing to realize is that, for any particular topic you will debate, there will be five or six incredibly common arguments that people regularly make in favor of the topic, and five or six common arguments people frequently make against it. For example, here are some of the most routine arguments for capital punishment: Capital punishment is just; capital punishment deters crime; capital punishment has been used widely throughout history and in all civilizations; most ethical and religious systems allow some form of capital punishment; most people are in favor of capital punishment for at least some crimes. Here are some of the most common arguments people use who argue against capital punishment: Capital punishment is inhumane; most progressive civilizations have abolished capital punishment; capital punishment increases crime through the brutalization effect; capital punishment is unjust because it targets the poor and disadvantaged. If you read several basic, introductory articles or encyclopedia entries about your topic, you will see a handful of arguments pop up consistently. (You will learn more about basic research strategies later.) In this way, although you do not know exactly which argument(s) your opposition will make, you can gain a relatively clear idea of the ones she is likely to make, and you can prepare a general critique of these types of arguments. In chapter twenty-three, you will learn about the most common ways you can critique arguments.

Furthermore, if you do your research well, you will notice familiar ways that people critique or disprove the arguments on either side of a topic. This is beneficial for you because, in one sense, people have already done the rebuttal work for you. In other words, they have constructed good arguments against the opposition. All you have to do is become familiar with the usual ways people disprove the opposing side of the topic. Be sure to do your own thinking as well, rather than just relying on everyone else's thinking all of the time. This is where logic comes in. In some of the following chapters, you will learn not only how to construct solid logical arguments but also how to detect and prevent the most common argument pitfalls (logical fallacies) that people make when they argue and debate. If you do your research, become familiar with the key opposing arguments, and have a basic understanding of logic, you will readily find ways to rebut your oppositions' arguments. Rebuttal is a matter of sound research, sensible listening skills, and careful, logical thinking.

Cross-Examination and Rebuttal in Informal Debates

As noted at the beginning of the chapter, informal debates are, generally speaking, loosely organized, and their format is largely directed by the interests and personalities of the people involved, as well as by the environment in which the informal debate is occurring. Imagine that Andrew and Isabel are eating dinner with their mom and dad, and the family has a debate about where they should go on their next family vacation. Here is how their conversation might develop:

Dad: Kids, your mom and I have some good news. We have some extra money in the family budget this year, and we think it would be good to go on a special family vacation this summer. After all, in only a few years, you will be graduating from high school and going to college, and it will be a lot harder to go on family vacations together. Your mom and I had some ideas about where we could go, but we were wondering if you had any ideas.

Isabel: I would love to go back to Bolivia. I really miss all my friends there. It would be great to see them again.

Andrew: But Isabel, that wouldn't feel like a real vacation because we lived there. It would kind of be like going home. I miss my friends, too, but I think we should go on a vacation to a place we've never been before—you know, broaden our horizons, learn new things!

Mom: Did you have any places in mind, Andrew? By the way, Andrew and Isabel, we have cookies and ice cream for dessert. Would you care for any?

Isabel: I'd love a cookie.

Andrew: I'll have ice cream—and if it's that chocolate–peanut butter stuff, I want loads! That stuff's amazing! I think we should go somewhere in the United States. After all, we've lived abroad so much that we haven't actually seen a lot of interesting places right here in this country. I think we should go to Alaska. I hear it's unbelievably beautiful!

Isabel: Alaska would be cool, but I've always wanted to go to Washington, DC, and that would definitely be a learning experience. I'd like to learn more about our government.

Dad: *(hears car horn honking loudly outside)* Is that for one of you? I didn't know you were going out tonight.

Andrew: No, that's one of our neighbor Jeff's friends. He does that all the time. I don't know why he can't just walk to the door.

Isabel: Maybe he's been eating extra helpings of chocolate–peanut butter ice cream.

Andrew: Very funny, Isabel. Going to a famous city would be fun. DC would be cool, but if we were going to go to a big city, I'd rather go to Portland, Oregon. There's really interesting culture there. There are also great historic sites, including Fort Vancouver. I've always wanted to see that. Plus, there's beautiful countryside to explore not too far from the city. That way, you get the best of both worlds.

Isabel: But Oregon is so far away. I'm concerned that it would be exhausting just getting there.

Mom: Well, we wouldn't have to drive. There is an excellent public transit system, so we could walk, take the bus, or even ride the MAX light rail. Plus, if we tire of the city, we could head out to the country, as Andrew mentioned. I think Oregon would be a wonderful choice!

Isabel: Yeah, I suppose it would be. It does have a little bit of something for everyone.

Dad: Oregon it is! That sounds like a fun vacation.

Note that with this informal debate, at times the argumentation, cross-examination, and rebuttal sessions tended to overlap. That is, one person shared an idea, and then another person asked a question or critiqued the idea. For example, Isabel first argued for going on a vacation to Bolivia, but then Andrew rebutted this by pointing out that it wouldn't truly feel like a real vacation. Andrew's mom then asked him if he had any specific vacation ideas, and Andrew proposed Alaska. The informal debate continued in this manner—someone would make an argument for one vacation spot, and then another person would critique that idea and present a counteridea. This informal debate is a great example of a very natural, free-flowing debate. It was interrupted by jokes, commentary about dessert, and a loudly honking car horn. In addition, this debate was very short, but it easily could have lasted for several days if Andrew, Isabel, and their parents had not been able to reach a consensus.

You can imagine that most informal debates will proceed like this. For example, let's say that two people are debating the existence of God in a coffee shop. One person may talk more than another. They might spend most of their time discussing just one argument for or against the existence of God, or they could possibly cover a variety of arguments. Furthermore, the discussion could be interrupted by one or both of the people in the debate placing food orders, purchasing coffee refills, or answering their cell phones. Consider Andrew and Isabel's informal cat and dog debate. Both Andrew and Isabel were on a debate team in their last school in Bolivia, so even though their debate is an informal one, in this ongoing pet debate they will still intuitively incorporate some of the formal debate elements and strategies they've learned. The siblings will certainly present arguments, ask each other questions, and rebut each other's arguments. However, these specific elements of their discussion will likely overlap rather than being formal, distinct sections in their discussion, and the debate will probably continue over several days. The point is, when you want to have an effective informal debate that thoroughly explores an idea, the people involved should both present arguments and critique opposing arguments—the main difference is that the way they do this will be looser and more unstructured than it would be in a formal debate.

Debate formats definitely vary, depending on the type of debate and the people who are organizing it. Nevertheless, it is common for every formal debate to have, at the least, the following elements: affirmative arguments, negative arguments, and affirmative and negative rebuttals. Many formal debates also include a cross-examination segment. Informal debates often have these elements as well, but they take a more fluid form and regularly overlap. Now that you have an idea of how a debate is structured, you will spend some time in the next chapter examining how to gather research for your topic.

Review Exercises

Define

Give an appropriate definition for each of the following terms:

1. Affirmative presentation:

____

____

____

2. Negative presentation:

3. Rebuttal:

4. Cross-examination:

5. Flowing an argument:

Discuss

Why should you use your presentation time to make your arguments?

Building Copiousness

Review

Review your old quotes.

Practice

Practice saying the quotes to someone in your class, or practice writing them down on paper.

Memorize

Memorize your new quote:

> It is better that ten guilty persons escape than one innocent suffer.
>
> —William Blackstone[5]

Everyday Debate

Develop

Develop arguments for and against this quote (resolution):

> A corrupt government will not endure.
>
> —Shelly Johnson

Rebuttal and Counterexample

Once you develop your arguments, tell your best argument *for each side* of the argument to your partner and then listen to your partner's arguments. Once you both have shared arguments for and against this quote, take a few minutes to contemplate ways to rebut each argument. One of the most common methods used to accomplish this is to think of a counterexample. For instance, let's say your neighbor argues that a corrupt government cannot last because eventually the people in the kingdom will rebel. Can you provide a counterexample of a corrupt government whose citizens did not rebel? If your partner argues that rulers of corrupt governments often hold great power over their subjects through fear and intimidation, think of a counterexample of a ruler of a corrupt government who seemed very powerful and ruled through intimidation but was eventually overthrown or assassinated.

5. Ratcliffe, *Oxford Dictionary of Quotations by Subject*, 265.

Learning from the Masters

Observe

One of the most debated topics of history and our times is the existence of God. A famous debate between philosopher Daniel Dennett and writer and cultural critic Dinesh D'Souza took place over this specific topic. The resolution that Dennett and D'Souza debated is this: Religion is a man-made invention. Watch the first part of this debate in which Dennett presents his arguments (Link 6-1), and then discuss the strengths and weaknesses of Dennett's presentation.

The Big Debate: Gun Control

List

1. To help you prepare for the gun control debate, first read Wikipedia's "Gun Control" entry.[6] From what you find in the entry, list at least two arguments for gun control, and two against it.

Provide arguments *for* gun control:

a. ____

b. ____

6. *Wikipedia*, s.v. "Overview of Gun Laws by Nation," last modified April 2, 2014, http://en.wikipedia.org/wiki/Gun_control.

PROVIDE ARGUMENTS *AGAINST* GUN CONTROL:

a. ______________________________

____

____

____

____

b. ______________________________

____

____

____

____

2. In addition, list four Internet sources on gun control or gun-related issues that you find at the end of the Wikipedia article (in the "External Links" section).

a. ______________________________

____

b. ______________________________

____

c. ______________________________

____

d. ______________________________

____

Chapter 7

External Resources

TRUTH, LIKE A TORCH, THE MORE IT'S SHOOK IT SHINES.
—WILLIAM HAMILTON[1]

Beginning Research

Once you know your debate topic, your debate format, and the particular side of the topic for which you will argue (affirmative or negative), it's time to start gathering your arguments. In the last chapter, you learned that to do well in a debate, you should gain familiarity not only with arguments that support your side but also with arguments that support the opposition's side. After all, if you don't know what these arguments are, you cannot critique them. Therefore, you need to conduct your research in a way that ensures you develop a well-rounded understanding of both sides of the arguments. For some people, researching can be an overwhelming task. After all, whenever you use a search engine to find information about a term on the computer, you come up with—literally—thousands of entries. How do you know which ones are helpful or worthwhile? When you go to the library, sometimes it is difficult to know the quickest way to find the resources you need and how to best organize them once found. In this chapter, you will learn helpful strategies for locating sources, finding arguments in these sources, and organizing this information once it is obtained.

First, note that you will save yourself a lot of hassle if you follow this simple principle at the beginning of your research: *Read a little to find out what you need to read in-depth*. Remember that when you are debating (and when you are doing any kind of persuasive research, for that matter), one of your primary goals is to gain familiarity with the key arguments on both sides of the issue. However, if you know nothing about the topic of the debate, you wouldn't even know what these arguments are, on either side of the issue, in order to research them. In this situation, it would be difficult, if not impossible, to know which books or articles would provide the information needed to understand both sides of the issue. Therefore, when beginning your research, it is ideal to first locate and read a short article that summarizes these key arguments for you.

Tracking Down Sources

Now I'm going to tell you something that may surprise you: Wikipedia is often a great place to find this type of article. Don't get me wrong—I am *not* telling you that Wikipedia is a great source to cite in your paper. In fact, generally speaking, you should never cite Wikipedia as a source in your research arguments because Wikipedia is not considered a credible or authoritative source. Wikipedia is not carefully scrutinized and edited by a trained editorial team in the same manner as is done for

1. Susan Ratcliffe, *Oxford Dictionary of Quotations by Subject*, 2nd ed. (Oxford: Oxford University Press, 2010), 487.

published works such as scholarly periodical articles, books, or regular encyclopedia articles. There are no identifiable persons who are accountable for the accuracy of the information presented on Wikipedia. Therefore, while many Wikipedia articles may be accurate and informative, it is possible for some to contain significant factual error. By and large, teachers and professors consider Wikipedia to be an unreliable source for information. Notice that I am *not* advocating that you use it as a legitimate source. Instead, I am advocating that you use it to *find* legitimate sources.

There are two reasons why it is usually a good idea to read a Wikipedia article to help you find out what you should further read to research your topic: First, many Wikipedia articles, especially those on important cultural issues, significant people, or major events, have a great deal of information organized in a user-friendly manner (this is the Internet, after all—people use it to find information quickly). Mr. Bennet, Josh and Christy's debate coach, encouraged both students to read Wikipedia's "Capital Punishment" entry to gain the big picture of their topic. Josh and Christy found an introduction to the basic topic of capital punishment at the beginning of the entry, and then they saw a box (the "Contents" box) that contained the outline of the whole article, including all of the subjects contained within it.

Most Wikipedia articles are organized in the same way.

Each article has a brief introduction, and then it has an outline that gives an overview. Once she and Josh had looked at this outline, Christy said, "I think the first part will be useful. I must get a better idea of how capital punishment has been used through history, and how it is used today."

"Yeah," Josh answered, "but we are just focusing on capital punishment in the United States, so we probably don't need to read all of that stuff about capital punishment in Iran and Somalia. Oh, and I think that the 'Controversy and Debate' section will be valuable. This is probably where we can read brief explanations of both sides of the issue, which Mr. Bennet told us we should do."

Christy responded, "I also think we should look at what all of the different religions think about capital punishment, because one of the aspects of capital punishment we are examining is whether it is ethical. So that would likely be good to read."

As you read through the Wikipedia article for your topic, you will notice the second helpful feature of Wikipedia articles. Most Wikipedia articles contain words or phrases that are in blue type (shown as underlined below), rather than the standard black, which signals a link to other Wikipedia articles that can provide an overview of the key topics on each side. For instance, when Josh and Christy reached the part of the article entitled "Controversy and Debate," they read the following summary:

> Advocates of the death penalty argue that it deters crime, is a good tool for police and prosecutors (in plea bargaining for example), makes sure that convicted criminals do not offend again and is a just penalty for atrocious crimes such as child murders, serial killers or torture murderers. Opponents of capital punishment argue that not all people affected by murder desire a death penalty, that execution discriminates against minorities and the poor, and that it encourages a "culture of violence" and that it violates human rights.[2]

2. *Wikipedia*, s.v. "Capital Punishment," last modified November 5, 2015, http://en.wikipedia.org/wiki/Capital_punishment#Controversy_and_debate.

They were excited about finding this because it gave them a clear, succinct overview of the arguments on both sides. Plus, there were a few links (words in blue type) to other Wikipedia articles they could read. The benefit of Wikipedia articles is that if you are doing research on any controversial topic, Wikipedia will likely have an article that offers a decent overview of the topic in general, a succinct summary of the views on both sides, and further articles or books to read that can give you background information on both sides of the argument.

As we found in chapter 6, there is a further benefit to Wikipedia—at the end of almost every Wikipedia article, there is a heading called "External Sources," which is a listing of other sources available, often locatable on the Internet, about this topic. Usually, many of the sources listed in this section are good, legitimate sources (you will learn more about how to determine this later in this chapter), and there are often links you can click to go straight to them. Although you will still need to double-check the legitimacy of these Web sources, normally they are valid ones that you can cite in your research.

The great thing about the "External Sources" section of a Wikipedia article is that it provides an at-a-glance list of some of the most informative, topic-specific Internet sources available. For example, at the end of the article on capital punishment, Josh and Christy found two very helpful lists (with links) of **external sources**: those in favor of capital punishment and those against it. Each list had about ten sources and saved these two researchers hours of wading through myriad Internet sources. The following is a sample of what was listed:

Opposing

- World Coalition Against the Death Penalty
- Death Watch International: International anti-death penalty campaign group
- Campaign to End the Death Penalty
- Anti-Death Penalty Information: includes a monthly watchlist of upcoming executions and death penalty statistics for the United States.
- The Death Penalty Information Center: Statistical information and studies
- Amnesty International—Abolish the death penalty Campaign: Human Rights organisation

In favor

- The REAL Death Penalty in the US: A Review
- Studies showing the death penalty saves lives
- Criminal Justice Legal Foundation
- Keep life without parole and death penalty intact
- Why the death penalty is needed
- Pro Death Penalty.com[3]

As you can see, these external sources will be advantageous for Josh and Christy in developing their arguments, and you also will certainly want to check Wikipedia's external source listings for your topic.

You may be asking the following question: *What if my topic doesn't have a Wikipedia article on it?* The simple answer is this: Use an encyclopedia. You may already have an encyclopedia set in your home. If you don't have a current encyclopedia, however, the local library will have several sets—and the librarians there will be able to assist you with finding reference books and encyclopedias for your research. Your best bet is to find and read an article about your debate topic in one of these encyclopedias to get a general overview of the subject matter. As an example, Isabel and Andrew could not find a Wikipedia article on pets because their Internet was down, but they were able to locate an article in their *World Book Encyclopedia* at home. Right at the beginning of this article, they read the following paragraph:

> The kind of home you live in, and where you live, have much to do with the kind of pet you choose. Dogs, cats, birds, and fish are easy to care for in almost any kind of home. Before choosing a dog as a pet, you should consider the size of both your home and the dog.
>
> For example, a collie needs a large home with a big yard for exercise. If you live in an apartment, you should be sure pets are allowed. Then choose a small dog, such as a cocker spaniel. A small dog can get most of its exercise by playing around the house, and needs only short walks outside for fresh air.
>
> Cats do not depend on their masters as much as dogs do. Many persons prefer them for

3. *Wikipedia*, s.v. "Capital Punishment."

> this reason. They are quieter and gentler than dogs. But they, too, need outdoor exercise. On pleasant days, a cat can run around in a yard. Cats should always be brought inside at night.[4]

Although Isabel and Andrew already had this basic idea about pets, this summary was beneficial in helping them think through the advantages and disadvantages of owning a cat or a dog. Furthermore, the article also gave information about choosing a pet, training a pet, and taking care of a pet, which encouraged them to consider the different aspects of owning a pet.

In addition, at the end of the encyclopedia article, Andrew and Isabel found a list of other articles related to pets, and they found two articles specific to cats and dogs, as well as recommended books, both basic and complex. One great aspect of encyclopedia articles is that, like Wikipedia, at the end they often include a list of related articles or books for further reading on the topic. When you research topics for your debates, be sure to read these related sources to broaden your understanding of your topics. Andrew and Isabel decided to go to their local library and see if they could find any of the sources listed to conduct a little more research on this issue.

Head to the Library!

Like Andrew and Isabel, you will want to take your recommended reading list to the library to do some research. (You will find out more on how to tackle library research below.) Having this list on hand will make your search much easier. For instance, when Christy and Josh were researching their topic in their *World Book Encyclopedia* at home, they found two books listed at the end of the entry that sounded intriguing. They wrote the titles down and decided to look for them on their trip to the local public library. While reading both a Wikipedia article and a basic encyclopedia entry on your topic is a great start, reading several basic articles and subject-specific books about your topic will give you an even deeper comprehension of, and better familiarity with, the topics on each side of the issue. In addition, you will find that your local library may have online catalogues or interlibrary loan systems that allow you to find books that are not at your library but are available at others. Interlibrary loan can be an invaluable tool for allowing you find the exact books you need for your research.

Now you have accomplished the first research step: You have conducted enough preliminary research to know what you now need to research more extensively. At this point in the process, you should have a fairly clear idea of the key arguments on each side of your topic. This doesn't mean that you know how to explain, or give evidence supporting, the arguments. However, you know what the basic arguments are about. This will assist you in further research. Additionally, you have likely discovered several key terms related to your debate. For example, as Christy and Josh read basic articles about capital punishment, the following words kept popping up in their research: "deterrence," "retribution," "brutalization," "discrimination," "innocent victims," and "right to life." When you begin to recognize familiar terms that recur in your initial basic reading, keep these terms in mind. These are terms that are related to specific arguments on either side.

When you grasp some of the basic arguments and terms of your topic, you are in an excellent position to move to the next step of research: looking for more books, articles, and Internet sources to grow your comprehension of the arguments.

One of the best places to go for this next phase of research is, of course, the library. In your debate, you will need to be both familiar with arguments that other people have made about a topic and able to form your own arguments. You will learn to craft your own arguments in the following chapters, but right now your focus is honing your research skills to find what other people have said about the arguments. If you have never been to your local library before, ask a librarian to help you get started. Librarians are happy to help people find books or articles. In fact, if you call ahead, many librarians will gladly give you a tour of the different print resources, as well as show you methods for finding information, such as the library catalog, searchable databases, and other tools for finding helpful magazine articles. Librarians want the library to be utilized well, so don't be afraid to ask questions!

4. Maxwell Riddle, "Pets," *World Book Encyclopedia* (Chicago: World Book, 1992), 319.

Each library has an organized catalog system that you can use to locate books and other works in its collection—most library catalogs are accessible online via a computer. Find an open computer at the library, which is sometimes called a search station, and locate the catalog, which is usually found on the library's home page. To find materials related to your research, type in your topic theme, or key words related to your topic, in the search function in the catalog. You can usually select options to streamline your search, for example, limiting the search to books only, or books published after a certain year. If the library has books related to your topic, the search results will provide you with not only the book titles and author names, but also the call numbers—this is important. Call numbers are necessary to track down the exact books you are looking for quickly, because titles are organized by this numbering system in the book stacks. If you don't know how to use call numbers to find items in the library, just ask your librarian. Once you successfully find a few books using this method, you'll find it becomes easier to research and quickly locate materials at your library.

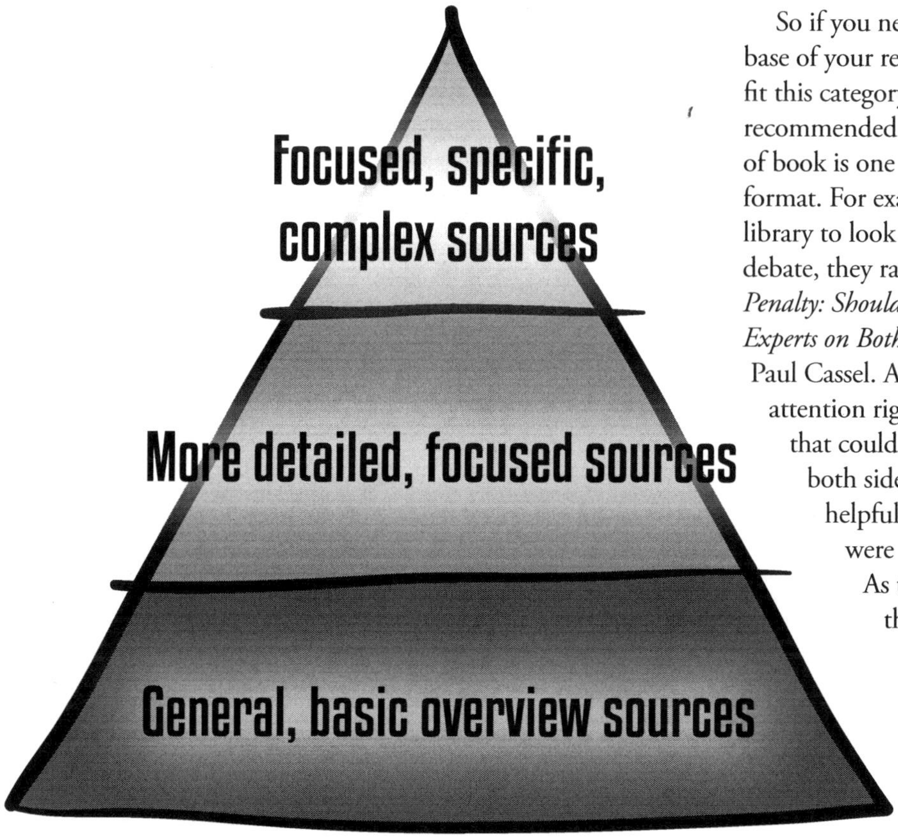

The Research Pyramid

For most students, finding books is the easy part; knowing which ones to use is the hard part. Here are a few tips to help you find books that will work well for you in your debate: First, think of the research-gathering process in terms of a pyramid. The base of your pyramid is very wide. The base of your research should be wide, too—this means you should try to find a lot of books to give you a general, basic overview of your topic. This is similar to what you did when you read the Wikipedia or encyclopedia articles. You read a broad overview of your topic in order to help you grasp its foundational elements. This is what you want to do with your books, and because books contain more information, they will help you fill in the foundation of your research pyramid a little more. The more you learn, generally, about your topic, the stronger your foundation will be. You can then narrow your research to more detailed, focused sources. As you continue to fill in the foundation of your research pyramid, you can finally move to focused, specific, complex sources, which will form the top of your pyramid.

So if you need to find general books to form the base of your research, how do you know which books fit this category? There are two types of books that are recommended at this stage of your research. The first type of book is one that is written, more or less, in a debate format. For example, when Josh and Christy went to the library to look for books for their capital punishment debate, they ran across this book: *Debating the Death Penalty: Should America Have Capital Punishment? The Experts on Both Sides Make Their Case* by Hugo Bedau and Paul Cassel. As you can imagine, this book caught their attention right away because it appeared to be a book that could easily help them grasp the arguments on both sides of the topic. Because this book was so helpful to their case, they decided to see if there were any other books structured in this way.

As they looked through the rest of the books that their library search brought up in the library catalog, they found two other books that appeared to be formatted like a debate: *Does Capital Punishment Deter Crime? (At Issue Series)* edited by Amy Marcaccio Keyzer and *The Death*

Penalty and the Disadvantaged (Ideas in Conflict) by Gary E. McCuen. You should be able to find a book for your topic that is structured in a debate format. This is the first type of book you should look for to fill in the foundation of your research pyramid because such books often present a basic view of the arguments on both sides of an issue.

The second type of book that can help you round out the base of your research pyramid is one from the juvenile section, or the young adult section, on your topic. It may seem odd for a middle or high school student to look at children's books for research. You may or may not want to cite a source from the juvenile section; however, bear in mind that a juvenile book will be an excellent resource for a *general* look at your topic, and it will help you determine what you need to research further. Some library systems allow you to easily identify juvenile books because in the system they have a "J" at the beginning of the call number. Not all libraries put a "J" at the beginning of juvenile books, however. Therefore, if you would like to find the juvenile books on your particular topic at your library, ask your librarian to show you how you can locate these sources.

When Christy and Josh went to the Lexington Public Library and searched the database, they found the following book in the juvenile section: *Capital Punishment* by Paul Almonte and Theresa Desmond. This book was quite useful because it presented an overview of the evidence both for and against capital punishment. Furthermore, it accomplished this in a basic manner that children and young adults (and, therefore, adults) could easily understand. If you start your research by looking at books from the juvenile and young adult sections that present an overview of both sides of the debate, you will strengthen the base of your research pyramid.

Finding the Useful Parts

Once you find foundational books for your topic, what should you do with them? Should you read the books in their entirety? If they are short and interesting, and you really want to read them, this is fine to do—but reading books from beginning to end just to research information for a debate usually isn't necessary (and is usually not be the best use of your research time). Instead, read the table of contents to find which parts of these books will benefit your research. You may be wondering, *How do I know which portions of a book will be most helpful?* The best sections are the ones that are easy to understand, that interest you the most, and that help you gain a better understanding of the key arguments on both sides of the debates.

Once you find these easiest, most interesting, and most informative sections, it is a good idea to spend some time skimming them. **Skimming** is a tool you can use to help you quickly find the information you need the most, and it will help you avoid spending a lot of time reading sources that are not helpful to your research project. When you skim a chapter, you move your eyes quickly across sentences and paragraphs, noting the key words and ideas in the sentence, rather than reading the sentences and paragraph in detail. When you skim, you are trying to get a quick, general idea of sentences and paragraphs, rather than a detailed understanding. You can also skim an entire chapter by looking at the section headings within a chapter (many books contain these headings, but not all). It is also often helpful to read the first and last sentences of paragraphs because these sentences often contain the main ideas of the paragraph. Remember, the purpose of skimming is not to remember everything in the book but rather to gain a quick overview of the main ideas and arguments of a book, chapter, or paragraph and whether certain kinds of information are contained there. Once you grasp what key ideas the author is discussing in the section in question, you will better know if you want to spend time exploring the chapter in depth. If the chapter contains the information you need for researching your topic, then you can read it more in detail. If the chapter does not, you can move on to another chapter.

Another tool that can help you with skimming your book is the index at the back of the book. The index of a book is a list of key terms, names, and events that show up in the book and on what page they occur. An index can be an invaluable tool because it can help you decide quickly if the information you need for your research is contained in the book you are reading. In other words, the index is a tool that allows you to determine quickly if the book you are looking at will help you in your research.

Let's return now to Josh and Christy and their search for good sources. In the book *Debating the Death Penalty*, Christy and Josh looked in the table of contents and found the following chapters:

1 *Tinkering with Death*
—*Alex Kozinski*

2 *An Abolitionist's Survey of the Death Penalty in America Today*
—*Hugo Adam Bedau*

3 *Why the Death Penalty Is Morally Permissible*
—*Louis P. Pojman*

4 *Close to Death: Reflections on Race and Capital Punishment in America*
—*Bryan Stevenson*

5 *Truth and Consequences: The Penalty of Death*
—*Joshua K. Marquis*

6 *Why the United States Will Join the Rest of the World in Abandoning Capital Punishment*
—*Stephen B. Bright*

7 *In Defense of the Death Penalty*
—*Paul G. Cassell*

8 *"I Must Act"*
—*George Ryan*

In looking at this table of contents, Christy and Josh realized that some chapters were more obviously helpful to them than others. Josh said, "I believe chapters 3, 6, and 7 are the most helpful to us in researching our debate because they talk about the morality of capital punishment and why it should or should not be abolished."

"I agree," Christy replied. "Those chapters definitely look the most helpful. But I'm curious about some of the other chapters, too. For instance, I can't completely tell what chapters 2 and 5 are about from the titles alone, but I have a feeling they might contain valuable information. Why don't you let me skim through them while you are looking for other books?"

Josh agreed, and while he ventured into the main book stacks, Christy sat at a table and skimmed through chapters 2 and 5. To do this, she read the first few paragraphs on the first page of each chapter, as well as the last couple of pages of each chapter, in order to determine the main points of the chapters. Based on those points, she was able to decide whether the chapters warranted further reading and research. Christy found that chapter 2 was a historical look at a supposed movement toward abolition of capital punishment in the world and in America, written from an abolitionist's perspective. In chapter 5, she discovered excellent information in favor of the death penalty written from the point of view of a prosecutor who had worked with many death penalty cases.

Upon Josh's return, she told him, "I'm glad I looked at these chapters more carefully. Chapter 2 really edifies your side of the debate, and chapter 5 supports my side, although we will probably want to read each other's chapters, too. I'm going to quickly scan the rest of the chapters as well, just to make sure that we don't miss anything."

After skimming the other chapters, Christy determined that she and Josh had already found most of the helpful chapters. Chapter 1 was interesting but was more a personal reflection on the death penalty and lacked the hard facts that she and Josh were looking for. Chapter 4 was also interesting and contained fascinating information, but it pertained more to capital punishment and race issues specifically, an area of the capital punishment debate that Christy and Josh could not consider due to the time restraints on their debate. Effectively utilizing the table of contents and the art of skimming helped Josh and Christy find the most useful information as quickly as possible.

Sometimes students make the mistake of assuming that in order to be a good researcher, you must choose the

It may not surprise you that, in the course of a debate, one key aspect is agreeing on what the most important and relevant issues are. If, for instance, Christy and Josh are debating as part of a class at school, they might be evaluated on their grasp of what the judge (in this case, a teacher) considers to be the essential issues. However, in a more competitive or advanced debate format, Christy and Josh might have the flexibility to argue for the significance of points that may not seem important to an issue initially. On one hand, the advantage of arguing down an unforeseen path is that you might catch your opponent off guard on a subject about which they may have had little preparation or thought. On the other hand, there is the potential disadvantage that your opponents could argue, or the judge might think, that your argument or point made is less relevant to the debate topic. It is always essential in a debate to weigh what the most critical issues are. It is also crucial to know and understand *who* decides (or *how* it is decided) what those critical issues are. Are they established by common agreement, a judge, or by one's own arguments? In most debates, it is usually a combination of these that decide the important issues. So consider carefully the range of ideas or topics that could be advantageous for you to be prepared to know and discuss, should the debate take an unexpected turn.

thickest, most incomprehensible and boring books to do your research. This couldn't be further from the truth. In most cases, any given topic has a wide variety of books available, written by a wide variety of people. Some of these books will be more interesting to you or written in such a way that is conducive to the way your brain works. Why not start with these books? Sometimes the reason a book is difficult to comprehend is because it is incredibly technical, and you may not have enough background information yet to understand all of the details in the book. However, if you start with less complex books, or books that are more suited to your personality, you will quickly gain a foundational knowledge of your subject, and then you will be in a better position to move on to more in-depth books later. The more you read and understand about a topic, the more momentum you build and the more easily you are able to comprehend complicated aspects of the subject matter.

Once you have found and skimmed basic books, you can move on to more complex books. Find the next book that looks fairly easy to grasp or understand. These books will be different from the basic books you have been reading. When you look for more complex books, you still want to find books that are interesting and comprehensible to you. However, you also want to find books that are a little longer than the basic books and that have more detailed paragraphs and chapters. Moving on to these more complex books will allow you to build your knowledge base of your subject gradually. Following the same process used for the basic books, look at the table of contents, skim, and read the chapters that help you (and ignore the ones that do not). If the table of contents for a book is daunting and appears incomprehensible, move on to another book that looks more accessible. Keep the pyramid research method in mind.

Both Josh and Christy used the pyramid method when they started by reading the books they found on capital punishment that broadly examined both sides of the debate. After they skimmed the most interesting chapters in these books, both of them found more complex and specific books that they decided to peruse. For example, Josh found the book *The Wrong Men: America's Epidemic of Wrongful Death Row Convictions* by Stanley Cohen, which discussed innocent men sentenced, by accident, to death. Christy found the book *The Death Penalty for Teens: A Pro/Con Issue* by Nancy Day, which discussed

How much do you need to research? Perhaps you're overwhelmed by the idea of researching a topic extensively. Maybe you're shocked by the idea of skimming through a book or article without reading the entire thing. In order to debate, you have to become a crash-course amateur expert about your topic. So what defines how much or how little research you need to do? There are no hard-and-fast rules; however, one important principle required to govern your research is *respect*. In other words, in determining how much research you should do for your debate, ask yourself the following question: *In order to respect my opponents, judges, and the topic at hand, what should I know?*

One way you can show this respect to your opponent is to follow a standard that many people refer to as the **principle of charity**. If you follow the principle of charity, you assume that your opponent is an intelligent, rational, and moral person, and you assume that she has legitimate reasons for believing what she does. The principle of charity does not demand that you accept your opponent's beliefs; it only demands that you assume she has good, though possibly flawed, reasons for what she believes. If you assume the principle of charity in your debates, you will be more likely to take your research seriously because you genuinely will want to know the reasons that compel your intelligent, rational opponent to believe what she does. This will make you a much better debater.

the pros and cons of sentencing teenagers to death. It was good for Josh and Christy to read these books later in their research, rather than at the beginning. These books deal with very specific aspects of capital punishment, and Christy and Josh were able to understand these specific issues better because they had already formed an overall view of the issue of capital punishment. Eventually, you will be able to read books that are very detailed and complicated (these are books at the top of the pyramid) because you have established this groundwork.

How to Evaluate Online Resources

Now you'll learn more about Internet sources. One reason why you were instructed to utilize books first is that many recently published books list viable Internet sources at the back, or at the end of each chapter, that you can consult them for further information. These are usually some of the best Internet sources available on the subject. However, let's say that you want to find your own Internet sources. What are the characteristics of suitable, credible Internet sources? A legitimate site is either written by a professional person or group (i.e., the person or group has professional expertise in the area in which they are writing, and/or have had work edited or reviewed by a professional), or constructed by a person who has included a list of the sources from which he drew the information and facts. Let's consider why each of these characteristics is important for establishing legitimate Internet sources.

First, identify the author of the Internet site and ascertain whether this person or group is a professional with expertise in the area covered on the site. It is important for you to find out what qualifications the author of the site has to confirm the legitimacy of authority on the subject. After all, you and your friends probably have very strong opinions on a number of subjects, for which you could construct a website and about which you could write a bunch of essays or blog entries. However, just because someone has strong opinions on a subject does not mean that what she writes is accurate, logical, or helpful. Therefore, it is vital for you to know about the author of the page, and to verify what authority the person has to write about the matter. In a best-case scenario, the ideal source is an author who has a degree related to, or who has experience working in a field related to, the topic about which he is writing. This demonstrates that he has had significant education, training, and/or experience pertaining to the subject matter about which he writes. In addition, in most cases a reliable author will have written several books or articles about the issue that have been edited and reviewed by other professionals. This adds an extra measure of expertise because the person has spent a significant amount of time researching and considering the subject matter.

It is important to note that many websites are set up by groups rather than by a single person. For instance, as Christy and Josh researched capital punishment, they found a website by a group called Amnesty International, which publishes information and statistics about human rights issues. Christy and Josh also decided to research murder and other crime statistics and came across a website by the Bureau of Justice, which is funded by the federal government. When you find a site that is published by a group, rather than a government, it is acceptable if it is constructed by a professional organization that has expertise in the area you are researching. Amnesty International is a group whose expertise is in human rights issues; therefore, their information on capital punishment is legitimate. The purpose of the Bureau of Justice is to collect data on matters pertaining to crime and the law. Therefore, their information on crime is authoritative. Furthermore, sites set up by professional organizations or groups often employ someone to be responsible for editing or reviewing the work on the site, or they draw their information from professional task forces or academic studies that have been reviewed by editorial boards or task force team members. Websites set up by nonprofit organizations or professional groups are common and can be excellent resources for your research.

It is important to realize that even if people do not have a degree in a subject, have not written a book on the topic, or do not work for an official organization, they can still post a helpful and legitimate site on an issue. For example, imagine a woman named Rebecca whose sister is murdered by a man who is later arrested

and convicted for this crime. Rebecca, who does not have any degree or related job experience in the area of criminal justice or law, becomes personally invested in the issue of capital punishment. Her gut reaction is that this man should pay with his life for the murder of her sister. Yet she is not sure that this is a moral action to take. Therefore, she reads numerous books about capital punishment and interviews other people whose family members have been murdered. Rebecca then constructs a website in which she posts essays and information about murder and capital punishment. She is meticulous in her research and always includes the sources from which she has gained her information. This site can be considered legitimate because Rebecca has accurately cited the sources from which she has gleaned her information and people can check her information to make sure it is valid.

It's important to note that a website created by a nonprofessional, such as the example of Rebecca's site, is more prone to error than a site constructed by a professional group or by person who has had work published about, or has had experience in, the subject area. This is because Rebecca has constructed information based on her own research, rather than based on formal education she has received or professional research she has conducted. In addition, it is likely that her essays are not being reviewed by an outside editor, whereas an author of a book or a professional group will have a book or website editor, or a person responsible for fact checking and editing their content. In addition, a website constructed by a nonprofessional person (i.e., someone who is not an expert or member of a particular profession, sometimes referred to as a **layperson**) such as Rebecca is only as good as its sources. For instance, if Rebecca cited the *National Enquirer* (a celebrity gossip magazine) as a source, this would not be considered an authoritative source and the legitimacy of her website would be in question. Therefore, while it can be acceptable to use sites that contain cited research by laypeople, it is important to note that these sites may have more errors than those organized by professionals, and they may base research on suspect sources.

Taking Good Notes

Another important skill to learn to hone your research skills is how to take excellent notes. As you skim and read your sources to gather information, you will need to take notes on information that you find to support your point. You can record notes on index cards, in paper notebooks, or on the computer. However you document your information, make sure you include four important items: (a) the *title* of the book (including chapter title, if it is an edited volume), or the article name and title of the periodical, or the article title of the website; (b) the *author* and/or editor name(s), or the author or organization name of the website; (c) the *page number* (or numbers) where you found this specific information, if available, or the specific web address; and (d) the *publisher details*—the publisher's name and the year the work was published. It is especially important to accurately record page numbers for any direct quotes you may use later. It is imperative to follow this process to record every source you may use, because one way to build a strong case in debate is to demonstrate that your sources and the authors of those sources have credentials or a great deal of expertise in the area. It will be very hard to accomplish this if you cannot remember from which source you obtained a piece of information. It is also a good idea to photocopy or use your phone to snap a picture of the copyright page of the book you are using, as well as the pages with the passages you are quoting, so that you can go back later and double-check a page number, a publication date, or a term you might have misspelled while taking notes.

As Christy and Josh began to take notes, they compared their note-taking strategies and realized that they did this in very different ways. Josh tended to take notes from one chapter or article at a time in a legal notebook. He would write the important information about the source mentioned above—the title, the author, the page number, and the publishing details. Alternatively, Christy liked to take her notes on index cards, and she preferred to use a system that she had been taught in ninth grade. In fact, her system is used by many people who write research papers. Whenever Christy starts taking notes from a source, she creates an index card for the source—she calls these master source cards her "bibliography cards" (a bibliography is a list of all of the works consulted in writing a research paper or book). She first assigns each bibliography card a number, which she writes in the top right-hand corner (e.g., the card for the first book is marked #1; the card for the second book is #2; the third book is #3, etc.). Then, she writes all of the bibliographic information for her source:

the title, the author, the publishing details, and the page numbers if it is a magazine or periodical article or an article from an encyclopedia.

Whenever Christy wants to record a quote or specific information from a source, she uses the following procedure: Using a new index card (which is separate from her bibliography cards), in the top right-hand corner of the card, she writes the number of the corresponding source—in other words, she writes down the number from the corresponding bibliography card—from which she obtained her findings. This way, she doesn't have to duplicate the bibliographic details (e.g., author and title of the book) for every single quote or fact she wants to jot down. Then, she writes the information in the middle of the card (one quote or piece of information per index card), and directly under the quote or findings she writes the page number from which she got the information. If she writes down the information word-for-word from the original source, she places the information in quotation marks—this reminds her that the text is a direct quote, the citation for which will definitely require use of the page number if used later. Lastly, in the top left-hand corner of the index card, she writes a general topic heading to describe the note details. For example, to make her life easier and to help her organize her notes, Christy decided to use these general categories of capital punishment research for her note cards:

General background information

Deterrence effect—proof for

Deterrence effect—proof against

Ethics of capital punishment—for

Ethics of capital punishment—against

Since Josh and Christy's proposition for the debate was "Resolved: Capital punishment is ethical, and it deters crime," Christy found these topics to be very helpful in organizing her research. Furthermore, Christy decided to organize her research even further, and she color-coded her index cards, using different colored cards for each of the different categories she decided upon. This way, she could easily identify to which general topic a fact belonged.

It is important to note that while both Josh and Christy's note-taking systems are effective strategies, you must develop or adopt a notation system that is best suited to your personality and research process. For instance, while some people prefer to take notes on paper or index cards in the same manner as Josh and Christy, others like to take notes directly on the computer. They find this method easier for organizing their thoughts and ideas. Feel free to use a system that works best for you, but however you choose to take notes, make sure that you keep track of the source, page number, publishing details, and author.

Let's revisit Isabel and Andrew to see how they are faring with their research. Isabel and Andrew agreed that for their debate about cats and dogs, they needed to explore some outside information to gain a full perspective of which type of pet would be best for their family. However, they also agreed that they didn't have enough time—nor was it necessary—to do lengthy, intensive research at the library. Therefore, they decided that they would check out only a few books from the library. When they arrived at their local library, they typed "pets" into the search function in the library catalog. Since this is a broad topic, the search results brought up some off-topic titles such as *How to Draw Dinosaurs and Other Prehistoric Animals* and *Alien Pets.* However, they kept reading down the list, and they found these two book titles that looked promising:

The ASPCA Guide to Complete Pet Care by David Carroll

Encyclopedia of Pets & Pet Care: The Essential Family Reference Guide to Pet Breeds and Pet Care by David Alderton

Although Isabel and Andrew will spend more time building arguments about pets from internal sources rather than from external sources, they decided that checking out these books and skimming them for any helpful information couldn't hurt.

In conclusion, whenever you research a topic, start with basic, general sources to build a strong foundation first, and then work up to focused, complex sources. Remember to look in the back of your books to find legitimate Internet sources. If you desire to find your own Internet sources, make sure that your sources have an author and cited sources, and that the work is an article in a legitimate magazine or part of a legitimate research group. If your Internet source is missing two or more of these characteristics, then you should not use it.

No matter what sources you use, make sure that as you take notes that you write down the title, the author, the page numbers you get your information from, and the correct publishing details.

Now that you know how to find credible research and arguments, you need to examine how to organize your research to create a solid argument, which you'll learn in the following chapters.

Review Exercises

Explain

Explain what Wikipedia is and is not good for.

Explain

Early in the chapter you read that you need to "Read a little to find out what you need to read in-depth." Explain what this phrase means in the context of researching your topic.

Explain

Explain what skimming is, as well as its purpose.

Describe

Describe two types of legitimate websites.

Define

Define the term *layperson*.

Consider

If you are consulting a website constructed by a layperson, what do you need to verify?

Practice Evaluating Website Legitimacy

List

In "The Big Debate: Gun Control" section, you will list various sources you can use in your debate. In addition to researching books, you will also look for Internet sources to help you in your debate. Review each of the following websites. In the space provided, for each site evaluate and explain whether it is a legitimate source, and give at least one reason for your answer.

1. GunCite (Link 7-1)

   Evaluation:

2. Just Facts: A Resource for Independent Thinkers (Link 7-2)

Evaluation: ______________________________

3. The Brady Campaign to Prevent Gun Violence (Link 7-3)

Evaluation: ______________________________

Building Copiousness

Review

Review your old quotes.

Practice

Practice saying the quotes to someone in your class, or practice writing them down on paper.

Memorize

Memorize your new quote:

> Courage is not simply one of the virtues but the form of every virtue at the testing point. —C.S. Lewis[5]

5. Ratcliffe, *Oxford Dictionary of Quotations*, 103.

Everyday Debate

Prove

Thus far, in your "Everyday Debate" exercises, you have practiced developing simple Toulmin arguments in favor of, or against, a proposition. Here are the basic parts of a Toulmin model of argument: claim, evidence, warrant, and reservations. It is important to note that while some arguments are very simple, many arguments contain myriad pieces of evidence and many warrants to prove this evidence. In upcoming chapters, you will read about some of the most common and useful types of evidence you can harness to prove your points in your arguments, and you will learn how to develop these arguments. For now, here are suggestions for different types of evidence you can use in a Toulmin argument: (a) specific examples from history, culture, or everyday life; (b) observations about how life works; (c) quotes or statements from authorities, such as doctors, persons who are experts in their respective fields, experienced researchers, and respected authors; (d) analogies (comparing two similar ideas to draw a conclusion); and (e) religious or ethical teachings. In the "Everyday Debate" section for this chapter, you will need to use at least three pieces of evidence to prove your statement.

A common debate in our society is whether children should receive an allowance. Develop an argument for both sides of this proposition:

Giving children an allowance teaches them responsibility.

(Note that this is not an allowance based on chores; it's just a set amount of money they get each month.)

Here are some types of evidence you could use for both sides:

Learning from the Masters

List

Watch the other half of the Dennett and D'Souza debate in which D'Souza gives his arguments (Link 7-4). List the strength and weaknesses of D'Souza's presentation.

Observe

In addition, watch the rebuttal section of this debate so that you can get a feel for how this process of rebuttals works.

The Big Debate: Gun Control

List

As you know, in this section throughout the book you will be preparing for a debate on gun control. To help you focus your research, here is a suggested resolution for your debate:

Resolved: Gun control is ethical and will make the United States a safer place.

To help you with this debate, go to the library and look on the Internet to find at least seven sources on this topic. List your sources below, in order of what you think will be the most helpful (1) to the least helpful (7):

1. ______________________________
2. ______________________________
3. ______________________________
4. ______________________________
5. ______________________________
6. ______________________________
7. ______________________________

Chapter 8

Inductive Logic: Introducing the Common Topics

> YOU CAN'T THINK RATIONALLY ON AN EMPTY STOMACH, AND A WHOLE LOT OF PEOPLE CAN'T DO IT ON A FULL STOMACH EITHER.
>
> —LORD REITH[1]

In the last chapter, you learned how to find credible books, articles, and Internet sources to help you develop a clear understanding of the basic information and key arguments about your topic. This is crucial because, obviously, you cannot start from scratch every time you need to research a subject. That is, you can't do all of the research yourself. You should use and build on information that other people have researched, developed, and collected over the years. You must develop techniques to evaluate the arguments you are reading; just because someone has written an argument that is published in a book does not mean that the argument is automatically a valid one. Therefore, learning the use of certain research tools is required to help you critique the arguments you read. You need tools that aid the construction of your own arguments.

After all, you will be bringing your own viewpoint to the discussion. This means that you will often construct new arguments based on your view of the evidence and the issue at hand. In a sense, what you require is a means by which you can evaluate arguments from external sources, such as the books and articles you read. You also will need tools to help you develop and critique arguments from **internal sources**, that is, your own personal logic and experience. In the next few chapters, you will learn tools and techniques for critiquing and developing arguments. You will learn how to effectively develop arguments from your own internal resources and critique arguments from external sources. In doing this, you will learn about three types of persuasion: logos, ethos, and pathos.

Inductive Arguments

The first type of argument we will be discussing is an argument from **logos**, or logic. You may remember from the overview of logic in chapter 4 that there are two main types of logic that people use in debates: inductive and deductive logic. In this chapter, as well as the next few chapters, you will focus on inductive logic. Later, you will examine deductive logic. Remember that inductive arguments are arguments based on generalizations. That is, when people make inductive arguments, they make observations from examples in life, research, and their own common sense. Based on patterns noted in these observations, they then make generalizations that represent general rules for how things work in the world. To get an idea of how inductive arguments work, read the following example of two friends chatting in a coffee shop:

1. Susan Ratcliffe, *Oxford Dictionary of Quotations by Subject*, 2nd ed. (Oxford: Oxford University Press, 2010), 290.

Jennifer: *(puts down a newspaper she has been reading)* I don't know what to think about education in America today. Schools seem to be getting worse and worse, and kids aren't learning anything.

Karen: What makes you say that?

Jennifer: I was just reading in the newspaper about how this school near me had to close down because a majority of the kids performed so poorly on standardized tests. And this isn't the only incident I've noticed like this. Last month, I read a newspaper article about how numerous businesses have to train their new employees, who just graduated from high school or college, basic math and communication skills because they simply did not know these fundamentals. Not only that, but my sister has been having tremendous difficulty with my nephew's school. He's in third grade and he still has problems with reading. My sister discovered that he doesn't know all of the sounds of the letters of the alphabet well. When she asked his teacher about it, the teacher said that they no longer drill the alphabet into kids' heads anymore, and instead spend a lot of time reading books. It just appears as though schools aren't what they used to be.

Karen: I disagree. I think there are some bad schools, but I think many schools are doing wonderful things. My niece goes to a really great school. She is in seventh grade, and this year she already has participated in science fair, has acted in a Shakespeare play, and has exchanged letters with a pen pal in Guatemala as part of her Spanish class curriculum. I know of other schools where kids are doing meaningful and thoughtful work. I think there are just a few bad apples in the bunch.

As you can see, both Jennifer and Karen have made some generalizations based on scenarios they have witnessed in everyday life. (**Generalization** is the process of extrapolating broad theories or ideas from consistent patterns we observe in life.) Jennifer observed negative stories in the newspaper and remembered the incident with her nephew, and from those observations she generalized that schools today must be getting worse. Alternatively, Karen took note of the positive influence of her niece's school, and remembered other schools she knew of that focus on thoughtful curricula, and as a result she generalized that many schools were doing a great job, and there were only a few that were not.

One of the most common ways that we argue is through the process of generalization. However, it's important to note that we make generalizations from several different sources. For instance, we generalize from everyday occurrences, just as Jennifer and Karen did in the previous dialogue. We generalize from studies and information provided by reputable and scientific organizations. We also generalize from the morality and ethics teachings of spiritual and philosophical leaders. Furthermore, we generalize from cause-and-effect relationships that we have observed in history and in life. These are just a few of the types of generalizations people regularly make. Because generalizations can be helpful to you when you construct arguments for a debate, you should know about a helpful tool that can help you discover as many of these types of arguments as possible: the **common topics**. Greek philosopher Aristotle wrote about the common topics, which he invented, in his book *Rhetoric*, one of the most influential books on the development of rhetoric.[2]

2. Christof Rapp, "Aristotle's Rhetoric," in *The Stanford Encyclopedia of Philosophy*, February 1, 2010, Edward N. Zalta, ed., http://plato.stanford.edu/archives/spr2010/entries/aristotle-rhetoric/.

Beware of Fallacies

The common topics are a list of categories for finding all of the available arguments for a given subject, and it can be extremely helpful when constructing arguments for debate. For each common topic, there are common argument pitfalls that people fall into when trying to make these kinds of arguments. These argument pitfalls, which Aristotle referred to as "argument pretenders," are called fallacies. A **fallacy** is a commonly recognized type of poor argument; an error in reasoning. An argument is poor when the conclusion does not follow from the premises with strong probability. For instance, the premises might not actually relate to the conclusion but may be irrelevant and related to something else. Another problem that could arise with an argument that contains a fallacy is that the premises may not be strong enough or contain enough evidence to support the conclusion. There are several different specific problems that a fallacy can have. The problem that all fallacies have in common, though, is that the premises do not support the conclusion.

Therefore, if you learn the basic common topics and the most frequent fallacies people commit when constructing these arguments, you will be well on your way to building a solid case in any debate. The common topics are definition, comparison, relationship, circumstance, and testimony. In this book, you will learn a strong overview of these common topics and fallacies. (To learn about these fallacies and common topics in depth, check out Classical Academic Press's publications *The Argument Builder* and *The Art of Argument*.)

Internal or External Arguments: How to Choose

Before you review the common topics, it is important for you to understand which sources you should consult to build these arguments. To better understand the range of sources available to you, next you'll explore the use of internal arguments and external arguments a little more, both of which are necessary in debate. Internal arguments are arguments that you can form from the knowledge and insight you possess right now. For example, when you are debating or discussing any topic, it is important to realize that you already possess numerous arguments at your fingertips because of your personal experience and/or common sense. In addition, people can also craft arguments from just plain logical deductive reasoning and rational thinking. (You will learn about how to construct deductive arguments in later chapters.) Personal experience, thoughts, opinions, and common sense are your internal sources, and they are the best place to start in any debate, though many

What limits are there to generalizing from personal experience? Assuming a general knowledge from an individual circumstance can be dangerous, especially in regard to people or people groups. General conclusions based on limited evidence are rarely justified, but making them is a typical human tendency. It could be tempting to assume, from one particularly terrible experience at a Bulgarian train station while on a European vacation, that Bulgarian people as a whole are rude—though clearly, the acts of one person are rarely, if ever, an accurate representation of an entire cultural group of people. If making judgments and assumptions are inevitable, then how can you make them more effective and accurate? How can you tell who or what individual, or action, is representative of a whole? There are some qualifications—a devotee to a certain religion will probably give you a fairer and more thorough account of the religion than a recent convert, though the devotee may not give you an accurate picture of the average person committed to that religion. By the same token, a football player ejected for unsportsmanlike conduct is unlikely to fairly or averagely represent the entire team (the players of which have not been kicked out). When you use examples, you want to aim at using an example that most represents the whole group it exemplifies. Hasty generalizations can lead one into unintentionally committing the **straw man fallacy**. The straw man fallacy occurs when a person draws a conclusion from a caricatured or otherwise distorted version of his opponent's argument. When you create a straw man version of your opponent's argument, you aren't actually fairly addressing your opponent's argument but rather creating a distorted version of your opponent's argument that is ridiculous and easy to defeat.

people are tempted to consult an external source first. The common topics will help you understand how to make the most of your own personal experience when building internal arguments.

External arguments, in contrast, are arguments you construct from sources outside of yourself. For example, books, magazine articles, documentaries, credible Internet sources, and interviews with experts are all excellent resources in which to find external arguments. In the last chapter, you learned how to use external sources to help you find the arguments people have written on a topic. Not only can you use these arguments to build your case, you can also combine them with your own internal arguments to create new arguments. Although external sources you use will vary for different debates, there are three external sources in particular that are useful for every debate you encounter: a dictionary, a thesaurus, and a quote book. These sources are invaluable tools for building a good foundation for your argument, as well as for adding entertaining and elaborative touches. Luckily, in this age of the Internet, you can easily find affordable versions of these sources for purchase online. I personally recommend *The Merriam-Webster Dictionary of Quotations*, as well as *The Merriam-Webster Dictionary* and *The Merriam-Webster Thesaurus*. You can even consult both dictionary and thesaurus online (Link 8-1). Although there is certainly a wide array of dictionaries, thesauri, and books of quotations from which to choose, these are good foundational external sources that will meet many of your debating needs.

Consider what you have learned about the common topics, as well as internal and external sources, thus far in light of Josh and Christy's capital punishment debate and Isabel and Andrew's pet debate. Both Josh and Christy should first consult their own experiences and reason so that they can make full use of their internal resources. For instance, they may have heard about capital punishment cases in their own state or other states from which they could draw conclusions. They may also be able to construct some arguments based on common sense. (You will examine these possible arguments in more detail in upcoming chapters.) They should spend some time mining these internal resources first. Because there has been so much written and researched concerning capital punishment, Christy and Josh will also have a wealth of external resources at their fingertips regarding this topic. For example, they can consult statistical studies, historical and modern examples of the use of capital punishment, and religious and ethical teachings pertaining to this issue. These are all external resources that will provide ample material from which Josh and Christy can make generalizations. Alternatively, as you can imagine, Isabel and Andrew will largely consult internal resources for their pet debate. Although they may read a few books to glean some specific information about these animals as pets, they will primarily form arguments from their personal observations about cats and dogs, and from watching other people's relationships and experiences with their pets. They will then evaluate how these observations apply to their particular family situation. Informal debates often take this form. Both informal and formal debates can use external and internal resources; however, people involved with a formal debate make more extensive use of external resources than those involved in an informal debate.

In conclusion, once you have established what it is that you are debating by forming the idea into a proposition, it is time to start constructing arguments. One of the best ways to form inductive arguments is with a systematic tool such as the common topics, which helps you to discover all of the available means of persuasion for a given topic. You can use the common topics to explore both internal and external resources. In the next chapter, you will look at the first common topic: definition.

Review Exercises

Define

Define each of the following words.

1. Inductive Logic ______________________________

2. Generalization: ______________________________

3. Common Topics: ______________________________

4. Internal Sources: ______________________________

5. External Sources: ______________________________

Practicing Generating Arguments from Internal Resources

Develop

Imagine that you are involved in the following debate: "Resolved: Lying is always wrong." This is a proposition for which you can generate several internal arguments. Choose a side of this debate—either affirmative or negative—and then generate three internal arguments for your position. You do not need to create a full Toulmin argument. A one-sentence argument claim will suffice for this exercise. After you generate your three arguments from internal sources, list two external sources you could consult to further develop arguments.

Building Copiousness

Review

Review your old quotes.

Practice

Practice saying the quotes to someone in your class, or practice writing them down on paper.

Memorize

Memorize your new quote:

Courage is the knowledge of what is and is not to be feared. —Nicias[3]

Everyday Debate

Consider

As discussed in previous chapters, Andrew and Isabel are still debating about which pet they should get. Although this is an informal debate between the twins, both of them have had experience on a debate team when they lived in Bolivia, and so they decided to focus their debate on the following proposition: "Resolved: A cat is the most practical pet for our family at this time." As you may have already guessed based on their earlier dialogues, Isabel is arguing the affirmative, and Andrew is arguing the negative. After they decided on the focus of their informal debate, these siblings had a casual conversation to better understand each other's points of view. Read their conversation and then answer the following questions:

Andrew: OK, Isabel. If we are going to present a proposal to Mom and Dad about which pet is ideal for our family, we might as well understand both of our perspectives. After all, that's probably the only way we will be able to come to any kind of agreement. Also, I know Mom and Dad will ask us lots of hard questions to make sure we've looked at the issue from all sides.

Isabel: You're right, Andrew. First, tell me why you think that a dog is the most practical pet for our family, and then I will tell you why I think a cat is more ideal.

Andrew: I think a dog is more ideal for several reasons. You know there have been several robberies in our neighborhood in the past year, right? Well, I noticed that none of the people who were robbed had a dog. That's because robbers don't want to break into houses with dogs because they bark loudly and are protective. If we got a dog, it could help guard our house. I think robbers are less likely to rob a house when there is a potentially noisy dog watching over the house. Also, do you remember Joe's dog, Samson? Joe taught him the coolest tricks. He even taught Samson to sing—well, howl, actually—along with the radio. A lot of my other friends who

3. Ratcliffe, *Oxford Dictionary of Quotations*, 103.

have dogs teach them amazing stunts and actions. Dogs can be taught tricks, and since we have wanted a pet for so long, I think it would be a good idea to get one that we can interact with—really actively engage with the animal. Those are my main reasons. Now you can tell me why you think a cat is an ideal pet.

Isabel: Well, one reason I think a cat is the ideal pet for us is because our house is kind of small, and I've noticed that all of our friends who live in diminutive houses either have no pets or small pets, such as cats or goldfish. If we got a large dog, such as a golden retriever—which is the kind of dog that I know you want to get, by the way—it would probably feel very crowded in our home. Our house is small, and a big dog like a golden retriever needs a lot of room to move around. Making such a large dog live in a small house would be unfair to the dog. Also, dogs have a tendency to be messy. They can chew and tear up things, and potentially can cause greater messes than cats. I know many dogs, such as Joe's dog Samson, can do neat tricks, but do you remember how destructive he was? He constantly dug in the trash, and he even ate part of the family's Christmas tree one year. Most of my friends with dogs have similar stories about their dogs occasionally ruining something in their houses. Since everyone in our family is usually busy with work and school, I think we need a pet we don't need to monitor as closely, or clean up after as much.

List

For both Andrew and Isabel, list two generalizations that each twin makes based on observations from everyday life.

Andrew's generalizations:

____

____

____

Isabel's generalizations:

____

____

____

List

List two other sources Andrew and Isabel could consult—either external or internal—to gather more inductive generalizations.

____

____

____

____

Learning from the Masters

Observe

Intelligence Squared, a public debate program started in 2006 by the Rozenkranz Foundation, gathers cultural leaders and intellectuals to debates issues of current public concern. Many of these debates are broadcasted on National Public Radio (NPR). For instance, the following are some of the topics that have been debated on Intelligence Squared:

Resolved: Churchill was more of a liability than an asset to the free world.

Resolved: The Catholic Church is a force for good in the world.

Resolved: Free-market capitalism is "so" twentieth century.

Resolved: The threat to our civil liberties from an over-mighty state has been greatly exaggerated.

As you can see, these debates cover a wide range of issues. If you look at some of the past debates, you will find other topics such as "Resolved: Too many people go to universities"; "Resolved: Hunting with hounds should be banned"; and "State education is a comprehensive disaster." Intelligence Squared will also occasionally sponsor humorous debates such as "Why can't a man be more like a woman?" and "The problem with this country is the daily mail." The basic format for an Intelligence Squared debate is based on affirmative and negative presentations followed by cross-examination/questions. Typically, there are three experts on the affirmative side and three experts on the negative side. One speaker on the affirmative side first presents arguments. Then, a speaker from the negative side presents arguments. The affirmative side presents again, followed by the negative side, until all three speakers on each side have presented. Each presentations lasts about six minutes. After all of the presenters on both sides have delivered their arguments, there will be several cross-examinations periods. During the first cross-examination period, the moderator of the debate generally asks the speakers questions. During the second cross-examination period, the audience members ask the speakers questions. In addition, sometimes there is another cross-examination time in which speakers on each side ask speakers on the opposing side questions. Lastly, there is usually time given at the end for each speaker to present closing arguments, lasting about two minutes each. There is no established rebuttal time in these debates; however, because speakers can respond at length to cross-examinations and because they have closing arguments, this often serves as a time when they can rebut points raised by the other team.

Intelligence Squared debates are great examples to learn about the debate format. They are especially interesting because they allow you to compare and contrast various speakers and speaking styles. You can gain a clearer picture of what is effective and what is not. Further, the people who speak at these debates are often, though not always, authorities on the matters they address, and they are competent, strategic thinkers. Because of this, they often craft proficient and thorough arguments, which serve as excellent models for students learning to develop arguments. In addition, the cross-examination times are enlightening because the moderator and audience members ask probing and intelligent questions that challenge the speakers to defend their arguments. You can gain a strong sense of how to ask first-rate cross-examination questions from these arguments.

Next, you are going to watch one of the Intelligence Squared debates on the following proposition: "Resolved: America should be the world's policeman" (Link 8-3). Begin by watching each set of two debaters—the affirmative and negative sides—and then discuss how they develop their arguments, and the strengths and weaknesses of their presentations.

Observe and Evaluate

Watch the first affirmative presentation by Max Boot and the first negative presentation by Ellen Laipson. Then, answer the following questions:

1. List at least three key arguments that Max Boot makes in his presentation:

2. What are some observed strengths and weaknesses of Boot's argument and presentation style?

3. List at least three key arguments that Ellen Laipson makes in her arguments:

4. What are some observed strengths and weaknesses of Laipson's speech?

5. Who do you think was the better speaker, and why?

____

____

____

____

____

____

The Big Debate: Gun Control

List

You have started to research the issue of gun control. To get you thinking about this argument, list two arguments in favor of, and two arguments against, the following proposition: "Resolved: Gun control is ethical and will make the United States a safer place." These preliminary arguments should be arguments purely from internal sources—that is, your own logic, common sense, and experience. Use the Toulmin model of argument to develop your two arguments on each side. For right now, because you are examining both sides of the argument, just complete the claim, evidence, and warrant parts of the argument.

Chapter 9

Inductive Logic: Definition

> 'WHEN I USE A WORD,' HUMPTY DUMPTY SAID IN A RATHER SCORNFUL TONE, 'IT MEANS JUST WHAT I CHOOSE IT TO MEAN—NEITHER MORE NOR LESS.'
> —LEWIS CARROLL[1]

The first common topic you will learn about is definition. This is an explanation or illustration of a word, and it is the first of Aristotle's common topics. It explores the meaning of a word in order to develop an argument. After you have established a proposition for a debate, one of the most important actions you should take to ensure your debate runs smoothly is to define the terms in your proposition. After all, if you and your opponent define the same key word in your proposition differently, then the debate will be confusing, as you would in fact be arguing two different propositions. This common topic provides you with some of the most common definitional devices for clarifying a word. Definition is useful for much more than merely clarifying the terms of a debate. It helps your audience grasp the big picture of, as well as the fine distinctions within, your debate topic. There is a wide array of definitional techniques people use when they employ the common topic of definition. Some of the most common methods are stipulative definitions, dictionary definitions, etymology, examples, synonyms and antonyms.

Stipulative Definition

You will learn about each of these techniques in more detail in this chapter. First, you'll learn about the stipulative definition, which is one of the most common, useful, and important definition techniques that you will use in informal debates. It is important to note that when you are in an informal debate, your main goal is to make sure that everyone in the discussion is on the same page. For instance, consider the following discussion between Isabel and Andrew:

Andrew: Isabel, I know that you are going to argue that a cat is the most practical pet for our family right now. But just to make sure I understand you correctly, what exactly do you mean by "practical"?

Isabel: I mean, given our family's busy schedule, that a cat is the easiest pet to care for and the pet that best matches our lifestyle.

When Isabel defined the word "practical" for Andrew, note that she did not consult a dictionary. Instead, she provided a definition for the word to indicate how she was using it in the debate. That is, she used a **stipulative definition**. A stipulative definition is a reasonable definition for a word that one or two people create on the spot—often in an informal discussion or debate—for the purpose of

1. Susan Ratcliffe, *Oxford Dictionary of Quotations by Subject*, 2nd ed. (Oxford: Oxford University Press, 2010), 517.

clarifying a term. Be aware that in an informal debate, you will likely use the common topic of definition in a brief way. Usually, one or both parties will provide a stipulative definition for the terms in their debate so that they know they are using terminology in the same way. Put another way, this method prevents potential confusion regarding the meanings of the terms used in the debate.

Alternatively, when you are involved in a formal debate, such as Josh and Christy's debate on capital punishment, it is far more likely that you will need to use several definitional techniques to provide an accurate definition for your word. For example, read the following discussion that Christy and Josh had in class:

Josh: I think we need to clarify exactly what we mean by *capital punishment*, Christy.

I *think* I know—I mean, usually when people talk about capital punishment, they mean the death penalty. But I'm not sure if capital punishment differs in other states and countries. I mean, do all countries and states have capital punishment? Also, do countries and states that practice capital punishment carry out execution in the same manner, or do they execute in different ways?

Christy: Those are good questions, Josh. I also wonder which crimes, specifically, are considered capital offenses, and which are punishable by death. Is it all instances of murder, or only some particular types of murder? And are there any other crimes, other than murder, that are punishable by death?

As you can see, Christy and Josh have a lot to clarify before they can jump right into their arguments. Whenever you are involved in formal debate, you will use the common topic of definition more thoroughly than you would in an informal debate. This is true for several reasons. First, one of the purposes of a formal debate is to inform as well as to persuade, whereas in an informal debate, there is less emphasis on informing one another; rather, the focus is on discovering both sides' viewpoints and reaching a conclusion about which position or argument is stronger, more logical, or more reasonable. In addition, there is a bit of a theatrical element to formal debate. In chapter 3, "Debate: The Janus-Faced Discipline," you learned that you while you want to gather logical arguments in formal debate, you should also strive to connect with, and even entertain, your audience. As such, in a formal debate you will likely use several definition techniques, all for the purpose of clarifying the proposition, and informing and entertaining the audience. It's important to study each of the different kinds of definitional techniques you can use to accomplish these purposes.

Dictionary Definition

Next, let's examine the other types of definitional techniques, as well as the sources we can use to develop these techniques. You may have noticed that stipulative definitions are created from internal resources—that is, from a person's existing understanding and familiarity with a term. The other definition techniques must often, though not always, utilize external resources such as dictionaries or encyclopedias. One of the most common types of definition techniques you will use is a **dictionary definition**. A dictionary definition is just that—a definition that comes from the dictionary. For instance, for Christy and Josh's debate, when Christy looked up the word "capital," she found the following definitions: "punishable by death; involving execution; most serious."[2] These definitions rounded out their notion of what capital punishment is. It is the most serious punishment, or the punishment involving execution.

In addition to providing a quick and clear explanation for the key words of your debate, dictionary definitions also often contain another common definition technique: **etymology**. Etymology is the study of the roots and origins of a word. For example, many of the words in our English language come from Latin and French because, historically, Rome and France had a significant impact on English civilizations, and so our language absorbed many words or word roots from these languages. For example, in the dictionary entry on "capital," Christy found that the word "capital" derived from, or came from, the Latin word *caput*, which means "head." Through a little extra research, she discovered, as she suspected, that capital punishment came to be named this because, originally, people who received the sentence of capital punishment

2. *Webster's Ninth New Collegiate Dictionary*, s.v. "capital."

were executed by having their heads chopped off—thus, the tie-in to "head." Josh also found a few helpful antonyms and synonyms for the term "capital" in a class thesaurus. As you probably remember, **synonyms** are words that have the same or a similar meaning to another word, and **antonyms** are words that have an opposite meaning to another word. Josh discovered some synonyms of the word *capital*: uppermost, most serious, and critical. He also found the following antonyms: trivial, insignificant, and minor. As you can imagine, using synonyms and antonyms can be valuable: If you are not familiar with a given term, then there is a good chance that you may be familiar with a word that is similar to, or opposite, the term. While synonyms tell us what a word *is*, antonyms can be especially helpful, since one common way to grasp a concept is by understanding what that concept is *not*.

After Christy and Josh researched and shared their information with each other, they felt they had a solid start to defining capital punishment and providing a clear picture of it for their audience. However, although the dictionary definition and etymology of "capital" were helpful, they still needed answers for their other questions, including which crimes were considered capital offenses, which countries and states practice capital punishment, and what types of execution techniques are used in capital punishment. Although seemingly small details such as these can sometimes appear to be irrelevant, they can actually be vital to a debate. Remember, Josh and Christy decided to debate that capital punishment is both ethical and an effective deterrent to crime. Details, such as the specific method used to execute a criminal, could be a strong determining factor in whether the practice is considered ethical.

Examples and Illustrations

As Josh and Christy discussed these questions, they realized that they needed specific examples of countries and states that use capital punishment, as well as examples of kinds of crimes that warranted the death penalty. In addition, they recognized that they should find examples of the types of capital punishment practiced around the world. For your debates, in defining the terms in your propositions, the use of **examples**—that is, instances or illustrations of a larger group or concept—is one of the best tools for clarifying terms. Of course, it is wise to start with dictionary definitions, but dictionary definitions tend to be somewhat abstract and "skeletal," so to speak, while examples help to put flesh on the bones of the skeleton. Furthermore, dictionary definitions often employ abstract words, while examples create vivid pictures of the term under discussion. To find valid examples, Josh and Christy looked up capital punishment in a *World Book Encyclopedia* that Christy had at home. Their teacher, Mr. Bennet, had told them that they were allowed to use one encyclopedia as a source for their debate, which was recommended for gaining background information on their topic.

In the encyclopedia entry for capital punishment, Josh and Christy found several facts that answered their questions. They discovered that in the 1990s, thirty-six US states allowed some form of the death penalty, but capital punishment was generally restricted to murder and other crimes that led to murder, such as "armed robbery, hijacking, and kidnapping."[3] Interestingly, they also found that most European and Latin American countries, and even Canada, had outlawed capital punishment at some point by 1976[4] because they believed it was inhumane.[5] To Christy and Josh's surprise, they discovered that, according to the encyclopedia, "in the early 1990s, the United States was the only Western industrialized nation where executions still took place."[6] They also discovered that all of the states that practiced capital punishment either used electrocution, the gas chamber, or drug injection.[7]

These examples aided to clarify and create Josh and Christy's shared picture of capital punishment. Furthermore, their research showed them that they needed to narrow their proposition even further. As a result, Christy and Josh changed their proposition as follows: "Capital punishment as it is practiced in the United States is ethical, and it is an effective crime

3. Franklin E. Zimring, "Capital Punishment," *World Book Encyclopedia* (Chicago: World Book, 1992), 193.
4. "Capital Punishment in Canada," CBCNewsCanada, last updated June 7, 2010, http://www.cbc.ca/news/canada/capital-punishment-in-canada-1.795391.
5. Zimring, "Capital Punishment," 193.
6. Ibid.
7. Ibid.

How do you decide which definition to accept in a debate? As in the case of most disputes, whichever side is shown to be most attractive is the one that wins the day. Definitions that possess accuracy and clarity are viewed in a positive light when they correspond to the reality perceived by your audience. Such definitions make immediate and clear sense to your audience. Attractive definitions also might be those that reveal a meaningful aspect or quality of the word in question (e.g., when one uses etymology to define a word, or uses a technical definition provided by a particular field of study or practice), impressing your audience with a depth of meaning or an intriguing quality of the word they might not have known before. Unless a particular dictionary has been adopted as an official standard by your debate organization, or the word has been defined in the brief or topic, definitions are decided by the arguments and consent of the debaters. Therefore, do not allow key terms in a debate to be defined in a way that is unfavorable to your position, and be sure to take strategic advantage of defining words that are favorable (either to your position, or to your judges and fellow debaters) and viewed as fair and accurate.

deterrent." They presented their new proposition to Mr. Bennet, who said, "Good work. I was wondering if you would eventually decide to narrow your statement. I think this is a good new proposition."

The common topic of definition is one that people often use as an introductory tool to become more familiar with a word and its background. In a formal debate, it can also provide a whole picture of a topic for an audience. For most of the definition techniques you will use, you will need to consult external sources, such as a dictionary, a history book, or an encyclopedia article. By establishing this information clearly, you will lay a strong foundation for the rest of your debate. Remember—in an informal debate, you will likely use a stipulative definition, but you won't commonly use the other definition techniques, because in an informal debate you don't have the requirement of providing background information or entertainment for an audience. Definitions are obviously important, but, certainly, there is so much more to a debate than definitions. In fact, definitions aren't even considered arguments; rather, they are tools for *clarification* (of an argument). In the next chapter, you will read about the next common topic on Aristotle's list: comparison. As you will see, this common topic helps our two sets of debating teenagers get head starts on developing their arguments.

Review Exercises

Define

Define each of these definition techniques:

1. Stipulative definition:

2. Dictionary definition:

3. Etymology:

4. Examples:

5. Synonyms:

6. Antonyms:

Discuss

Why is definition important?

Building Copiousness

Review

Review your old quotes.

Practice

Practice saying the quotes to someone in your class, or practice writing them down on paper.

Memorize

Memorize your new quote:

> Cowards die many times before their deaths;
> The valiant never taste of death but once.
>
> —William Shakespeare[8]

Practicing Definitions

Write

Later in this book, you will learn that it is quite common for debaters to define the terms in the debate at the beginning of a debate speech. In fact, in the exercise from chapter 8's Learning from the Masters section, you saw Ellen Laipson do this when she defined the word "police" in the Intelligence Squared speech. In order to practice this skill, write an argument based on the quote you memorized in the Building Copiousness section—"Cowards die many times before their deaths; / The valiant never taste of death but once" by William Shakespeare—and make sure that as a part of this argument, you define the word "cowardice" using three definition techniques (e.g., dictionary definition, synonyms, and examples). In addition, make sure your argument, in addition to definition, follows the Toulmin model of argument. The following is a sample order of information for your paragraph, to help you get started:

- Introductory sentence
- Three definition techniques to define "cowardice"
- Toulmin model
- Conclusion

8. Ratcliffe, *Oxford Dictionary of Quotations*, 104.

Everyday Debate

Debate

In the last chapter, you considered the following debate topic: "Resolved: Lying is always wrong." Hold a minidebate for this topic using your internal arguments from the last chapter as the basis of your debate. As a part of your affirmative argument, include a definition of lying that uses at least three definitional techniques. Recommended techniques for this exercise are a dictionary definition, a synonym, and an antonym.

Learning from the Masters

Observe

Watch the next set of speeches from the Intelligence Squared debate: "Resolved: America should be the world's policeman." Then, answer the questions that follow. The next two speakers in this debate are Michael Mandelbaum and Matthew Parris (Link 9-1).

List

List three of Michael Mandelbaum's key arguments.

Discuss

What are some strengths and weaknesses of Mandelbaum's speech?

List

List three of Matthew Parris's key arguments.

Discuss

What are some strengths and weaknesses of Parris's speech?

Discuss

Which speaker did you think was more effective and why?

The Big Debate: Gun Control

You are now starting to take notes in these exercises that will later help you when you debate. Therefore, make sure you take complete notes by recording the sources (remember to note the title, author, page number, and publisher details) from which you find the information for the exercises in these sections at the end of each chapter. If needed, review the different note-taking styles mentioned in chapter 7 and pick the style that best fits your researching habits and personality.

Debate

In order to gain a clear idea of our preposition "Resolved: Gun control is ethical and will make the United States a safer place," write a dictionary definition for each of the following terms: "gun," "control," and "ethical."

Gun:

____

____

Control:

____

____

Ethical:

____

____

Chapter 10

Inductive Logic: Comparison

> 'CONTRARIWISE,' CONTINUED TWEEDLEDEE, 'IF IT WAS SO, IT MIGHT BE; AND IF IT WERE SO, IT WOULD BE: BUT AS IT ISN'T, IT AIN'T. THAT'S LOGIC.'
>
> —LEWIS CARROLL[1]

Do you remember the purpose of Aristotle's common topics? The purpose of the common topics is to provide a framework for creating all of the available arguments for a given topic. In the last chapter, you examined the common topic of definition, which, as you learned, is a foundational tool for ensuring that everyone understands the topic at hand. Use of this common topic also provides clear examples of the key terms, as well as some history and development of those terms.

Comparison and Analogy

Before you study the next common topic, *comparison*, look at another conversation that Christy and Josh had concerning their debate:

Christy: Well, Josh, now that we have a better picture of what capital punishment is, tell me why you think capital punishment isn't just and doesn't deter crime.

Josh: That's a good question. I was thinking of an analogy the other day. Capital punishment is like screaming at someone to get him to stop screaming at you. That hardly ever works. It just breeds more bad feelings. That's why most ethical systems teach that a soft answer stops anger, and a peaceful response conquers violence and hatred.

Christy: Hmm. I think your analogy about a person screaming at someone to get him to stop screaming breaks down, because when people scream at each other, it is usually out of anger and rage. I think authority figures can put someone to death without rage and anger; instead, they do it as a remedy for murder. In fact, I think capital punishment is more akin to doctors using chemotherapy or radiation to remove cancer. Of course, those medical treatments are severe procedures with serious effects, and no one would use such treatment lightly—rather, only to treat a life-threatening illness. In the same way, capital punishment, which should never be used lightly, is a very serious treatment that is necessary for eradicating the disease of violence and murder.

Josh and Christy's dialogue about capital punishment illustrates the next common topic: comparison. The common topic of **comparison** can be used to help you draw conclusions about your topic based on its similarities and dissimilarities to other topics. One of the most frequently used tools for using the common topic of comparison is an analogy. An **analogy** is an argument tool that compares an abstract idea to a similar, simpler concept that is more common and clear. The simpler concept illustrates

1. Susan Ratcliffe, *Oxford Dictionary of Quotations by Subject*, 2nd ed. (Oxford: Oxford University Press, 2010), 290.

the more abstract idea. For instance, note that Josh compared capital punishment to someone screaming at another person in order to get him to stop screaming. The point of Josh's analogy was that two people screaming at each other is not an effective strategy to halt the act of screaming, just as killing someone to get people to stop killing is not an effective strategy. Christy disagreed, however, and said that capital punishment is like using chemotherapy or radiation treatment to eradicate cancer. Just as chemotherapy can have good results but should not be used lightly, so too can capital punishment have good results but should not be used lightly. The power of analogies is that they compare a less familiar topic (such as capital punishment) to a simpler, more familiar topic (such as screaming or chemotherapy). Analogies help people understand the nuances of a subject in a way that hard facts and explanation cannot.

False Analogy

When you are using the common topic of comparison, you must avoid the fallacy of **false analogy**. Remember, a fallacy is a poor argument because its premises do not adequately support its conclusions. When you commit the fallacy of false analogy, you compare two things that are too dissimilar—or, conversely, too similar—for any appropriate conclusion to be drawn.

As an example of false analogy, consider the following comparison, which attempts to argue in favor of capital punishment: "Capital punishment is like using gasoline to get a stain out of your clothes. Gasoline smells awful, and it can be dangerous, but it technically gets the job done. In the same way, no one really likes capital punishment, but it gets the job done." This is a weak or false analogy. As you may have noticed, getting stains out of clothing is a rather trivial matter compared to executing someone. It is important to remember that when you are using an analogy, the two items being compared must match each other in tone and level of seriousness. You don't want to compare a serious matter (such as capital punishment) to a trivial matter (such as getting stains out of clothes). The purpose of capital punishment is to discourage crime or provide retribution (justice payment for a crime)—removing stains from clothes does neither of these things. Therefore, it is a poor comparison. Use of poor comparisons could undermine your credibility as a presenter, and it could also have an unintended (negative) comic effect. (Humor is good in a debate when you intend to be funny, but it can be detrimental if people laugh at you when you don't mean for them to do so.)

Christy's analogy about using medical treatment for cancer was effective because the two items she was comparing—capital punishment and radiation treatment—were of a similar seriousness. In addition, although radiation differs from capital punishment in that it does not seek to provide retributive justice, it is like capital punishment because it attempts to discourage further recurrence of cancer, just as capital punishment attempts to discourage further recurrence of murder and other violent crimes.

As another example of a false analogy, imagine if someone argued this way: "Capital punishment is right because it is like a person killing a neighborhood gang leader so that leader won't kill any more people in the neighborhood." This analogy is a poor analogy. If the gang leader is dead, of course he won't be able to kill anyone else. However, preventing a murderer from murdering again is not the only purpose of capital punishment. It's certainly true that a person can't kill someone else if he is dead, but it is also true that a murderer can't kill any more people if he is locked up for life. Therefore, preventing a murderer from further murders cannot be the only goal of capital punishment, for this purpose can be accomplished through other, less extreme measures. In reality, most proponents of capital punishment agree that the main purpose of capital punishment is to perform justice and to discourage others from killing. The analogy of the gang leader is missing any similar retributive or justice-oriented element. Therefore, it is not as analogous as it should be to be considered a good comparison. Also, this analogy of the gang leader is too similar to what capital punishment actually is. In fact, in at least some elements—killing to prevent further killing—it is the same thing. In other words, it compares killing to killing. Remember that the point of an analogy is to compare two *different* things (often a familiar, simple concept compared to a less familiar, abstract concept) so that one can shed light on the meaning of another.

You can also commit the fallacy of false analogy if the two items in your analogy are too similar. While Josh's analogy of screaming to prevent further screaming may not be perfect, it does work because even though screaming at someone is not as serious as capital punishment, it is serious and it doesn't trivialize capital punishment. If your analogy isn't serious or if it trivializes the topic under discussion, it weakens your argument. Furthermore, Josh's analogy is dissimilar enough that it sheds some light on the topic of capital punishment. In order to construct an ideal analogy, you should strive to compare two different items that share key similarities of seriousness and purpose, and you should use a more familiar concept to shed light on a less familiar one.

It is important to understand that analogies are primarily drawn from your own internal resources. In other words, when you construct analogies, you usually do this by thinking through what your topic is like and what interesting conclusions these similarities could imply. You can sometimes find analogies in external resources as well. One of the most common places to find these is in books or articles you are reading for your own research. Because analogies can be such an effective tool, you will likely run across one in an external resource you are reading, since writers and researchers regularly use and create analogies in their work. As long as you give proper credit, it is fine to use other people's analogies, just as you might use a quote or fact from someone else.

One way to learn how to construct analogies is to draw a simple table. Draw two columns (vertical) with four rows (horizontal). Above the first row, label the top left column "Original" (the thing you're talking about) and the top right column "Analogue" (the thing you're saying the original is like, through analogy) as column headings. Then, fill in the first row with the appropriate content (left column: what the original thing is; right column: what the corresponding analogue is). In the second row, write the characteristic(s) that makes the original and the analogue *similar*. Then, in the final row, write the characteristic(s) that makes the original and analogue *different*. This way, you can check your thought process to ensure the analogy you craft doesn't form a false analogy through either too much dissimilarity or too much similarity.

	Original	Analogue
	Life	Box of chocolates
(similar)	One can't know what will happen.	One doesn't know what kind of chocolates one will get.
(different)	Animate, full of totally unexpected and surprising things	Inanimate object, full of similar things (chocolates)

You may be wondering how Isabel and Andrew have been getting along in their discussion about cats and dogs since you last read about their debate progress. While Andrew drove them to a basketball game, they had the following conversation:

Isabel: I have been thinking about what you said about dogs being highly interactive, Andrew, but the more

I consider this, the more I think dogs are just like the Cat in the Hat in the Dr. Seuss story.[2] You know how the Cat in the Hat convinced the two children who were home alone to let him come in and play on a rainy day? Remember how he meant well and certainly had a kind heart, but then he made a complete and utter disaster of their house? Well, I think a dog is just like this. Dogs are friendly and loving and interactive, I agree. But they are just like the Cat in the Hat from the Dr. Seuss story—they create huge messes and even disasters wherever they go; it just seems to be their nature.

Josh: OK, Isabel. I do agree with you that dogs are naturally messier pets than cats. However, I think that comparing dogs to Dr. Seuss's Cat in the Hat is a false analogy. It's pretty clear that the Cat in the Hat is incurable in his state of chaos. Creating disasters is a part of his nature, after all. But this is different from dogs. I think dogs are more like little children. Young kids are bursting with energy, and if you don't discipline them and set proper boundaries and guidelines, they can be nuisances and create disasters continually. If they are trained and disciplined, children actually can become pleasant, amusing, and even helpful. Dogs are similar in this way: Untrained, they are a disaster; trained, they can become a great source of pleasure.

2. Dr. Seuss, *The Cat in the Hat* (New York: Random House, 1957).

Another effective tool for constructing analogies is using **parallel syntax**. The term "syntax" refers to the arrangement of words in phrases, clauses, or sentences. Parallel syntax means that two phrases, clauses, or sentences have the same structure and arrangement of words. Consider the proverb "Stupid is as stupid does." You can break this sentence into two halves that are joined together. The same word ("stupid") that has the same grammatical function (i.e., subject noun) is located in the same position (in this case, as the first word) in the two parts. For both halves, the word that follows the subject is the verb that goes with the subject (i.e., "is" and "does," respectively). The halves are connected by the conjunction "as." By having similar syntactical structures, analogies with parallel syntax help emphasize the similarity in content.

Similarity in how you say something can reinforce the concept of similarity in what you say. We could use this method to rephrase Isabel's analogy a little more concisely (albeit in more complex sentences) in the following manner: "Just as Dr. Seuss's Cat in the Hat—though friendly, fun-loving, and well-intentioned—ultimately causes a mess that someone else has to fix, so, too, can a dog—though friendly, fun-loving, and well-intentioned—ultimately cause a mess that someone else has to fix."

Notice that while Isabel's Cat in the Hat analogy may seem like a strange choice because it is comparing a dog to a cat, the Cat in the Hat is actually a unique, one-of-a-kind creature that isn't like a normal cat at all. Dr. Seuss, the author of the story, created him to be more like a "person" than a cat, and he is a very destructive, chaotic "person" indeed. Therefore, this is a good analogy because it compares a dog to a different animal—a person-like creature—and both creatures have similar, readily acknowledgeable, destructive tendencies. This analogy is effective because a dog and the Cat in the Hat are dissimilar enough to provide a legitimate comparison, but they do have similar traits that work to Isabel's argumentative advantage. By the same token, Andrew's analogy also works well because dogs and little children are different enough that one concept can shed light on the other, and yet they both share a common trait of "trainability," which works to Andrew's argumentative advantage. Both of these analogies are effective.

Developing the skill of creating solidly structured analogies is an invaluable tool to possess. Human beings respond well to specific, pictorial images. After all, one of the best teaching techniques a teacher can use is to provide a specific, vivid image of a difficult concept she is trying to teach. This vivid image or example becomes a reference point to which students can compare and interpret the difficult concept. This is what an analogy does. It provides a precise, familiar, concrete image that serves as a reference point to which someone can compare and interpret a more difficult, or less familiar, concept. Have you ever heard of the saying "A picture is worth a thousand words"? In the same way, a good analogy is worth a thousand words. Now that you've learned about comparison, it's time to move on to the next common topic: relationship.

Review Exercises

Define

Define the term "analogy."

Explain

Explain how to construct a good analogy.

Define

Define the term "false analogy."

Building Copiousness

Review

Review your old quotes.

Practice

Practice saying the quotes to someone in your class, or practice writing them down on paper.

Memorize

Memorize your new quote:

Love seeketh not itself to please,
Nor for itself hath any care;
But for another gives its ease,
And builds a Heaven in Hell's despair.
—William Blake[3]

Practicing Analogies

Develop

Imagine you are involved in a debate on the following issue: "Resolved: Every child should have to do daily chores." Develop an effective analogy for the affirmative and negative sides of this proposition. To do this, state the two sides of the analogy—your point and the point to which you are comparing it. Then, explain the comparison. Finally, explain how the comparison and your point are alike.

Everyday Debate

Debate

In the last two chapters, you have been watching speeches on the following debate topic: "Resolved: America should be the world's policeman." So far, several speakers have compared the US policing of the world to the New York City police force policing their city. What are some strengths and weaknesses of this analogy?

Learning from the Masters

Observe

Watch the third set of speakers—Douglas Murray and Ian Bremmer—in the continuation of the debate: "Resolved: America should be the world's policeman" (Link 10-1). Then, answer the questions that follow.

3. Ratcliffe, *Oxford Dictionary of Quotations*, 293.

List

List three key arguments that Douglas Murray makes in his presentation:

Discuss

What are some strengths and weaknesses of Murray's speech?

List

List three key arguments that Ian Bremmer makes in his presentation:

Discuss

What are some strengths and weaknesses of Bremmer's arguments?

The Big Debate: Gun Control

Develop

To continue building arguments for the gun debate, develop an analogy for each side of the debate: "Resolved: Gun control is ethical and will make the United States a safer place."

Chapter 11

Inductive Logic: Relationship

> LOGICAL CONSEQUENCES ARE THE SCARECROWS OF FOOLS AND THE BEACONS OF WISE MEN.
> —T.H. HUXLEY[1]

Have you ever noticed that when people are trying to decide whether they should take a certain action, they commonly, and immediately, think about the potential positive or negative effects of taking (or not taking) that action? For example, let's say that a senior in high school is debating with himself about whether he should take a year off of school before he goes to college. He considers both the negative and positive effects this could have on him. On the one hand, he hypothesizes that delaying college could cause negative results, such as finishing college later than many of his friends. He also hypothesizes that it could cause him to work in a job he didn't enjoy for a year. On the other hand, he thinks that delaying college might cause some positive results, such as earning money to pay for college later and gaining life experience. He reasons that it would give him a break from schoolwork for a year and provide time to think about what he wants to do with his life. Ultimately, the student will need to decide whether this decision has more positive or negative effects, and his opinions about this matter will strongly influence the decision.

Causal Links: Relationship

This high school senior, though he may not realize it, is using the common topic of relationship to make his decision about college. When people use the common topic of **relationship**, they examine causal links between two factors (i.e., how one factor influences another). They do this to determine whether a certain factor has a negative or positive result. Another area where you commonly see use of this common topic is in academic studies—for example, doctors attempting to figure out the causes of certain diseases, such as cancer or diabetes. If they can find the *cause* of the disease, then they can try to eliminate the cause or help their patients to avoid or prevent it.

Consider how Josh and Christy might use the common topic of relationship for their debate. Christy has chosen to argue that capital punishment deters or discourages murder, while Josh is arguing that capital punishment either has no effect on murder or might actually encourage it. As you can see, both Josh and Christy are using the common topic of relationship. Over the phone one night, Josh and Christy discuss capital punishment using the common topic of relationship:

Josh: It doesn't make sense to me that capital punishment discourages murder. It seems that it could cause more negative emotions, which would lead to more violence. For example, let's say someone named Hal was killed for murdering his neighbor. Let's also say that Hal has a younger brother named Joseph. Joseph could be so traumatized by his brother's execution that it instills in him

1. Susan Ratcliffe, *Oxford Dictionary of Quotations by Subject*, 2nd ed. (Oxford: Oxford University Press, 2010), 290.

a hatred and fear of the government, which could encourage him to live a life of violence and crime. This may result in him causing harm to other people. In other words, when he sees the government executing people, it could desensitize him and teach him to value life less, which could lead him to commit murders. Perhaps if Hal had been disciplined and punished in a manner that reformed and rehabilitated him, instead of executing him, then not only would Hal be restored to society safely, but also his brother Joseph wouldn't be affected and changed in such a negative manner.

Christy: I understand what you are saying, Josh, but I think that when people know that killing someone could cause their own execution, it causes them to think twice about killing. In addition, this causes people to view life as sacred. For example, just imagine a world where people could kill others at any time without any punishment. This environment would lead people to think that human life is trivial, and it would result in more killing. When convicted criminals receive the maximum punishment for killing other people, it causes them and the rest of society to realize that human life is of utmost importance.

Using Statistics to Establish Relationship

Note that Josh and Christy used internal resources to develop their causal arguments. That is, they both used common sense and the common topic of relationship to create an argument. Because they both had good arguments, Josh and Christy decided that they needed to research capital punishment further by using external resources to determine whether it actually increased or decreased crime. Interestingly, they both found statistics supporting their separate arguments. A **statistic** is a numerical representation of examples. For example, Christy found a statistic from George E. Pataki, a former governor of New York. Pataki stated in 1997 that after New York reinstated the death penalty, murders dropped to nearly one-third of their previous rate.[2] Alternatively, Josh found the following information online: A September 2000 *New York Times* survey "found that during the last 20 years, the homicide rate in states with the death penalty has been 48 to 101 percent higher than in states without the death penalty."[3] How can it be that there are statistical studies supporting opposite claims? In order to answer this question, first you must learn how to construct a solid causal argument.

Remember that when you are making a causal argument, generally, your goal is to prove that a factor (Factor X) leads to either a positive result (Result P) or a negative result (Result N). For example, researchers have thoroughly documented that excessive smoking leads to lung cancer. It may not happen every time, but the causal scenario is so common that smoking is now commonly accepted as a causal factor for cancer. In addition, researchers have also documented a causal correlation between consuming large amounts of fast food and obesity and health problems. There are some exceptions, however. For instance, Don Gorske from Wisconsin has eaten seven to eight McDonald's hamburgers every day since 1972, and he maintains a healthy weight and has reasonable blood pressure and cholesterol levels.[4] This, however, appears to be an unusual example—an **anomaly** (an exception to the rule)—which is not representative of how a diet high in fast food normally affects people. When something is anomalous, it is an atypical example that does not fit the existing, common pattern. When you are making an inductive generalization, be sure to generalize on a consistent pattern demonstrated through many examples; you should not make a generalization based on an anomaly. In the case of fast food, the connection between high consumption of fast food and obesity is so well documented that it is a generally accepted causal relationship.

2. Richard C. Dieter, "The Death Penalty Is Not an Effective Law Enforcement Tool," in *Does Capital Punishment Deter Crime?* ed. Stephen E. Schonebaum (San Diego: Greenhaven Press, 1998), 11.
3. Raymond Bonner and Ford Fessenden, "Absence of Executions: A Special Report; States With No Death Penalty Share Lower Homicide Rates," *New York Times*, September 22, 2000, http://www.nytimes.com/2000/09/22/us/absence-executions-special-report-states-with-no-death-penalty-share-lower.html.
4. See Morgan Spurlock and Steve Horowitz, *Super Size Me*, directed by Morgan Spurlock (2004; New York: Hart Sharp Video, 2004), DVD.

Have you been able to figure out from these examples what constitutes a strong causal relationship? You probably have. In order to establish a strong causal connection, you need to find many examples of Factor X leading to Result P, or Factor X leading to Result N. The more examples you have that illustrate this causal relationship, the stronger the likelihood will be that that causal relationship is legitimate. Think about what is represented when you see a statistic about a causal relationship, such as the data found by Josh and Christy's research. When you see statistics illustrating causal relationships, you are looking at the percentage of examples consulted in which this causal relationship was present. For instance, Christy's study only examined the effect of the death penalty in New York. Josh's study examined the effect of the death penalty in twelve states.[5] Josh's study is more reliable than Christy's because it includes more examples (more states) than Christy's study (it was based solely in one state, New York). This doesn't mean that Josh's study proves that capital punishment is bad, once and for all; rather, this simply means that his study is stronger in this case because it is based on more examples.

It is important to note that statistics can be very deceiving. For example, let's say that I have three friends that come to my house for lunch, and we eat chicken salad sandwiches. Then, all three of them, as well as myself, get violently ill. I could create a statistic in which I state that 100 percent of people who eat chicken salad sandwiches have violent reactions. While this statement may be true as it specifically applies to lunch with my friends, it is nonetheless a distorted statistic. After all, I based this conclusion on my friends and me only, and there could be many different reasons to explain why we got sick. For example, perhaps the mayonnaise, or the chicken, in the salad was bad. Or, though it seems unlikely, it could be that all of us have developed an allergy to bread and are reacting to it. Of course, most statistical studies that you read are much more sophisticated than my silly statistic about chicken salad. However, sometimes these studies make similar mistakes that lead to distorted statistics: Namely, they use a small number of people (a small sample) to construct their statistic, or they fail to notice other causal factors. A **sample** is the number of examples considered in a statistic or the number of examples used to create a statistic. The more examples you have in a sample that demonstrate a certain effect, the more likely you are indeed observing a legitimate causal scenario. The fewer examples you have in a statistic, the more likely it is that you are not actually observing a causal scenario but rather just an apparent one. A small sample (the number of examples considered in a statistic) can lead to two common fallacies. They are the fallacies of hasty generalization and false cause. **Hasty generalization** occurs when someone bases a conclusion on too small a sample size, or too few examples. **False cause** is a fallacy someone commits when he reasons that because A happened before B, A caused B.

5. Bonner and Fessenden, "Absence of Executions."

For example, look at how these fallacies could occur in statistical studies about capital punishment. Let's say that a researcher conducted a study in which he measured crime in a certain state after it legalized capital punishment. Imagine that he documented that homicides (murders) increased 30 percent over a three-year period after capital punishment was legalized in this state. From this statistical study, it seems obvious that legalizing capital punishment leads to an increase in homicide rates. Therefore, one could easily surmise that capital punishment increases violence. However, if you think critically about this study, it should raise a few red flags in your mind. First, this researcher sampled just one state; therefore, the sample size is very small. If he had researched ten states and noticed a similar pattern, these results would be much more convincing. In this example, the researcher made a hasty generalization because he based a broad conclusion on one example—his one state that legalized capital punishment. While this study might have some force when dealing with the issue of capital punishment within his state (e.g., there might be unique factors, such as the ones addressed in the next paragraph, contributing to specific conditions), to apply it beyond that state is generalizing too hastily.

In addition, this statistic fails to demonstrate that capital punishment is the key cause of the increase in crime; after all, it is highly possible that other factors are involved in this crime increase. For example, it is plausible that the same year that capital punishment was legalized in the state, unemployment also increased, and the frustration over unemployment led to the rise in crime over the next three years. Or, as another possibility, perhaps the same year that capital punishment was legalized, a sociopath was paroled from prison and committed a series of violent murders that distorted the otherwise normal homicide statistics. It is important to note that social phenomena, such as crime rates, play a part of a larger, complex social system with many variable factors; therefore, it is important to investigate a variety of possible causal factors, or else your study may lack credibility. In other words, you may be guilty of committing false cause and attributing a causal relationship to factors that are only tangentially or coincidentally related. It would be wise, then, for Christy to think twice about using such a study to bolster her argument.

Andrew and Isabel Use Relationship in Discussing Pets

Now that you have a better understanding of how people can use the common topic of relationship in a formal debate, examine the following discussion that Isabel and Andrew had about pets:

Andrew: Isabel, I know this isn't a formal debate or anything like what we did in Mr. Garcia's class last year, but I think we need to do some more research. After all, you are pretty convinced that dogs cause messes and even disasters, and I've been arguing that the two are not necessarily always related. I'm concerned that we will just keep arguing back and forth unless we find some outside information to shed light on the issue.

Isabel: OK, that makes sense. How about we each interview five people with cats and five people with dogs about the messes their pets make.

Andrew: That's a lot of people, but I guess we probably should—I mean, if we are going to even attempt to have some kind of legitimate statistic. I can just hear Mr. Garcia saying, "Don't commit the fallacy of hasty generalizations. Don't commit the fallacy of false cause. Do your research!"

Isabel: Yeah—I was thinking the same thing. So, do you want to give it a shot?

Andrew: Sure, why not? Boy, sometimes I can't tell whether taking that debate class was a blessing or a curse. I sure have to think a lot harder now than I used to before I took it.

Isabel: I know the feeling. How about we take the weekend to call people and discuss this again on Monday?

Note that Isabel and Andrew did not use statistics in their informal discussion about cats and dogs. As you can imagine, it will certainly be difficult to find legitimate, scientific statistics about whether cats or dogs are more practical pets. It is likely that no such definitive statistics exist. However, Isabel and Andrew are still attempting to make legitimate inductive generalizations because they have decided to call ten of their friends (five with cats and five with dogs) each to find out their opinions about how they are as pets. If this were a more formal scientific study or academic research, Andrew and Isabel would need to interview many more people to create a more credible and legitimate sample size. However, for their purposes in this informal debate, their sample size of ten people is adequate. In other words, Isabel and Andrew just want to know, in general, some of the experiences their friends have had with cats and dogs to better determine which pet choice causes more messes. This will be helpful for them because their friends are similar to them, that is, they are similar in age, interests, and schedules.

Furthermore, Isabel and Andrew need help figuring out which pet would be best for *them*, personally—not which pet would be best for every teenager in America or in the world. Therefore, for their purposes, interviewing ten people who they know personally is adequate. By the way, it is probably no surprise to you that all the dog owners Isabel and Andrew interviewed admitted that though they loved their dogs, they often had to clean up large messes that their dogs had made. On the other hand, only one of the interviewed cat owners could remember any serious mess their cat had made—one girl's cat had attacked a bird cage containing the family's pet bird, knocking over the cage and scattering feathers and bird food everywhere. Therefore, Isabel appeared to be justified in her claim that dogs cause more messes. It is important to realize that the more academic your study is, and the more generally you wish to apply your conclusion, the more examples you should consult to make your generalization.

In conclusion, both sets of debaters were able to use internal sources to generate arguments with the common topic of relationship. That is, they could hypothesize about some likely cause-and-effect relationships just by using their common sense. However, both pairs of debaters eventually decided that they needed to consult external sources as well. You will begin to regularly notice that the more in depth you research a subject, the more likely it is that you will need to consult both types of sources as well.

Review Exercises

Define

For each of the following terms, please provide a brief but complete answer.

1. Relationship:

____

____

2. Statistic:

____

____

3. Sample:

____

____

4. Anomaly:

____

____

5. Hasty Generalization:

____

____

6. False Cause:

____

____

Building Copiousness

Review

Review your old quotes.

Practice

Practice saying the quotes to someone in your class, or practice writing them down on paper.

Memorize

Memorize your new quote:

> Hope is definitely not the same thing as optimism. It is not the conviction that something will turn out well, but the certainty that something makes sense, regardless of how it turns out. —Václav Havel[6]

6. Ratcliffe, *Oxford Dictionary of Quotations*, 230.

Practicing Evaluating Causal Relationships

Discuss

Learning how to determine which factor causes another can be very tricky. To practice this skill, read each of the following exercises, which discuss possible causal relationships. Then, answer the questions that follow.

1. Possible Causal Relationship between Playing Video Games and Violence

   In a study published in early 2014 in the medical journal *JAMA Pediatrics*, a team of scientists "found hints that violent video games may set kids up to react in more hostile and violent ways," basing their conclusions on two years of detailed surveying of over 3,000 boys and girls in Singapore across a variety of grade levels. The children who played violent video games more often were more likely to score higher on standardized questionnaires measuring their attitudes about violence and their own aggressive behavior, and "the more long-term gamers were also more likely to fantasize about hitting someone they didn't like."[7]

   Perhaps even more alarming, a 2011 study by Indiana University School of Medicine suggests that the brain may actually be changed by playing violent video games. Twenty-eight healthy young men participated in the study, with half of the group playing a shooting game on a laptop at home, and the other half playing no games. A comparison of brain images of the two groups demonstrated "sustained changes in the region of the brain associated with cognitive function and emotional control," and this effect was noticeable after only one week of daily gaming. One researcher in the study concluded that "these effects may translate into behavioral changes over longer periods of game play."[8]

   A. What are the strengths and weaknesses of the causal claim made in the first study?

   ____

   ____

   ____

   ____

   ____

   ____

   ____

7. Alice Park, "Little By Little, Violent Video Games Make Us More Aggressive," *Time.com*, March 24, 2014, http://time.com/34075/how-violent-video-games-change-kids-attitudes-about-aggression/.
8. Indiana University School of Medicine, "Violent Video Games Alter Brain Function in Young Men," *ScienceDaily*, December 1, 2011, www.sciencedaily.com/releases/2011/11/111130095251.htm.

B. What are the strengths and weaknesses of the causal claim made in the second study?

2. Researchers James D. Wright and Peter H. Rossi surveyed felons and found that:

> "Most criminals are more worried about meeting an armed victim than they are about running into the police." When felons were asked what they personally thought about while committing crimes, 34 percent indicated that they thought about getting "shot at by police" or "shot by victim." The data suggests that criminals may be a little more concerned about being caught by police and imprisoned than about being shot, but meeting the armed citizen clearly elicited fears of being shot.[9]

A. What is the causal claim being made in this study?

B. What are the strengths and weaknesses of this claim as it is currently worded?

9. Paul Blackman, "The Armed Criminal in America," NRA-ILA, September 9, 2003, https://www.nraila.org/articles/20030909/the-armed-criminal-in-america.

3. Several gun control studies have been done comparing Seattle, Washington, in the United States and Vancouver, British Columbia, in Canada because these cities are alike in many ways—except for their gun control laws. Here is a description of what some researchers have found:

   A team of scientists led by Dr. Henry Sloan conducted a comparative study of Seattle and Vancouver in order to draw conclusions about the effect of gun laws on gun violence. Although these two cities are neighbors, more or less, and although their populations have similar economies and demographics, the researchers noted that Seattle has many more gun-related deaths than Vancouver. The researchers concluded that the key difference in the two cities is that gun control is much more lax in Seattle than in the other city. Canada has much stricter laws concerning handguns. Therefore, a person is far more likely to be shot in Seattle than in Vancouver.[10]

   A. What is the claim in this argument?

   B. What are the strengths and weaknesses of this study?

10. Richard Reeves, "Seattle-Vancouver Figures Prove Gun Control Does Work," *Sun-Sentinel*, September 27, 1992, http://articles.sun-sentinel.com/1992-09-27/news/9201240223_1_colin-loftin-homicides-and-suicides-gun-control-laws.

4. Purdue University economist John Umbeck did a study on California in the gold rush and discovered something very interesting about gun ownership and violence in this historical time period. Umbeck noted that in the high Sierra gold fields in Californian, gold was discovered in Sutter's Mill in 1848. As a result of this discovery, thousands of prospectors rushed into this area of California, staking their claims. There was no government in place at this time; there were no laws to speak of, but almost all the prospectors owned guns. What is especially interesting is that hundreds of millions of dollars' worth of gold were being discovered in gold fields, but there was little violence.[11]

   A. What is the claim being made?

   B. List a couple of strengths and weaknesses of Umbeck's argument.

11. John Umbeck, "Might Makes Rights: A Theory of Formation and Distribution of Property Rights," 9 *Econ. Inquiry* 38 (1981), cited in Clayton E. Cramer and David B. Kopel, " 'Shall Issue': The New Wave of Concealed Handgun Permit Laws," Independence Institute, 1994, footnotes 158–159, http://rkba.org/research/cramer/shall-issue.html.

Spotting Fallacies

At this point, you have learned about the fallacies of false analogy, hasty generalization, and false cause. Six arguments are listed below. Three contain fallacies, and three do not contain fallacies. If an argument contains no fallacy, circle the words "No Fallacy." If an argument does contain a fallacy, however, then circle the word "Fallacy" and write the specific fallacy (or fallacies) being committed in the blank provided.

1. Smoking causes lung cancer. I once knew this guy who smoked a pack of cigarettes every day for fifty years. Then, he got lung cancer and died.

    No Fallacy Fallacy ______________________________

2. It appears that there is a very strong correlation between eating large amounts of fast food and obesity. For instance, I was reading this study put out by the USDA Agricultural Research Service. They surveyed 9,000 US citizens over two days and found that those who ate fast food on those days drank "twice as many sugary drinks" and more "fats, carbohydrates, added sugars, and protein" than those who did not eat fast food. In addition, they found that those who ate fast food on one or both of those days had a higher BMI that those who did not eat fast food on either of the days.[12]

    No Fallacy Fallacy ______________________________

3. It is clear that capital punishment actually increases crime. For example, the state of Texas, which leads the nation in executions, has also led the nation for years at a time in the number of its police officers killed. And in 1994, the state of New York, which did not have the death penalty saw one-third the number of its police officers killed as did the state of Texas.[13]

    No Fallacy Fallacy ______________________________

4. It is wrong to lie. Lying is like forgetting to take out the garbage. When you keep forgetting to take out the garbage, eventually it makes your whole house stink. In the same way, when you lie, lying eventually "stinks up" your life because lying eventually causes you to get into trouble.

    No Fallacy Fallacy ______________________________

5. It's really dangerous to lie. Lying is like skiing down a really steep slope that has a lot of rocks and trees in your path. You keep going faster and faster, and you lose control and eventually you will crash into something and damage yourself. In the same way, once you lie, you start telling more and more lies to cover the old lie. Pretty soon, you are constantly telling lies to hide your past dishonesty, and you feel out of control, and eventually, your lies cause a huge catastrophe or a breakdown in trust that seriously damage your reputation and your relationship with others.

    No Fallacy Fallacy ______________________________

---

12. "Fast Food Consumption Increases Obesity Risk." *FoodNavigator.com*, May 24, 2004. http://www.foodnavigator.com/Science-Nutrition/Fast-food-consumption-increases-obesity-risk.
13. Dieter, "Death Penalty Is Not an Effective Law Enforcement Tool," 31.

6. A study done at Harvard University, which tracked 84,129 healthy women, found that women who ate high levels of whole grains, polyunsaturated fats, folic acid, fish, and alcohol in moderation, and reduced their levels of saturated and trans fats, reduced their risk of getting a heart attack by as much as 80 percent when they "combined these healthy eating habits with non-smoking, getting regular physical activity, and maintaining a healthy weight."[14]

No Fallacy Fallacy ______________________________

Everyday Debate

Debate

So far, we have discussed how to use the common topics of definition, comparison, and relationship. It's time to practice these skills in a minidebate. The topic for your minidebate is "Resolved: Everyone should own more houseplants." As you develop the arguments for your debate, make sure you include a definition, an argument from comparison, and an argument from relationship. It is fine to include more arguments than this, but make sure you at least include these three types of arguments. In addition, try to include at least one quote from your "Building Copiousness" exercises.

Learning from the Masters

Observe

Now that you have listened to all of the presentations on the topic "Resolved: America should be the world's policeman," listen to the question-and-answer sessions by the moderator, presenters, and audience (Link 11-1). What, in your opinion, was one of the best questions and why?

The Big Debate: Gun Control

List

As you can probably imagine, both sides of the gun control debate list numerous statistics and/or arguments from cause-and-effect relationships to support their ideas. You have already read some of these in your previous exercises. Now it is your turn to find and evaluate cause-and-effect arguments about gun control. In the space provided, list two cause-and-effect arguments pertaining to gun control—one for the affirmative side and one for the negative side. Evaluate the strengths and weaknesses of these arguments.

---

14. Mollie Katzen and Walter Willett, *Eat, Drink, and Weigh Less: A Flexible and Delicious Way to Shrink Your Waist without Going Hungry* (New York: Hyperion, 2006), 3.

Chapter 12

Inductive Logic: Circumstance

> NO MAN IS AN ISLAND ENTIRE OF HIMSELF; EVERY MAN IS A PIECE OF THE CONTINENT, A PART OF THE MAIN.
> —JOHN DONNE[1]

Introduction

You can probably complete the following quote: "He who does not learn from history is . . ." Did you guess the rest of it? You may have heard this quote before. The phrase is finished by "doomed to repeat it." This quote, which your history teachers have probably repeated to you regularly, holds a lot of truth. Sometimes we make the mistake of believing that because we are more modern and more technologically advanced today than people from history, the people in the past have nothing to teach us. This belief would indeed be a mistake, and as you shall see, circumstance—or, specifically, past and future fact—is the next common topic that can help you develop inductive arguments.

Before you learn how to construct this type of argument, let's first discuss what you can learn from the past. It's important to understand that it is challenging to be objective about the particular time and circumstances in which you are living. That is, when we make decisions and accept beliefs, it can be difficult for us to see the flaws or errors of our specific beliefs or practices because they grow out of a specific culture and set of circumstances. For example, when the scientists Copernicus and Galileo began talking about a heliocentric, or sun-centered, theory of the universe, it was very hard for the people around them to accept this theory because their culture was steeped in the geocentric, or Earth-centered, theory of the universe. The beauty of history is that people and cultures have been involved in shifting political situations and belief systems.

Comparing our modern culture's current beliefs to what people in the past have believed can sometimes help us recognize weaknesses and viewpoints in our own belief systems. For example, cultural analysts have noted that modern American culture is an extremely individualistic culture. We tend to be wrapped up in our personal lives, goals, and career aspirations. And, in fact, contemporary American life can be so busy that it can be challenging to make meaningful connections with people on a regular basis. However, this lifestyle is a relatively new development in history. Historically, individuals' lives were centered around a close group of people, like their family and neighbors in a small community, and they had very close connections with the people in this group. When we compare this community-oriented aspect of some past societies with our modern, individualistic culture, it can help us gain a better perspective on both the strengths and weaknesses of that mind-set. In other words, when we are confronted with lifestyles or ideas that are very different from our own, we can compare them with our current ideas or lifestyles. This exposure to other ways of thinking can help us gain a better understanding of history's changing norms.

1. Susan Ratcliffe, *Oxford Dictionary of Quotations by Subject*, 2nd ed. (Oxford: Oxford University Press, 2010), 442.

When we study the past, we have a better understanding of why things have developed the way they have—that is, why we believe or act in the ways that we do today. For example, many people know that American democratic tradition has historical roots that go back as far as the time of ancient Greeks and Romans. American democracy certainly did not spring to life out of thin air. It was highly influenced by philosophies, persons, and events dating back many centuries. One such event occurred in AD 1215 when a group of English noblemen dragged King John, the despotic king of England, to a nearby meadow and made him sign a significant document called the Magna Carta.[2] King John was a selfish ruler who enjoyed an extravagant lifestyle and wanted the English people to fund his standard of living, no questions asked. The king would continue to raise taxes on his people, never caring that they were unfair, unnecessary, and, in many cases, devastating for many of his subjects.[3] Finally, a group of his subjects became so tired of this practice that they decided they would force John to change. They made him sign the Magna Carta, a document that required the king to not raise taxes without the consent of his people. The signing of this charter was a pivotal event that weakened the long tradition of absolute rule by a monarch and paved the way for rule by the people, or constitutional law.[4] By understanding historical events such as this, we can grasp more fully why we are where we are today.

2. Bryce Lyon, "Magna Carta," in *World Book Encyclopedia* (Chicago: World Book, 1992), 53.

Circumstance

So how does the study of history help us? Well, have you ever heard of the phrase "Don't reinvent the wheel"? This phrase alludes to the idea that people in the past have gained relevant knowledge just from being alive and experiencing the world. It's not that they know everything, but rather that they might know more than we do because of their experiences. Therefore, when we look to the past and learn from what they discovered, we can avoid learning things the hard way—in other words, we can prevent needing to relearn lessons that people in the past have already learned and are able to teach us. Because the past has so much to tell us about the present, it is always wise to examine the historical development of a topic you are researching. When people research and comprehend elements of the past so they can apply that knowledge to current situations in the present, they are utilizing the fourth common topic: **circumstance**. When you use the common topic of circumstance to develop inductive arguments, you ask questions such as the following: How did this situation develop? Why did this situation develop? What can we learn from this? What have people believed in the past about this situation? How is this different from what people believe today? What can we learn from this?

At first glance, these may look like hard questions to answer, but you are likely able to answer them more easily than you think. You have probably accumulated a lot of information about historical events or people that pertain to your topic, without even realizing it. As an example to

3. Ibid.
4. Ibid.

illustrate this point, let's revisit Josh and Christy's debate about capital punishment. There are some key historical issues about capital punishment that could help them with their debate. The following are questions they should consider: How long has capital punishment been around? Why did it develop? Why have people been in favor of it? Why have people opposed it? How have views of capital punishment changed over the years?

Josh and Christy had already checked out several books from the library during their last visit, so they set about researching these questions in the pages of their borrowed materials. A few classes later, they had the following conversation:

Josh: Christy, did you realize that the United States is the only Western industrialized nation that still uses capital punishment? Over the past few decades, almost all European nations, as well as Canada and Latin America, have abolished capital punishment?[5] Many people claim that the more enlightened, mature, and industrialized a country becomes, the more it moves toward the abolition of the death penalty.

Christy: I did read those quotes, but I think they can be kind of misleading. After all, some of those countries, such as Canada, only abolished the death penalty recently. Furthermore, just because they have abolished it now doesn't mean it will stay abolished. For example, for a period of time in the United States, the Supreme Court ruled that the way capital punishment was being practiced was arbitrary and unconstitutional.[6] Because of this, capital punishment drastically decreased in America for a while. But then, only a few years later in 1976, the Supreme Court ruled that capital punishment was not unconstitutional per se, and states started using the death penalty again.[7] So a state or a country can change its mind on the matter. It's not as if all states or countries that abolish capital punishment maintain that decision indefinitely.

5. Franklin E. Zimring, "Capital Punishment," in *World Book Encyclopedia* (Chicago: World Book, 1992), 193.
6. Gary E. McCuen, *The Death Penalty and the Disadvantaged (Ideas in Conflict)* (Hudson, WI: Gem Pubns, 1996), 28.
7. Zimring, "Capital Punishment," 193.

As you can see, Josh and Christy's research has given them a lot of material that will help them analyze the historical nature of capital punishment in their debate. Consider the role of history in informal debate and discussion. One difficulty with using circumstance for informal arguments is that history often requires some research to develop it, and for the most part, the setting of an informal argument doesn't allow for this type of research. Instead, informal discussions are often spontaneous and occur without prior warning. If the common topic of circumstance usually requires research, it may not seem like a very useful tool to use in an informal debate because that type of spur-of-the-moment discussion often occurs in places and at times where there is little, if any, opportunity to research. So what should you do with the topic of circumstance in an informal discussion? First, keep this topic in mind because you may be able to use it more than you think. For example, you may already know about the history of a topic without needing to look it up. If you do, then, by all means, make it part of your consideration in your debate. However, even if you don't know the history of your topic offhand, you can still access a tool, sometimes even at your fingertips (e.g., via a cell phone or laptop) that enables quick historical research: the Internet. As you have already learned, not all websites on the Internet are legitimate or credible, and you should be extremely careful when you use Internet sources in formal research. Nevertheless, if you have a brief question about the history of your topic, you can type your query or subject into a search engine and, possibly, find the answer in a matter of seconds. As an example, let's say you are at a coffee shop with a friend, and your friend claims that whenever the federal government intervenes during times of economic crisis, this intervention produces very little benefit to the economy. One thing you could do is use the Internet to research the economic effects of federal involvement during the time of the Great Depression, as this is one of the most severe economic crises of history. Researching this information would allow you to verify or to critique your friend's claim.

There is another important point regarding circumstance when it comes to informal discussion. Sometimes in your informal debates and discussions, you may be in a position to continue the debate over several days or weeks. In fact, on the Internet and in social media (e.g., Facebook), you are probably aware that there are websites and online groups set up purposefully for the debate of certain issues. Of course, some of these are more formally organized than others. But the point is that sometimes an informal debate can carry on for quite some time. If this is the case, take the time to conduct extra research so that you can present an informed and knowledgeable case. Understanding the history of your topic is a very important part of this.

Let's return now to Andrew and Isabel and their debate about pets, and let's examine how research plays a part in their debate. Andrew and Isabel have both became interested in the history of people owning cats and dogs as pets. Each of them, without the other knowing it, consulted the "Cat" and "Dog" entries in the *World Book Encyclopedia* set they had in their house. Later in the week, they had the following conversation:

Andrew: Isabel, did you know that dogs were the first domesticated pet and that they have been highly valued throughout history for their abilities to guard people and to help keep campsites clean?

Isabel: Wow! You've been reading the encyclopedias, too. I just read that today. Mom and Dad are going to be shocked when they find out that we're actually reading the encyclopedias, rather than using them for doorstops or footrests. Ha ha! Well, did you know that cats, too, have also been domesticated pets for a long time, and that—unlike dogs—cats were believed to be sacred, and even worshipped, by many cultures?

Andrew: As a matter of fact, I did know that. But did you know that many people in the Middle Ages considered cats to be evil and had massive cat purges to get rid of their diabolical influence? You don't see people conducting dog purges anywhere in history, do you? I'll tell you what, those people in the Middle Ages were on to something—maybe the Dark Ages weren't so dark after all.

Isabel: Oh, good grief![8]

8. Andrew's information was taken from M. Fox, "Cats," *World Book Encyclopedia* (Chicago: World Book, 1992), and Isabel's from Sean McGinnis, "Dogs," *World Book Encyclopedia* (Chicago: World Book, 1992).

Isabel and Andrew's historical information about cats and dogs is more entertaining and enlightening than it is truly persuasive for either side. This is normal in the course of debate. Sometimes, as seen in the case of Josh and Christy, the history of your topic will be integral to setting up and strengthening your argument. For instance, the fact that throughout history most civilized cultures have moved toward abolishing capital punishment will likely be very helpful for Josh's side of the debate. Alternatively, the fact that capital punishment has been practiced in almost every country under every religious system will likely be helpful to Christy's side of the debate.

Before you read about the common fallacies people commit with the common topic of circumstance, you need to learn about one other source that is good to use when you are looking at the historical development of a topic. Remember that recommendation to obtain a book of quotations for research purposes? This is a great place to make use of that resource. Quote books are great tools to use because they are usually arranged by topics, and for a given topic they often provide a grouping of various quotes from many different kinds of people throughout history. Therefore, if you want to look at what people have thought about a topic throughout the ages, a book of quotations can be a great place to start. However, be aware that these kinds of quotations rarely prove a point; instead, they serve to illustrate, embellish, or amplify your arguments. (In rhetoric, "amplification" refers to a process of expanding on a point to give additional information or emphasis, usually by repeating words and then adding onto them. Here, we use the word to mean strengthening the force of your argument.) You won't use them as much in informal debates, but they are extremely useful in formal debates because they can put the finishing touches on your argument, or they can be an entertaining or humorous addition to your speech. Effective quotes can serve as the "icing on the cake," so to speak, when you are developing a historical look at your argument.

Beware of False Analogy

Once you have developed a good argument from history, you'll want to be aware of four common fallacies that people commit when using the common topic of circumstance. Be especially mindful of these arguments when you use circumstance because you could easily commit one of them. Also, someone could commit one of these fallacies as they attempt to argue against you. Remember how we discussed at the beginning of the chapter that people have a tendency to look down on people from the past, whom they view as less advanced and not enlightened? Well, the more an opposing debater feels this way, the more she is likely to commit this fallacy against you during her arguments.

The first fallacy is a fallacy with which you are already familiar: *false analogy*. You've learned that someone commits false analogy when he draws a conclusion from two items that are too dissimilar for any comparison to be made. If you think about it, you will see how someone could easily commit this fallacy when arguing from circumstance, for when you argue from circumstance, you usually draw a conclusion from a historical situation that you believe to be analogous to a current situation. For instance, in Josh's research about capital punishment, he found that throughout history, countries tended to punish criminals in extremely harsh ways. He discovered that for a variety of crimes England, criminals could be hanged, drawn and quartered, boiled, or burned by authorities.[9] In his studies, Josh noted that as time went on and people became more humane and enlightened, punishment for crimes became less severe. Josh planned to use this fact from history to argue that even though capital punishment had been common in the past, more and more people have abandoned this practice as they become more humane and enlightened. In this argument, Josh is drawing a conclusion from a comparison between past and current events. In other words, he is making a type of analogy.

When you draw a comparison between analogous past and current events, it is important that the two events have more similarities than dissimilarities. Otherwise, you could easily commit the fallacy of false analogy. For example, Josh could try to argue the following: "Just as people abandoned the geocentric (Earth-centered) theory of the universe as they became more educated, so, too, will people abandon capital punishment if they become more educated and enlightened." The problem with this comparison is that the items are too dissimilar to warrant any conclusion. One pertains to scientific views (of geocentric theory), while the other pertains to moral and ethical views (of capital punishment). While science is certainly affected by ethics and moral ideas, and moral and ethical views are affected by science, the two areas of study are dissimilar enough that a change in one does not automatically necessitate a change in the other. Therefore, this is a false analogy. Whenever you draw a conclusion from comparisons between past and current situations, make sure that the comparison is truly warranted.

Beware of Bandwagon

The second fallacy you need to watch out for is a fallacy called *bandwagon*. This is a fallacy that you might accidentally commit when you are constructing an argument from history or past circumstances. When someone commits the **bandwagon** fallacy, he reasons or argues that because many people are doing or believing something—or have done or believed it—then it should be done or believed. When a large number of people believe something, however, it doesn't automatically make that something true. For instance, if you recall, when Josh had researched capital punishment (see chapter 9) he had discovered that after 1990, the United States was the only industrialized, modern country that practiced capital punishment. All of the other modernized countries such as Canada and many European countries had outlawed the practice.[10] Josh would be committing the bandwagon fallacy if he were to argue "Capital punishment must be wrong because every other industrial country besides the United States thinks it's wrong." As you have observed from everyday experiences and interactions, just because many people think, believe, or do something, that doesn't mean it is necessarily the right thing to think, believe, or do. The number of believers says nothing significant about the validity, or fact, of a practice or belief. Of course,

9. "Introduction to the Death Penalty," Death Penalty Information Center, 2015, http://www.deathpenaltyinfo.org/part-i-history-death-penalty.

10. Zimring, "Capital Punishment," 193.

if a large number of credible, intelligent people believe something, then it is certainly worth checking and considering. You should endeavor to learn from the wisdom and experience of others. However, although the number of people who believe something might make its truth more *likely*, large numbers of believers never *guarantee* the truth. Masses of people have been known to be deceived. And when the bandwagon fallacy comes into play, there may be pressure to engage in some activity that is morally questionable or outright wrong, simply because many others are doing so. For example, during the Second World War, many Europeans found it easier to turn a blind eye to the persecution of Jews because so many people in their society maintained prejudiced views about this people group.

Beware of Appeal to Tradition

In addition to bandwagon, be wary of another common fallacy: **appeal to tradition**. This fallacy occurs when someone argues that because something has always been believed or practiced, it must be the right thing to believe or do. For instance, Christy would be committing the fallacy of appealing to tradition if she argued the following: "Capital punishment is reasonable. After all, until recently, capital punishment has been practiced by every nation and culture around the world." This may sound like bandwagon, and the two fallacies certainly have some similarities. However, instead of arguing that someone should do something because *many people* are doing it (bandwagon), a person who makes an appeal to tradition argues that a practice or belief is right because it always *has been* believed or practiced. In other words, bandwagon tries to falsely justify a position by noting the *number* of people doing or believing something, and an appeal to tradition tries to falsely justify a position by noting *how long* people or cultures have been doing or believing something.

Beware of Appeal to Novelty

A fallacy that is nearly the opposite of an appeal to tradition is the **appeal to novelty**. When someone makes an appeal to novelty, she believes that whatever is new is always better, wiser, or more advanced than the technology, concept, practices, or belief systems of the past. It is certainly true that new developments or beliefs *can* be better. For instance, in the 1800s, developments in our understanding of hygiene improved hospital practices dramatically.[11] Copernicus and Galileo revolutionized our understanding of cosmology with the aid of a particular advance in technology, the microscope. Sometimes new *is* better. However, the newness of something does not guarantee its wisdom or effectiveness. Some new things are just trendy, faddish, and superficial. For instance, how many clothing styles, singing groups, movies, and toys have been touted as the "next hot thing," only to be cast aside as trivial rubbish the following year, if not within the month or week. Therefore, we cannot deem some action, belief, or practice wrong or right based merely on its age or currency. Rather, the belief or practice itself must be examined and judged for its own merit.

In summary, the common topic of circumstance is extremely helpful because it directs us to past people, events, and ideas to see what we can learn from them, and how to apply those observations to our current situation or debate. Although contemporary people are certainly advanced in many ways because of our ever-expanding technology, science, and learning, we can also be blind to our modern faults and misconceptions. When we look to the past, we can gain a more objective picture of who we are and the place from which we come. In using the common topic of circumstance, it is important to avoid the fallacies of false analogy, bandwagon, appeal to tradition, and appeal to novelty. In the next chapter, you will examine the last—and one of the most frequently used—common topic: testimony.

11. Kenneth F. Manning, "Florence Nightingale," in *World Book Encyclopedia* (Chicago: World Book, 1992), 424.

Review Exercises

Define

Give an appropriate definition for each of the following words:

1. Circumstance:

____

____

2. Bandwagon:

____

____

3. Appeal to tradition:

____

____

4. Appeal to novelty:

____

____

5. False analogy:

____

____

Explain

1. Explain why it is so important to learn from history.

____

____

2. Explain why quotes found in quotation books are often only illustrative for your arguments.

____

____

____

____

Building Copiousness

Review

Review your old quotes.

Practice

Practice saying the quotes to someone in your class, or practice writing them down on paper.

Memorize

Memorize your new quote:

> Those who cannot remember the past are condemned to repeat it. —George Santayana[12]

Practice Evaluating Arguments from Circumstance

Explain

Read the following argument, which pertains to the Bosnian/Serbian/Croatian conflict in the Balkans, which led to the genocide of Bosnian Muslims. Then, answer the questions that follow:[13]

> In the initially lethal skirmishes between Serbs and Croats in the north . . . after some fighting, Serbia cut a deal, settling for a relatively small share of Croatia. The Croats' military power was nowhere near enough

12. Ratcliffe, *Oxford Dictionary of Quotations*, 354.
13. You can read more on this conflict in the article "Bosnian Genocide" at this site: http://www.history.com/topics/bosnian-genocide.

to conquer the Serbs. It was merely enough to make the Serbs appreciate the advantages of peace. Guns did not so much win a war as avert one.

The Bosnian Muslims were not so fortunate. For the most part they were unarmed, and the arms embargo left them helpless against Croat and Serb enemies who wanted their land. Margaret Thatcher . . . had warned for several months that the embargo spelled disaster for Muslim people of Bosnia. Until . . . "ethnic cleansing" proved her point, respectable opinion was very much against her views.[14]

1. What is being claimed in this argument?

____

____

____

2. What are the strengths and weaknesses of this argument?

____

____

____

____

____

____

Explain

Many arguments for and against gun control center on the Second Amendment, which includes language about the right to bear arms and the right to have a militia. Read the following argument about the Second Amendment and historical interpretations of it. Then, answer the questions that follow:

> Based on the first clause of the Second Amendment, the ACLU suggests the Second Amendment guarantees only a state's right to maintain a militia. This, too, is a misinterpretation of the history and meaning of the Amendment.
>
> During the Revolutionary era, every city and township maintained its own militia. There were also private militias. In Lexington, Massachusetts, it was the town militia which squared off against the British regulars.
>
> Historically, and under current law, militias consisted of "citizen-soldiers." This meant all able-bodied males between 18 and 45 years old were expected to muster, bearing their own arms, during times of threat. Today, all able-bodied citizens of either sex would probably be expected so to appear.

14. Daniel D. Polsby, "Private Ownership of Handguns Leads to Lower Rates of Handgun Violence," in *Gun Control: Opposing Viewpoints*, ed. Tamara L. Roleff (San Diego: Greenhaven Press, 1997), 27.

Since a militia consisted of all the armed citizens, it could exist only if all the citizens were armed. For this reason, the ACLU's assertion that the reference to a "well regulated Militia" confers a right upon states is, again, ludicrous.[15]

1. What does this argument claim?

2. What are the strengths and weaknesses of this argument?

15. Steven Silver, "Private Gun Ownership Is Protected by the Second Amendment," Roleff, *Gun Control*, 80.

Spotting Fallacies

So far, you have studied the fallacies of false analogy, hasty generalization, false cause, bandwagon, appeal to tradition, and appeal to novelty. Read each of the following arguments and identify one fallacy being committed, writing this in the space provided. Some arguments commit more than one fallacy; in this case, you only need to write down *one* of the fallacies in the space provided.

1. I can't believe you are quoting Benjamin Franklin to support your ideas about gun control. He wrote in the 1750s. His ideas are hardly relevant today.

   ____

2. The majority of Americans believe that guns should be restricted. We need to enact strict gun control legislation now.

   ____

3. We have to allow private gun possession. Guns are like seat belts—you never know when you'll need them, but when you do, they can save lives.

   ____

4. Handguns should be made illegal. Two of my friends have been seriously wounded with handguns their family or friends owned. Handguns in the possession of private people are extremely dangerous!

   ____

5. Back in colonial times, people owned guns, and there weren't a lot of deaths. So guns aren't the problem. We shouldn't outlaw them.

   ____

6. I knew this family that was really happy and successful. Then they bought a handgun. The next year, their dad was laid off from work and the mom got stomach cancer. Not only that, the son found the gun and accidentally shot the next-door neighbor in the leg. He had to do community service. Guns are obviously bad news.

   ____

7. Americans have always possessed guns. You can't argue with hundreds of years of American heritage!

   ____

8. In the last city I lived in, they lowered gun restriction laws, and the next year, criminal activity increased quite a bit. Guns obviously need to be restricted.

   ____

Everyday Debate

Debate

Here is a topic for a good minidebate: "Resolved: It is wrong to kill spiders." Your teacher will divide you into teams. Choose a side, then develop arguments for your side using (a) at least two historical examples to support your point, (b) a definition, (c) an analogy, and (d) a cause-and-effect argument. In addition, incorporate one quote from the "Building Copiousness" sections from previous chapters.

Learning from the Masters

Observe

To finish up the Intelligence Squared debate, "Resolved: America should be the world's policeman," watch the closing arguments of the speakers (Link 12-1). Then, explain which arguments you think are the most effective. Be sure to clarify why you believe they were effective.

The Big Debate: Gun Control

Develop

Because people have regularly owned and used guns throughout history in different cultures, you can develop many arguments from circumstance for the gun control debate. Now that you have read a few examples of these types of arguments in the previous exercises, find and evaluate two arguments from circumstance: one for gun control, and one against it. Write these arguments in the space provided.

Chapter 13

Inductive Logic: Testimony

FOOLS NEED ADVICE MOST, BUT
WISE MEN ONLY ARE THE BETTER FOR IT.
—BENJAMIN FRANKLIN[1]

The last common topic you will examine is testimony, which is one of the most frequently used common topics people utilize to construct inductive arguments. The common topic of **testimony** refers to the testimony, or witness, of everyday examples, ordinary people, and expert authorities. You have already been introduced to this topic in chapter 8, where Isabel and Andrew were talking about their friend's dog, Samson. Andrew had said that Samson was really good at doing tricks. When Andrew discussed this, he was taking an example of everyday experience, and he let this experience "testify" about the point he was trying to make. The word "testimony" derives from the Latin word *testificari*, which means "to bear witness." A witness, of course, is a source to support a belief or argument. Therefore, a testimony bears witness to the fact or idea you are trying to support.

Common Facts and Examples

There are a lot of different kinds of testimony, and when we are looking for information to prove our point, we often seek a variety of testimonies. One of the most common types of testimony is the testimony of common facts and examples. In other words, you should consult what well-known facts and standard examples reveal about a topic.

Just like having a witness take the stand in a courtroom case, bringing testimonies is intended to summon other voices to help your own in support of a claim or point of view. What makes a witness worth listening to? They have experience in the subject under question (such as an eyewitness to a particular event). They have knowledge or skills unique to the topic at hand. Or they have demonstrated a trait—honesty, wisdom, eloquence—that disposes an audience or judge to listen to what they're saying.

Testimony of Authorities

Another commonly used testimony type is the testimony of authorities. Authorities are experts or people who have conducted extensive research, or have had a lot of hands-on experience, in a particular field. For example, an acceptable authority on education would be a teacher or principal with many years of educational experience, and he would likely have a degree, or several degrees, in education. An expert on capital punishment would likely have a degree in a related field such as sociology, psychology, law, or possibly even theology or ethics. She could have performed studies in this area and, possibly, have written a book about it.

1. Susan Ratcliffe, ed., *Oxford Dictionary of Quotations by Subject*, 2nd ed. (Oxford: Oxford University Press, 2010), 8.

We consult experts because they know a great deal about their area of expertise, and we can discover a great deal of important information about a topic without doing the research ourselves. Experts are certainly a common type of testimony that people consult, but there are others as well. In addition to the testimony of experts, we also often consult the testimony of everyday people. It is important to note that while everyday people certainly don't have the credentials and research experience of experts, their opinions can still be valuable. For example, let's say you want to go to a movie on the weekend. To help you decide which film to see, you will likely ask your friends and family if they have seen any good movies lately. If you have a friend who has movie tastes similar to yours, you'll probably rely on his testimony to make your decision. It's not that your friend is a movie "expert"—you just know that he likes a lot of the same movies as you; therefore, his testimony is valuable in helping you choose which movies you may like.

Proverbs

There are several other common types of testimony that people rely on to prove their points. Another form of an everyday testimony is a *proverb* or wise saying, such as the kind that you find in a quote book. Though they are not always spoken by experts in the field, the wisdom and cleverness of a quotation or speaker can stand out authoritatively. By now, you have certainly noticed the quotes at the beginning of each chapter. These are proverbs. Not all of them have been authored by experts in the field of debate; however, they are wise or clever sayings, often worded in a catchy manner, that relate to, or highlight aspects of, the subject of debate.

Which kinds of witnesses are the most effective? Often, the answer to this question depends on your audience, or judge. Which kinds of persons are they most likely to believe? Experts with impressive credentials? Epic historical figures? Popular heroes? Sages? Artists and creators? If you know that your audience or judge has a particular inclination, then you can provide the kind of testimonies most desired. If not, or if it's a large, mixed group, you should seek to provide testimonies from an assortment of sources. This also strengthens your argument by showing just how wide a range of witnesses support, or have a similar idea to, the claim you're arguing. For the same reason, in debates when there are clearly defined opposing "sides" (whether political, religious, philosophical, or other), bringing in testimonies from sources who typically are part of the opposing side can be a powerful proof. Examples of this would be when an advocate of pacifism quotes a high-ranking military official expressing his misgivings about war, or when a student arguing against school uniforms cites an executive of a school uniform company admitting that the cost of their products is a burden on families.

Religious Teachings or Sayings

Yet another common type of testimony is the use of religious teachings or sayings. People may rely on various scriptures such as the Bible, the Talmud, the Koran, the Bhagavad Gita, or other religious texts as testimonies or examples for their arguments. These

Short, clever, and clear sayings have a variety of names: proverbs, aphorisms, apothegms, commonplaces, adages, maxims, dictums . . . and on and on the list goes. They are rarely more than a sentence in length and usually feature a witty turn of phrase (perhaps a rhyme, pun, or repetition), or a powerful image. Above all, the clarity and simplicity of the proverb contrasts with the deep, profound wisdom that, supposedly, underlies it. You have likely realized at this point that this is exactly the type of saying you've been memorizing in the "Building Copiousness" exercises in this book thus far. As an exercise, take out a piece of paper and write out as many proverbs as you can remember—these could be sayings you have memorized from this book, or they could be sayings you've heard in day-to-day discussions. (Here's one to help you start: "Slow and steady wins the race.") How many did you come up with? Are you surprised? These testimonies are designed to stick deeply with you. Look at the list you've made. Are there any common features among them? What might that reveal about the kinds of things that stick in your memory? Now, using your list as a series of models for imitation, try to create a few of your own proverbs. This can be difficult at first. If you practice this, being concise, clear, and pithy won't feel so intimidating, and this skill can help refine your own speech to be more persuasive and compelling, particularly in a debate.

documents provide helpful testimony because they can offer moral or ethical insights on an issue that may not have been considered. It is important to note that while sacred scriptures can shed light on many issues, from seemingly trivial issues to major problems, they tend to address some issues more than others. For instance, most religious texts speak about animals and our care of them. However, they don't necessarily speak about pets a great deal. Therefore, Andrew and Isabel probably won't choose to consult any scriptures concerning their pet debate. However, Josh and Christy will likely consult scriptures a great deal for their debate because the various scriptures say quite a bit about life, killing, murder, punishment for murder, and other themes related to capital punishment. In fact, their proposition itself even mentions the moral or ethical aspect of the topic: "Capital punishment is *ethical*, and it deters crime." Therefore, in order to argue this thesis effectively, they will need to consult various scriptures. Consulting scriptures can be an effective tool to use when you are researching a topic because, as you will read about in the next chapter, another kind of topic (a special topic) is the good. That is, one way we often demonstrate that an idea is right is to prove that it is morally worthy or ethically correct.

Beware of the Fallacy of Accent

It is important to note that although the common topic of testimony is very helpful, if you are not careful, it can easily be abused by committing fallacies. One of the most common ways to misuse testimony is with the fallacy of **accent**. This fallacy occurs when someone emphasizes the words of someone or a sacred scripture in a way that supports *his* point but distorts the meaning of the original statement. For example, let's say that a mother, as she is leaving for work in the morning, tells her son, "You can go to the movies when your room is clean." Later, even though his room is still a mess, the son informs his father that he is going to the movies with his friends, adding, "Mom said I could go." Did you see what happened here? The son emphasized—accented—the first part of his mother's words, "You can go to the movies," but he conveniently left out the second part of her statement ("when your room is clean"). He has distorted his mother's original intention and the meaning behind her words. When you state someone else's words, it is imperative that you state all the pertinent parts—the quote in its entirety, so intended meaning is upheld—so that you are using the words with context and are not distorting them.

When should you use sacred texts in an argument? After all, what is holy to one group of people is often heresy to another. Using support from sacred texts can be dangerous, as they might have credibility only to members of the religion or philosophy that believes in that particular book. Use of text from a particular scripture might also alienate those from another religious or philosophical group. However, it can be very persuasive if you are able to show how testimonies from a variety of sacred texts share agreement about aspects of a given idea, or how a sacred text that is relatively unfamiliar to your audience agrees with an idea they might honor.

Beware of Bandwagon (Again)

Another common fallacy people commit when using testimony is one you have learned before: bandwagon. Remember that someone is bandwagoning when he argues that because many people are doing or believing something, then it should be done or believed. Though it is natural to give credence to something that a lot of people do or believe, it is important to realize that, throughout history, large groups of people have done and believed the wrong—even destructive—thing. During World War II, thousands of German citizens were caught up in the waves of anti-Semitism (hostility and discrimination against Jews). At the same time in the United States, many Americans fell prey to anti-Japanese sentiment. These examples clearly demonstrate that a high number of people believing in an idea does not guarantee its truth or worth. Be especially careful of this when you discuss what everyday people believe or what authorities believe. Just keep in mind that although large numbers may believe something, it could still be false or inaccurate.

Beware of Appeal to Illegitimate Authority

The last fallacy often committed with testimony is **appeal to illegitimate authority**. This fallacy occurs when someone uses the authority of an expert in one field to prove a point in another field. We see this occur in the media when celebrities pitch products or causes. In these scenarios, advertisers are hoping that we will transfer our respect for someone's authority or fame in one field to the product they are advertising. It is important to realize that, although someone may have a lot of expertise in one area, this does not mean that they automatically know about other areas outside of their expertise. Though an actor or athlete might be visible and familiar to us, what reason do we have to trust their expertise in insurance companies, shaving razors, or political candidates?

When you are building copiousness, the danger of appealing to illegitimate authorities often rears its sinister head. Particularly when you are drawing sources from the Internet, always be careful to verify your source. Sometimes, quotations are attributed to the wrong person, or they've been distorted from the original meaning. Sometimes, the author of the found quote might turn out to be someone who would not be a beneficial source for your argument: an infamous tyrant, a discredited authority, or the advocate of an idea or viewpoint that actually disagrees with your argument. Don't be seduced by the pithiness or cleverness of a saying you've come across—always make sure to do a little sleuthing first before you decide to use a quote in your argument.

Both Isabel and Andrew remembered that testimony was a good common topic to use for supporting their arguments; this is why they interviewed owners of cats and dogs to learn about other people's experiences with their pets. Furthermore, they also knew that an impactful testimony could be found by consulting with authorities on their subject. After discussing this, they decided that they would call a few veterinarians to determine which factors they should consider in selecting the most practical pet. They had the following conversation the very next day:

Isabel: Andrew, I called Dr. Peterson, the veterinarian at Gainesway Veterinary Clinic. He said that many dogs he sees in his practice are overweight and unhealthy because they just don't get enough exercise. I think we need to take that into consideration because our family is very busy.

Andrew: I was told the same information when I spoke to a few other veterinarians. I went in and visited that clinic by Xavier the other day—you know, the one back on Brannon Road? The vets there also said they were seeing many dogs who needed more exercise than they were receiving. So I asked them what people could do if they wanted a dog but had very busy lifestyles. They had a lot of good suggestions and said that busy people can still own dogs, but they just have to be more thoughtful in planning times for exercise for their dog's daily schedule.

These testimonies were extremely helpful to both Andrew and Isabel, because they helped them see a larger view of the issue than just their own perspectives. By the same token, Josh and Christy also looked for testimonies about the issue of capital punishment. Neither of them, fortunately, knew anyone who had experienced the murder of a relative, or whose relative had experienced the death penalty, so they could not ask friends and everyday people about their personal experiences with this issue. However, they both found excellent testimony in books. For example, Josh found a quote by a convicted murderer on death row who claimed that many murderers do not fear the death penalty because they do not think they will be caught. Furthermore, Christy found an excellent testimony from a prison director who stated that it is logical to come to the understanding that the only thing that disciplines many convicted murderers in prison for life is the fear of the death penalty. After all, if there were no death penalty, prisoners in jail for life could kill people in jail without any further punishment, as they would already have the worst punishment possible—prison for life.

Using testimonies can be a great support for your case—whether these testimonies are the testimonies of common people or the testimonies of authorities. However, you should be careful not to commit several common fallacies of testimony when you use this common topic. The first easily used fallacy is one you have already studied: the bandwagon fallacy. Remember—someone commits the bandwagon fallacy when he argues that because everyone, or the majority of people, believes something, it is true (or should be done or believed). For instance, in his research, Josh ran across a study that shows that a majority of police officers and lawyers don't believe capital punishment deters crime.[2] Just because a majority of police officer and lawyers believe this doesn't make it true. They could be mistaken or biased. However, the fact that lawyers and police are—through their experience—authorities on crime to a certain extent, we certainly put a lot of stock in what they believe. Therefore, although the fact that a majority of these authorities believe capital punishment does not deter crime doesn't *prove* this belief to be true, it may make it more likely that the belief is based on credible and sufficient evidence. (It is also important to note that this is just one study.) When you construct arguments from testimony, recognize that majority opinion may make something more likely to be credible or true, but it does not guarantee that it is true. Testimony, after all, is only one kind of argument among many, and needs to be supported by other kinds of proofs.

When using arguments from testimony, it is also important to avoid committing appeal to illegitimate authority. A person commits this fallacy when she appeals to the expertise of an authority whose expertise is irrelevant to the field under discussion. For instance, many movie stars have vocalized their stance against capital punishment. Film notables certainly have an area of expertise; however, unless an actor also happens to have a specific degree or relevant experience in researching and studying capital punishment, his celebrity status is irrelevant to an argument about capital punishment. Unfortunately, many advertisers often appeal to the opinion or ideas of movie stars to support a product or point. The public recognizes, likes, and trusts these stars. They may impress and wow us, but they lack credibility within the field or question under debate.

Another common way people commit appeal to illegitimate authority is to cite someone who has an academic degree but who is not certified in the area under consideration. For example, a person with a PhD in physics is certainly knowledgeable in the field of physics, but this does not mean she has expertise in the field of capital punishment. Therefore, Josh and Christy would be committing appeal to illegitimate authority if they cited a physics professor's ideas on capital punishment as testimony or proof to argue whether it is right or wrong.

In conclusion, using the testimony of everyday people or experts is a good way to develop your argument. In doing so, however, you must avoid the fallacies of bandwagon and appeal to illegitimate authority. Now that you have examined all of the common topics, which are common inductive arguments, you will learn how to make deductive arguments in the next chapter.

2. Richard C. Dieter, "The Death Penalty Is Not an Effective Law Enforcement Tool," in *Does Capital Punishment Deter Crime?* ed. Stephen E. Schonebaum (San Diego, CA: Greenhaven Press, 1998), 56–69.

Review Exercises

List

List at least two different types of testimony.

____

____

____

Explain

1. Explain the bandwagon fallacy.

____

____

____

2. Explain the fallacy of appeal to illegitimate authority.

____

____

____

Discuss

Discuss why the common topic of testimony is an especially beneficial way to develop an argument.

Practice Evaluating Arguments from Testimony

Evaluate

Throughout history, people have long had a fascination with mysterious creatures that appear to be half-man and half-animal, which lurk in remote regions such as the heavily forested Pacific Northwest or murky swamps such as the Florida Everglades. These human-animal hybrids go by many different names—Bigfoot, Sasquatch, Yeti, and even "the Swamp Monster." Many people have claimed to have seen such creatures and even to have had close-up encounters with them. Some have even brought back evidence from these encounters, including pieces of hair or plaster casts of tracks. While many people, especially some scientists, are skeptical of reports of such creatures, others, including foresters, biologists, anthropologists, and other persons of sound reputation and academic standing, give credence to such reports. Reading about reports of these creatures can be a great way to study the common topic of testimony because, in these reports, you will encounter personal testimonies of people who claim to have seen Bigfoot, descriptions of encounters with Bigfoot, and statements from authorities both for and against the existence of such creatures. In addition, you will also find people arguing from faulty or biased evidence, or using fallacies such as bandwagon and appeal to illegitimate authority.

Read the article about a sighting of a Bigfoot-like creature and the ensuing investigation (Link 13-1). Once you have read the article, answer the following questions.

1. Harlan E. Ford and Billy Mills were two hunters who claimed to have seen Bigfoot at one time, and also to have later run across Bigfoot tracks. What kind of testimony do their claims represent?

____

____

2. What facts about Ford's life lend added strength to his testimony?

____

____

____

____

____

3. Joe Nickell, the author of this article, has investigated this so-called swamp monster. You will notice at the end of the article that there is a note that says that Nickell is a CSICOP. Do some research on CSI and CSICOP to determine the credibility of Nickell. Is he a legitimate authority? Why or why not?

4. While Nickell was in Louisiana, he spoke with Paul and Sue Wagner, a husband-and-wife wetlands ecologist team that heads up Honey Island Swamp Tours. What did the Wagners say about the swamp monster? How legitimate is their authority?

5. Find two other testimonies in this article and evaluate how legitimate they are. Provide support for your evaluation.

Building Copiousness

Review

Review your old quotes.

Practice

Practice saying the quotes to someone in your class, or practice writing them down on paper.

Memorize

Memorize your new quote:

O tempora! O mores! (Translation: Oh, the times! Oh the manners!) —Cicero[3]

Everyday Debate

Develop

Develop an argument using testimony for this resolution: "Civil disobedience is a moral weapon in the fight for justice." Use at least two historical examples, a definition, an analogy, an argument from cause and effect, and an argument from testimony. In addition, incorporate one quote from the "Building Copiousness" sections from past chapters.

Note: "Civil disobedience" refers to the act of breaking the law in order to protest the harmfulness of that law, or another injustice.

Learning from the Masters

Observe

Watch the last debate (chapter 23, "The Harvard Debate," on the DVD) in the movie *The Great Debaters*.[4] Identify at least three common topics that each side uses to develop its arguments.

3. Ratcliffe, *Oxford Dictionary of Quotations*, 41.
4. Todd Black, et al, *The Great Debaters*, directed by Denzel Washington (2007; New York: Weinstein Co., 2008), DVD.

The Big Debate: Gun Control

Explain

Find at least two types of testimony from authorities for both sides of the gun control issues. In the space provided, list these authorities, explain why they are credible, and describe what they believe.

Chapter 14

The Special Topics

TAKE CARE OF THE SENSE, AND THE SOUNDS WILL TAKE CARE OF THEMSELVES.
—LEWIS CARROLL[1]

As you read about and study the common topics, a few more ideas for persuasion may come to your mind. For instance, you may ask, "What if I just want to prove that something is good? Is that a topic?" or, "What if I just want to prove that something is bad?" These questions suggest other possible tools of persuading people. To understand these tools better, it is important to understand three different branches of classical rhetoric: (a) deliberative or legislative rhetoric, (b) judicial or forensic rhetoric, and (c) epideictic or ceremonial rhetoric.[2]

Let's look at each of these branches more closely. In classical rhetoric, judicial or forensic rhetoric is the type of rhetoric or oratory you use when you want to argue that an act is or is not against the law, or is wrong or right. This is the type of oratory that a lawyer would use in the courtroom to argue that an action is or is not lawful, and it is also the type of oratory someone might use if he wanted to defend his actions to someone.[3] The second type of discourse, deliberative or legislative oratory, is the type of oratory you use when you want to prove that a course of action is good or advantageous (or the opposite). For example, you might use deliberative discourse if you want to persuade someone to study philosophy, take up exercise, or buy a certain type of technology.[4] Finally, ceremonial oratory is the type of oratory you use when you want to praise or blame someone. For instance, this is the type of oratory you would use to praise or blame a politician, a public figure such as a movie star, or even a character in a book.[5]

With each type of discourse, there are *special topics* you can use to develop that discourse. If the common topics are topics you to use to find all the available means of persuasion for any situation (or most situations), what do you think special topics are? You may have guessed that the **special topics** are topics you can use for special or unique types of situations—deliberative, judicial, and ceremonial discourse. If you guessed that, you are correct. Let's take a look at each of these discourses in order to understand in which particular situations they are most helpful.

1. Susan Ratcliffe, ed., *Oxford Dictionary of Quotations by Subject*, 2nd ed. (Oxford: Oxford University Press, 2010), 447.
2. Gideon O. Burton, *Silva Rhetoricae*, Brigham Young University, page last updated February 26, 2007, http://rhetoric.byu.edu/.
3. Edward P.J. Corbett and Robert J. Connors, *Classical Rhetoric for the Modern Student*, 4th ed. (New York: Oxford University Press, 1999), 124.
4. Ibid., 123.
5. Burton, *Silva Rhetoricae*, s.v. "epideictic oratory," http://rhetoric.byu.edu/.

- Deliberative discourse (persuasion directed at doing—or not doing—a certain action)
- Judicial discourse (persuasion directed at rightly judging someone or something according to law)
- Ceremonial discourse (persuasion directed at rightly praising or blaming someone or something)

Deliberative Discourse

Deliberative discourse ends with a decision to take action, or not; this is the type of persuasion someone might use when she is urging someone to think about (or deliberate) a specific action to take. For instance, in an earlier chapter, you reviewed a hypothetical scenario in which parents at a parent-teacher group meeting were discussing which type of fund-raising methods the school should adopt. In this case, they were deliberating upon the right action to take. As another example, consider a recent political situation that took place in Lexington, Kentucky. The Kentucky Water Utilities Company was considering selling their company to a German company. There was great deliberation in the news and in the newspaper about whether this was the right thing to do.[6]

6. Andy Mead, "Lexington, KY Voters Reject Take-Over of American Water of KY," *Water Industry News*, ed. Larry Chertoff, November 8, 2006, http://www.waterindustry.org/New%20Projects/American-19.htm.

Whenever you consider and discuss which action you should take in a matter, you are engaging in deliberative discourse. When you engage in deliberative discourse, there are two topics you can use to show whether an action should be taken: the good and the advantageous or their opposites, the bad and disadvantageous. That is, you can show why it is good or advantageous to take a certain action, or why it is bad or disadvantageous to take a particular action.

Let's look at this in light of Josh and Christy's capital punishment debate. Their topic is especially suited to the deliberative topics because the reason that people debate about this issue is because they are deliberating about whether capital punishment should be allowed. After doing some research on this matter, Josh and Christy had the following conversation:

Josh: It seems clear to me that capital punishment is never good. The best-case scenario is that it is a necessary evil. That is, it's an evil we must do because of another evil. But I don't really think that is the case. I think we should create a prison system that honors the dignity of human beings and rehabilitates criminals.

Christy: Josh, what you are talking about may sound nice, but, even if it were possible—which I doubt—it would be disadvantageous to American citizens. I means, just think about how much a system like that would cost. Our prison system, which I admit is not very nurturing, already costs us an arm and a leg. To accomplish what you are suggesting would be exorbitantly expensive. Not only that, but is it even fair or good? I mean, many murderers have committed horrible atrocities. Is it truly good to, in a sense, "reward" their heinous actions with a wonderful, rehabilitative environment that, in some cases, may be much better than the average living conditions of people who have committed no crimes? I think that scenario may actually encourage more murder because people would want to live in a place like that—and that certainly would be disadvantageous.

In their discussion, Josh and Christy have used both of the special topics for deliberative discourse. The special topic, or argument, of "goodness" directs us to consider what is desirable, or what is morally good, and its opposite, what is bad or unworthy. The special topic of "advantage" directs us to consider what will be advantageous or useful, and its opposite, what is disadvantageous. These two topics are connected, as things are only advantageous if they can help us, or be used by us, toward things that are desirable or morally good. Both Josh and Christy used an argument from goodness and an argument from advantage. Josh argued that killing another human being is morally bad, or unworthy, and that rehabilitative punishment will bring advantages in transforming the bad into good. Christy argued that it is morally bad to *not* give criminals something bad as punishment. Further, she argued that failing to punish murder in a certain way will have the consequence of making murder more attractive (a disadvantage), thus leading to more evil.

As you can see from this example, the deliberative topics can be very useful because most people have a desire to do what is good and advantageous. We may disagree about what is good and advantageous, but rarely will people advocate something they know is disadvantageous. We usually advocate what we believe is advantageous in some way, even if we disagree about what exactly that is. The special topics people usually use to develop an issue in deliberative discourse are the good, the worthy, and the advantageous.

Judicial Discourse

The next special topic is the topic of judicial discourse. In the United States, the debate over separation of church and state frequently pops up in the news. For instance, one common debate present in public schools is over whether these schools have the right to hang the Ten Commandments on their walls. Some people say that hanging the Ten Commandments is a violation of the establishment clause of the Constitution, while others argue that hanging the Ten Commandments is an exercise of freedom of religion. This topic was, and is, still hotly debated among school administrators, parents, students, and American citizens in general, and it was even debated in the Supreme Court. This debate was especially important in the Supreme Court because when the Supreme Court makes a judgment on an issue,

In thinking through what things might be desirable, or thought proper, by a majority of people, the philosopher Aristotle developed a lengthy list of qualities that belonged to the categories of the good and the useful. When you make arguments using this special topic, try to prove that something will either bring about, or exclude, one of the following: happiness, health, fame, respect, beauty, strength, justice, courage, self-control, and/or knowledge.

they interpret law, and often their decision becomes law. Therefore, the unique type of debate or discourse in which they engage is called **judicial discourse**, which is discourse pertaining specifically what laws should be made. Unlike deliberative discourse, which focuses on what future actions will be best to take, judicial rhetoric focuses on what decisions are right to make—in light of the law that exists. Obviously, Supreme Court justices are not the only people involved in understanding and applying the law—lawyers, policemen, school administrators, theologians, and even competitive debaters engage regularly in judicial discourse.

Some people are involved with judicial discourse daily as a part of their job, but realize that ordinary people often engage in judicial discourse as well as a part of their everyday life. For example, whenever we discuss whether something is just or unjust, we engage in judicial discourse, because the heart of judicial discourse is determining what is just or unjust, or fair or unfair, or deciding whether an action or idea conforms to a principal or law. The law to which we are comparing an action, practice, or belief can be a government, school, household, ethical, or moral law. For example, let's say that a student who attends a private school signs a code of conduct in which he pledges to avoid certain activities such as underage drinking. Later, when he is off campus, he does, indeed, go drinking—even though he is underage and had pledged not to do this. Someone from campus who knows about the pledge sees the student and reports him and soon after, he is suspended from his school. The boy argues that his suspension is unjust because these activities took place off campus, rather than on campus, and that he believes the code of conduct applies to campus activities only.

Or as another example, consider a teacher who decides to assign a student detention for the student's bad behavior. Suppose that the student later complains to her parents that the detention was unjust. It is not likely that this situation would ever be a matter that would go to court, but it is very possible that the teacher might have to explain to the parents why the punishment of detention was just.

When you are attempting to show that something is just or unjust, keep in mind three questions that ancient rhetoricians used to develop this topic:

- *What is it?* (That is, *What happened?*) This question seeks to describe and classify the action that is alleged to have taken place. For instance, in the first example, the boy in question might admit to the action of drinking a beer, while he might be accused of *underage drinking*, a legal term that has official power and force.[7]
- *Did it happen?* This question seeks to measure the action that actually took place. For example, the boy in the first example might argue that he was only carrying a case of beer that a family member had purchased and that he did not drink any of the beer or purchase it himself. Or the boy might argue that he did indeed go out with friends who were drinking but that he did not actually drink himself.[8]
- *What kind is it?* (That is, *What law did it break?*) The boy might admit to breaking the civil law against underage drinking, and could be found guilty if civil authorities, such as the police, arrested him with evidence and charged him in a court of law. However, he could argue that he did not drink on campus, and thus did not break an additional law (the school's code of conduct), and therefore cannot be judged guilty of that particular offense.[9]

It is important to note that this will not work for every subject about which you write or debate. For example, Isabel and Andrew would use deliberative and not judicial discourse in their pet debate. Subjects with an ethical angle, where some code of rules or justice is enforced by a judge or judges, will utilize judicial rhetoric. These subjects all involve judging an action by appealing to some accepted rule or standard. For example, if you were debating abortion or immigration laws in America, both topics involve ethical issues and can only be resolved by interpreting the law of the land (in this case, the US Constitution) in order to make a judgment. Therefore, the special topics specifically related to judicial discourse—the just and the unjust—would be especially helpful in these cases.

In their capital punishment research, Christy and Josh explored various laws in the United States regarding capital punishment, and they discovered some interesting facts. Josh learned that capital punishment appears to be applied in an arbitrary manner. For example, he found that a person is more likely to receive the death penalty if the victim is white rather than black. Christy found that although the death penalty process is imperfect, in general it is a very just system, as the average death penalty case takes ten to twelve years to be carried out, and both lawyers and criminals have many opportunities to make appeals if the sentence is unjust.[10]

Josh and Christy should emphasize these ideas in their debate to develop the idea of whether capital punishment is just. In some debates, such as the Lincoln-Douglas debate, the entire debate may revolve around whether an idea is just. The Lincoln-Douglas debate style is inspired by the 1858 debates between Abraham Lincoln and then Illinois Senator Stephen Douglas.[11]

For instance, a Lincoln-Douglas debate resolution for capital punishment might be formatted as follows: "Resolved: Capital punishment is unjust." In a debate such as this, judicial discourse is the primary mode of persuasion.

Ceremonial Discourse

Now that we've looked at deliberative and judicial discourse, let's take a look at **ceremonial discourse**, which occurs whenever someone praises or blames

7. Corbett and Connors, *Classical Rhetoric*, 124–125.
8. Ibid.
9. Ibid.
10. Deborah Fins, "Death Row USA," Fall 2013, A Quarterly Report by the Criminal Justice Project of the NAACP Legal Defense and Education Fund, Inc., 7, http://www.deathpenaltyinfo.org/documents/DRUSAFall2013.pdf.
11. Deborah Bush Haffey, Jeffrey B. Molter, and Christy L. Shipe, *Argumentation and Debate: Taking the Next Step* (Percellville, VA: Homeschool Legal Defense Association, 2004), 262–263.

others, highlighting their accomplishments or criticizing their failings. To better understand this special topic, consider George W. Bush's presidency. President Bush certainly had a roller-coaster ride of a presidency. During his first term, 9/11 occurred when terrorists attacked the United States in New York and Washington, DC. Bush was generally praised for his handling of the 9/11 crisis, and his approval ratings were generally high. He was praised for his boldness, his courage, and his compassion. Later in his presidency, Hurricane Katrina struck New Orleans, and the United States entered the War on Terror in Iraq. While some people continued to praise Bush for his handling of these crises, others censured his actions, calling him headstrong and impetuous for his handling of the war in Iraq. Many also criticized his handling of the crisis in New Orleans as haphazard and irresponsible. When people praised or blamed President Bush, they were engaging in ceremonial discourse and using the specific special topics of ceremonial discourse—praise and blame.[12] With ceremonial discourse, unlike deliberative discourse, we are no longer considering what actions to take in the future when evaluating the president and his actions. Nor are we placing him under the law's judgment. Rather, we are debating over how best to evaluate and think of the man and his actions.

You have actually encountered this special topic of ceremonial discourse more often than you may realize. For example, if you have ever gone to a funeral, it is likely that the pastor or officiant of the funeral was praising the deceased. If you have ever gone to a graduation ceremony, you probably have heard students giving speeches praising their classmates, their school, or their past teachers, and have heard commencement speakers praising the seniors' accomplishments and exhorting them to excellence. Political figures regularly engage in ceremonial discourse, praising people in their party or past political figures, and censuring the opposition. Pastors even do this regularly when they praise biblical figures they believe the congregation should emulate and censure other figures who serve as a cautionary tale.

The special topic of ceremonial discourse is especially helpful when you are debating a topic that centers on a specific person or group of people. For example, people might debate whether Napoleon was more helpful or harmful to France, or whether President Franklin Delano Roosevelt's New Deal policies were more beneficial or damaging to the United States.

> For the debaters and rhetoricians of old, ceremonial discourse was called **epideictic rhetoric**. The word "epideictic" comes from two Greek words: *epi*, meaning "for" (as in, for a particular purpose) and *deiknumi*, which means "I show."

The special topics for ceremonial discourse are praise and blame, and as you have probably figured out, there are specific categories you can use when you want to praise or censure someone. One of the main ways to do this is by demonstrating that the people possess or lack virtues. The following is a list of some of the most common virtues, and their opposite vices:[13]

- Bravery or cowardice
- Self-control or indulgence
- Justice or injustice
- Generosity or selfishness
- Prudence or rashness
- Gentleness or brutality
- Loyalty or disloyalty

Consider Josh and Christy's capital punishment debate. Will the oratorical branch of ceremonial discourse, along with its special topics, be relevant to their topic? Yes and no. They will not dwell on it as much as they would if their speech was about a person, but they could use elements of ceremonial discourse in their speech. For instance, Christy wrote the following paragraph praising America as a possible conclusion for her debate:

> America, you are a just and virtuous nation. You value the life of the individual. Everyone counts in your eyes. You mete out the death penalty with care, but when you do, you are just, and you show that all people's lives are valuable.

Alternatively, Josh used blame and censure ceremonial discourse to write the following possible conclusion:

12. Burton, *Silva Rhetoricae*, s.v. "epideictic oratory," http://rhetoric.byu.edu/.

13. Corbett and Connors, *Classical Rhetoric*, 128.

> America, you are hailed as the land of the free, yet this promise rings hollow for those who have been innocently put to death, or for others who killed and yet could have lived to see a change of heart.

In both cases, Josh and Christy use virtues that people like to think are true of America (and Americans) to show how, by making a certain judgment, America and its people succeed or fail in living up to the standards they have set.

The special topics are topics you can use to explore what is good, advantageous, just, or praiseworthy, as well as what is bad, disadvantageous, unjust, or blameworthy. We use these topics in deliberative, judicial, and ceremonial discourse. Sometimes you may organize your entire debate around one of these topics; other times, you will just use it as one topic of many to develop arguments. Either way, the special topics can be very helpful, just as the common topics are effective in developing your ideas.

Review Exercises

Define

Provide a definition for deliberative discourse.

____

____

Define

Provide definitions for the following terms:

Judicial discourse: ______________________________

____

____

Ceremonial discourse: ______________________________

____

____

Explain

Explain the special topics—what they are and how they are used.

____

____

____

____

____

____

List

List three kinds of discourse and the special topics you can use to develop each discourse type.

____

____

____

____

____

____

____

Building Copiousness

Review

Review your old quotes.

Practice

Practice saying the quotes to someone in your class, or practice writing them down on paper.

Memorize

Memorize your new quote:

Mistakes are a fact of life.
It is the response to mistakes that counts. —Nikki Giovanni[14]

Everyday Debate

Develop

The following are three debate topics; each represents a different type of discourse. Your teacher will divide your class into three teams and assign each group one of the following topics. Develop your argument using a variety of common topics, as well as the special topics specific for your topic.

1. Deliberative Discourse:

   "Proposition: Corporal (physical) punishment is an effective form of discipline in elementary schools."

   The Special Topics:

   a. How is corporal punishment in elementary schools advantageous? How is it disadvantageous?

   ____

   ____

   ____

   ____

   ____

   ____

   b. How is corporal punishment in elementary schools good for the school? How is it negative for an elementary school?

   ____

   ____

   ____

   ____

   ____

   ____

14. Ratcliffe, *Oxford Dictionary of Quotations*, 321.

c. How is corporal punishment in an elementary school worthy of an elementary school? How is it unworthy of an elementary school?

____

____

____

____

____

2. Judicial Discourse:

"Proposition: We should tighten immigration laws so that illegal immigrants are deported from the country."

The Special Topics:

a. What is it? (Example: What kind of problem is illegal immigration?)

____

____

____

____

____

b. Did it happen? (Example: Is illegal immigration happening now?)

____

____

____

____

____

c. What kind is it? (Example: What kind of law is it breaking?)

____

____

____

____

____

3. Ceremonial Discourse:

"Proposition: Napoleon Bonaparte was more harmful than helpful for his country."

The Special Topics:

a. Bravery or cowardice
b. Self-control or indulgence
c. Justice or injustice
d. Generosity or selfishness
e. Prudence or rashness
f. Gentleness or brutality
g. Loyalty or disloyalty

Which of these topics can you use to praise or blame Napoleon?

____

____

____

____

____

____

____

Learning from the Masters

Observe

This Intelligence Squared debate on universal health care is an interesting one to watch because this, historically, has been such a controversial issue in the United States. This debate is also especially well structured because the different speakers are doctors, researchers, and writers who have spent a great deal of time researching this issue. Not only that, some of the speakers are US citizens, some of whom are for universal health care and some of whom are against it. A few speakers are Canadian or former Canadian citizens, who bring a unique perspective to the debate since Canada is a country with universal health care. This variety of speakers brings a lot of insight to this debate.

Watch the introduction and the first two speakers of the universal health care debate, and flow their arguments (Link 14-1). Then, discuss the following questions. Keep in mind the proposition under consideration: "Resolved: Universal health care coverage should be the federal government's responsibility."

Discuss

1. What are three arguments that Paul Krugman makes?

2. What analogy does Krugman use in his arguments?

List

What are one weakness and one strength of Krugman's arguments?

Explain

Explain three arguments that John Stossel makes to support his point.

Discuss

What analogy does Stossel use?

List

Name one strength and one weakness of Stossel's argument.

The Big Debate: Gun Control

Discuss

How is gun control advantageous? How is it disadvantageous?

Explain

What law could you recommend?

Discuss

What is one way you can use ceremonial discourse in the gun control debate?

Chapter 15

Deductive Logic: Categorical Syllogism

15

> IT IS USELESS TO ATTEMPT TO REASON A MAN OUT OF WHAT HE WAS NEVER REASONED INTO.
>
> —JONATHAN SWIFT[1]

At this point, you have learned some of the most typical common topics and the special topics, and you now have several tools of persuasion in your argument toolbox. In the previous chapters you have spent quite a bit of time on logos, and at this point you might be wondering, "What about pathos and ethos?" Don't worry—you'll get there. But before you do, you need to look at one more very important part of logic: deductive logic. That's right, up to this point, you've been looking at the inductive arguments (i.e., generalizations based on examples).

Syllogisms

Now you need to take a minute and look at deductive logic—that is, reasoning from already established, *a priori* truths to new truths. If the foundation argument type of inductive logic is the example, the foundation argument type of logic is the syllogism. Before syllogisms are explained, look at two examples of this argument technique:

All heroes are admirable.
Theodore Roosevelt was a hero.
Therefore, Theodore Roosevelt was admirable.

And here is another:

No war is peaceful.
The American Revolution was a war.
The American Revolution was not peaceful.

This will help you understand syllogisms. Did you notice anything in particular about these syllogisms? First, observe that each of the syllogisms has three statements. In a syllogism, the first two statements are called the **premises** (or the proof) and the last statement the **conclusion** (i.e., the point of the whole argument). A **syllogism**, then, is an argument that contains a conclusion that is implied by two premises.

Second, the premises in both syllogisms are statements about which everyone agrees, for the most part, or for which a strong, reasonable case could be made. For example, no one would dispute that heroes are admirable, and Theodore Roosevelt is one of our most widely respected presidents, who is generally considered to be a hero. Furthermore, in the second syllogism,

1. Susan Ratcliffe, ed., *Oxford Dictionary of Quotations by Subject*, 2nd ed. (Oxford: Oxford University Press, 2010), 291.

everyone would agree that no war is peaceful, and no one denies the American Revolution was a war. Therefore, the premises in both of these syllogisms are either widely accepted or *a priori* truths.

Truths that are *a priori* are truths that are discovered without investigation into the world. They are true because they are a matter of reason. For instance, the truth "A=A" is an *a priori* truth. It is not something anyone has to investigate in the world to figure out. Rather, just by logically considering the sentence, a person knows it is true because A is the same thing as A. As another example, consider the phrase "All mothers are female." You can determine the truth of this statement by logically considering the meaning of the words "mother" and "female" and considering whether or not it is true that they are synonymous. Therefore, the phrase, "All mothers are female" is also an *a priori* truth because you can figure it out, just by using your reason, without any investigation. By contrast, consider the phrase "Some butterflies are yellow." You don't know whether this statement is true or not unless you investigate its truth in the world. That is, the truth of the statement "Some butterflies are yellow" cannot be determined through reason alone. It can only be determined by investigation.

Let's relate this exploration of *a priori* truths back to syllogisms. If the first two premises of your syllogism are not *a priori* truths or widely accepted truths, it weakens your syllogism because you are arguing from premises that not everyone accepts as true, and you may have to do quite a bit of work to prove that your premises are indeed true. If you believe you can prove your premises fairly easily, you may decide to argue from premises that are not true *a priori* after all. People often include an argument for their premises as they are constructing a syllogism, so this is a common enough practice. However, it is certainly the case that if your premises are *a priori* truths, it will be easier to convince people of the truth of your syllogism right away. The other thing you should note is that in both syllogisms, the premises imply the conclusion. In other words, the truth of the conclusions is contained in the premises. Given that the premises are true, the conclusion follows necessarily. For instance, notice in the first syllogisms that if all heroes are indeed admirable, and Theodore Roosevelt is, indeed, a hero, then it must be the case the Theodore Roosevelt is admirable. And in the second syllogism, if no war is peaceful, and the American Revolution was, indeed, a war, then it must be the case that the American Revolution was not peaceful. For these syllogisms, the conclusions are contained in, or implied by, the premises in such a way that if the premises are true, the conclusion must be true. In a way, the conclusion should not even need to be stated, if the premises are true. This is how syllogisms work.

To summarize what you have just learned, the following are three characteristics of a syllogism:

a. They have two premises and a conclusion.

b. The premises are usually statements that everyone accepts as true.

c. The premises imply the conclusion, or the conclusion is contained in the premises.

The fact that a syllogism's conclusion is implied by the premises illustrates the beauty of the syllogism. The best way to use a syllogism to support your argument is to develop two uncontroversial premises that lead deductively to your conclusion. If you accomplish this, you will have crafted a syllogism that has premises with which your opponent agrees, and these premises will imply your conclusion, which supports your side. Your opponent may say that he doesn't agree with your conclusion; however, if your premises are true, and the syllogism is structured correctly, then your conclusion is undeniable. If you can construct a syllogism in this way, this is ideal. Frequently, however, it is not possible to construct a syllogism with premises that everyone agrees upon. In this case, you can construct a syllogism with premises for which you can make a reasonably strong case. Here's an example with Josh and Christy's capital punishment debate. A possible syllogism someone could write against capital punishment is the following:

> No practices that take a person's life unnecessarily are good practices.
>
> Capital punishment takes a person's life unnecessarily.
>
> Therefore, capital punishment is not a good practice.

Please note that advocates of capital punishment will likely not agree with the second premise; however, someone could make a reasonably strong case for it. For instance, someone could argue that it is possible to imprison someone for life instead of killing them, and so capital punishment takes a person's life unnecessarily because there is at least one other alternative to capital punishment. This syllogism is effective because the two premises are premises that most people would agree with or for which someone can make a reasonable case. In addition, the premises automatically imply the conclusion because the syllogism is **valid**. "Valid" is a term used to describe an argument (or syllogism) in which the conclusion is implied by the premises. Therefore, in order to disprove this syllogism, an advocate of capital punishment would need to demonstrate that one of these premises is actually false. This will be difficult because, once again, the premises are truths with which most people agree, and so the person who wants to argue against this syllogism—someone who is against capital punishment, for example—needs to show why one of these premises is false.

Constructing a Syllogism

It's important to understand that there are many right ways to construct a syllogism—and there are a lot of wrong ways to construct them, too. When you write a syllogism incorrectly, the premises do not imply the conclusion; another way to state this is to say that in an incorrect syllogism, the conclusion states more than is contained in, or implied by, the premises. It isn't difficult to write a correct syllogism, but you need to know a few "tricks of the trade," as they say. While an in-depth lesson on syllogisms isn't covered in this book, you can find a comprehensive review of syllogisms in Classical Academic Press's *The Discovery of Deduction*. In this lesson, you'll be shown four syllogism forms that will always work. That is, if you use these specific syllogism forms, your syllogisms will always be structured correctly.

To teach you these four valid syllogism forms, you should first understand four important terms related to syllogisms: proposition, terms, mood, and figure. As you have already learned, each valid syllogism contains three statements: two premises and a conclusion. These statements are actually called propositions in deductive logic. A proposition is a factual statement that can be proven true or false.[2] For instance, in our syllogism examples at the beginning of the chapter, propositions such as the following were used: "All heroes are admirable," "Theodore Roosevelt was a hero," "No war is peaceful," and "The American revolution was a war." Propositions are statements that can be proven true or false. Therefore, sentences that are questions, commands, and statements of feeling or preference (e.g., "I like cheese," or "I think it is going to rain today") are not propositions. Propositions are the basis of categorical, deductive logic.

Propositions within syllogisms should have a subject, a predicate, and a being verb that links the two. A proposition within a syllogism must make a statement of identity to work: *S is P*, or *S is not P*. The *S* in the proposition stands for **subject term**, as in the subject of the proposition. The *P* stands for **predicate term**, as in the predicate of the proposition—the word that comes after the being verb *is* in the proposition and renames the subject. For instance, consider the proposition "All mice

2. In chapter 5 you learned that a proposition is a carefully worded statement that makes clear the positions of both the affirmative and negative sides. This definition pertains to the proposition that is the focus of a particular debate. However, it is important to note that a proposition is also a factual statement that can be proven true or false. Therefore, while debates are certainly centered around propositions, propositions are certainly found outside of debates as a part of arguments.

are small." The word *mice* in this proposition is the subject term of the proposition because it is the subject of the proposition, so it fulfills the role of *S* in the above formula. The word *small* in this proposition is the predicate term of the proposition because it comes after the being verb and renames the subject. So, it is the *P* in the above formula.

We have discussed in this chapter that the predicate term of a proposition comes after the being verb and renames the subject. The being verb "is" commonly occurs in propositions. However, it might be helpful for you to see a complete list of being verbs because they often show up in propositions, connecting the subject term and the predicate term: "am," "is," "are," "was," "were," "be," "being," "been."

Four Propositions

In addition, it is important to know that in deductive logic, we talk about four basic propositions: *A*, *I*, *E*, and *O* propositions. The *A* and *I* propositions are named thus because they are affirmative propositions, and they get their name from the Latin word *affirmo*, which means "I affirm." (The *a* and *i* in *affirmo* supply the names for the *A* and *I* statements.) The *A* statement is a statement such as "All men are mortal." (Note that it affirms something about an entire class of things and starts with the word *All*.) The *I* statement is a statement such as "Some men are mortal." (Note that it affirms something about part of a class and begins with the word *Some*.) While the *A* and the *I* statements are positive and affirm something, the *E* and the *O* propositions are negative propositions. They get their name from the Latin word *nego*, which means "I deny." (The *e* and *o* in *nego* supply the names for the *E* and the *O* statements.) The *E* statement is a statement such as "No men are mortal." (Note that it denies something about an entire class of things and begins with the word *No*.) The *O* statement is a statement such as "Some men are not mortal." (Note that it denies something about part of a class and contains the words *some* and *not*.)

To understand how the propositions in these syllogisms work, it is helpful to understand another syllogistic term: **mood**. The mood of a syllogism refers to what kind of proposition it is: an *A*, an *E*, an *I*, or an *O*. Mood is one half of the equation when you are structuring syllogisms properly.

Moods require **quantifiers**—words that tell us just how much of a given thing we are talking about. Ultimately, there are only three quantifiers: all, some, or none. For this kind of logical statement, words such as *few*, *most*, or *many* should be represented by the quantifier *some*. Whether we are talking about 99 percent of a category, or only 1 percent of a category, we are still talking about "some" of that category. Although there are ultimately only three quantifiers—all, no, and some—in order to distinguish between positive and negative quantifiers that talk about part of something, we use "some" and "some not." In other words, "some" pertains to partial quantities positively, and "some not" pertains to partial quantities negatively.

While mood is one half of the equation, the other half of the equation is **figure**. Figure pertains to how the words, or **terms**, of a syllogism are arranged. To better understand what we mean by figure and terms in a syllogism, it will be helpful for you to know that in every valid syllogism, there are three terms: the *major* term, the *minor* term, and the *middle* term. The **minor term** is the subject of the conclusion. The **major term** is the term that comes after the verb in the conclusion. The **middle term** is the term that appears twice in the premises but not in the conclusion. It connects the other two terms in the premises. In this book, we won't worry too much about the minor and major terms. Instead, focus on the middle term, because the middle term of a syllogism is the term that determines the figure of a syllogism. The figure of a syllogism refers to how the middle term in a syllogism is arranged.

There are four figures: first figure, second figure, third figure, and fourth figure. In this book, we are not going to go through all of the different figures. Instead, you will focus on the first figure.[3] When a syllogism is in the first figure, the middle term is the subject of the first premise and the predicate of the second premise. For instance, consider the syllogism in the first figure (the middle term is in boldfaced type).

3. If you would like to know more about mood and figure, please check out Classical Academic Press's book *The Discovery of Deduction*, which covers this topic thoroughly.

Here is the diagram for first figure:

Syllogism	Categorical Syllogism	Type of Categorical Proposition
All men are males.	*All M is P.*	*A*
All boys are men.	*All S is M.*	*A*
Therefore, all boys are males.	*All S is P.*	*A*
All rectangles are four-sided figures.	*All M is P.*	*A*
All squares are rectangles.	*All S is M.*	*A*
Therefore, all squares are four-sided figures.	*All S is P.*	*A*

First Figure:

M P

S M

M = Middle Term
P = Predicate Term
S = Subject Term

All **men** are mortal.

Socrates is a **man**.

Therefore, Socrates is mortal.

Now that you understand mood and figure, and you understand what a syllogism in first figure looks like, you can now learn four moods of syllogisms that are always valid: AAA, EAE, AII, EIO. All of these syllogisms are in the first figure, which means that the middle term is the subject of the first premise and the predicate of the second premise.[4] In order for these syllogisms to be correct, however, you need to make sure they have the right mood.

Look again at the first example syllogism in this chapter. The major term is "admirable." The minor term is "Theodore Roosevelt." The middle term is "hero(es)."

Let's take a closer look at each of the correct moods. For example, here is an *AAA-1* syllogism. The "one" at the end of the AAA stands for "first figure":

All practices that promote justice are good practices.

(All) Capital punishment is a **practice that promotes justice**.

Therefore, (all) capital punishment is a good practice.

All of the propositions in this syllogism are *A* propositions (therefore, the mood is *AAA*). Also note that the middle term is in first figure, which is why we say that the mood and figure of this syllogism is *AAA-1*.

Check out the following *EAE* syllogism:

No practice that deprives a human of life unnecessarily is a good practice.

(All) Capital punishment is a practice that deprives humans of life unnecessarily.

Therefore, no capital punishment is a good practice.

The first premise is an *E* statement, the second premise is an *A* statement, and the last statement is an *E* statement. Also note that this syllogism is in first figure. Therefore, it is an *EAE-1* syllogism.

Thus far, you have learned the AAA-1 syllogism and the EAE-1 syllogism. It may be helpful for you to know that these are two of the most common syllogisms you will encounter in arguments. In other words, when you run across a syllogism in arguments, it is frequently either of the AAA-1 variety or the EAE-1 variety. Now let's look at the other two valid syllogism types.

The following is an *AII-1* syllogism:

All practices that deprive an innocent person of life are unjust.

4. Please note that there are valid syllogisms in figures other than first figures. In this book, I am showing you a few of the more common valid syllogism forms, which all happen to be in first figure. For a more in-depth discussion of mood and figure, see Classical Academic Press's book *The Discovery of Deduction*.

Some capital punishment is a practice that deprives an innocent person of life.

Therefore, some capital punishment is unjust.

Lastly, look at the following *EIO-1* syllogism.

No practices which deprive an innocent person of life are just.

Some practices of capital punishment are practices that deprive an innocent person of life.

Therefore, some practices of capital punishment are unjust.

There are many other valid syllogisms not detailed here, but in order to learn about those, you will need to study deductive logic more thoroughly than we are able to cover in this book. Therefore, until you have time to study deductive logic more thoroughly, simply understand that if you construct an *AAA*, *EAE*, *AII*, or *EIO* syllogism in first figure, it will be a correct syllogism.

Review Exercises

Define

Define each of the following terms.

1. Deductive logic: ______________________________

____

2. Syllogism: ______________________________

____

3. Mood: ______________________________

____

4. Figure: ______________________________

____

5. Valid: ______________________________

____

List

List two frequently used valid figures described in this chapter.

Building Copiousness

Review

Review your old quotes.

Practice

Practice saying the quotes to someone in your class, or practice writing them down on paper.

Memorize

Memorize your new quote:

> To respond to evil by committing another evil
> does not eliminate evil but allows it to go on forever. —Václav Havel[5]

Practicing Syllogisms

Develop

Take one of the topics of your past minidebates, such as cell phone usage, students doing chores, or corporal punishment. Develop both *AAA-1* and *EAE-1* syllogisms for this topic.

Everyday Debate

Debate

Facebook is a ubiquitous cultural phenomenon. Everywhere you look, people are on Facebook or talking about Facebook. Some people say that Facebook is a really good tool because it allows people to maintain ties across the country and even around the world. Many people view Facebook as a valuable social networking tool. Despite these positive views of Facebook, others see it as a distraction and a technology that promotes only the most superficial and trivial communication. What do *you* think? Hold a debate on the following proposition: "Resolved: Facebook improves social relationships."

---

5. Ratcliffe, *Oxford Dictionary of Quotations*, 160.

Learning from the Masters

Observe

Watch the second set of arguments from the Intelligence Squared debate on universal health care (Link 15-1). These are the arguments delivered by Michael Rachlis and Sally C. Pipes. As a reminder, here is the proposition under consideration: "Resolved: Universal health care coverage should be the federal government's responsibility."

Flow the arguments and then answer the following questions.

1. What are three main points made by Michael Rachlis?

2. Rachlis spends a lot of time looking at health coverage in Canada and other countries with universal health insurance, and health coverage in the United States. What common topic is this?

3. What are some strengths and weaknesses of Rachlis's argument?

4. What are three main points made by Sally Pipes?

5. What common topics does Pipes make?

6. What are some strengths and weaknesses of Pipes's argument?

The Big Debate: Gun Control

Develop

Write *AAA-1* and *EAE-1* syllogisms for each side of the gun control debate.

Chapter 16

Internal Resources: Ethos

16

> TALENT DEVELOPS IN QUIET PLACES, CHARACTER IN THE FULL CURRENT OF HUMAN LIFE.
> —JOHANN WOLFGANG VON GOETHE[1]

Now that you have learned about appeals of logos, you will also look at ethos and pathos. In this chapter, you will specifically learn about ethos. You may be familiar with the English word "ethics," which is related to the Greek word *ethos*.[2] "Ethos" refers to a person's custom or character. A person's ethics are the principles of right conduct by which she lives. Therefore, when someone uses **ethos** to support his argument, he convinces the audience that he is good, right, and moral. Aristotle claimed that in order to properly establish ethos, "one needs to appear both knowledgeable about one's subject and benevolent."[3] It is important to note that there is certainly a difference between seeming knowledgeable and benevolent and actually *being* knowledgeable and benevolent. Unfortunately, people can sometimes appear to be kind and generous without actually being so, and can still reap the rewards of their "appearance." In fact, in Plato's famous book *The Republic*, Socrates discussed with some friends whether it is better to be just, or better to appear to be just. Socrates's friends argued that the best scenario is to appear just without actually being so.[4] That way, you can have all the benefits that a just reputation brings you, but you can also have all the benefits that being unjust can bring you. Having a righteous reputation, for instance, would lead people to trust you, which you could then exploit through lying, cheating, and other devious means.

Socrates's friends weren't the only ones who felt this way. In fact, in ancient Greece, there was a school of rhetoricians called the Sophists, many of whom reasoned in this manner.[5] They taught people how to win any argument, regardless of whether the argument was true or false. They learned how to appear logical, ethical, and sympathetic, even if they or their cause weren't actually any of these things. Of course, the strategies that they examined weren't necessarily bad; rather, the harm was in the way they could apply them. Therefore, while you should learn these tricks or techniques, you should make a point to use them in the right manner.

---

1. Susan Ratcliffe, ed., *Oxford Dictionary of Quotations by Subject*, 2nd ed. (Oxford: Oxford University Press, 2010), 74.
2. *Webster's Ninth New Collegiate Dictionary*, s.v. "ethics."
3. Gideon O. Burton, *Silva Rhetoricae*, s.v. "ethos," Brigham Young University, page last updated February 26, 2007, http://rhetoric.byu.edu/.
4. Plato, *The Republic*, trans. George Maximilian, Anthony Grube, and C.D.C. Reeve, 2nd ed. (Indianapolis, IN: Hackett Publishing Company, 1992), 37.
5. See William Turner, "Sophists," in *The Catholic Encyclopedia* (New York: Robert Appleton Company, 1912), http://www.newadvent.org/cathen/14145c.htm.

Establishing Ethos with Anamnesis

The first technique that the ancient rhetoricians taught people to establish ethos was something called **anamnesis**. This is recalling past events or even words of an authority from memory. If you have watched public speakers, you have often seen them use this **rhetorical device**. (Rhetorical devices are techniques for arranging words and phrases to increase the beautiful sound of language.) For instance, you have probably noticed politicians in the past making a point and then stopping, saying something such as "Winston Churchill once said . . ." and then they would recite a quote from a noted famous person (in this example Churchill) or from some other leader along the lines of George Washington, Susan B. Anthony, Queen Elizabeth I, or Mahatma Gandhi, to support their point. When a speaker is able to use quotes of significance, especially from memory and without using notes, it often causes the audience to place more trust in her. This is because when presenters cite authors from memory, it communicates that they are widely read, knowledgeable, thoughtful, and that they have gained wisdom from wise leaders. As another example, Robert F. Kennedy (John F. Kennedy's brother) once delivered an address to the University of Kansas. In this address, he encouraged his audience not to give up hope that the United States could be a better place to live, and he urged them to dream about how the country could be better. Kennedy used anamnesis when he said, "George Bernard Shaw once wrote, 'Some people see things as they are and say why? I dream things that never were and say, why not?'"[6] Using anamnesis in this way increased Kennedy's ethical appeal by making him appear widely read, thoughtful, and knowledgeable. You may not have realized it yet, but you have been working on developing **ethical appeal** as you've been reading lessons from this book. An ethical appeal is an argument technique that builds the speaker's credibility with the audience.

Do you know how? You probably guessed it—you've been learning how to do this in the "Building Copiousness" sections that have been included at the end of each chapter. In each chapter, you've memorized famous stories or quotes that illustrate major conceptual opposites, such as love and hate, bravery and cowardice, justice and injustice, righteousness and evil. Of course, the ability to remember these quotes and stories does not ensure that you are a well-read, thoughtful, wise person. Instead, these "Building Copiousness" sections should be treated as a springboard to help you cultivate the habit of reading widely and internalizing what you learn. This may mean that you develop a collection of your favorite quotes that you can recite from memory. Or it may mean that you develop a collection of stories that you can easily narrate to illustrate certain concepts. In any case, know that the more seriously you read meaningful things, the greater supply of *copia*[7] you will have from which to draw for establishing ethos. The Latin word *copia* means "abundance" or "supply." In other words, one of the things you want to work on to help you become a good speaker is developing a plenty and abundant supply of quotes, stories, and other material you can use to prove your point. Incidentally, Robert Kennedy, the brother of former president John F. Kennedy, often quoted from Greek plays and literature during his speeches. Although this may have turned off some people, it usually increased his credibility and ethos because it made him appear knowledgeable.

---

6. Robert F. Kennedy, "Remarks at the University of Kansas, March 18, 1968," John F. Kennedy: Presidential Library and Museum, Boston, MA, http://www.jfklibrary.org/Research/Research-Aids/Ready-Reference/RFK-Speeches/Remarks-of-Robert-F-Kennedy-at-the-University-of-Kansas-March-18-1968.aspx.
7. John C. Traupman, *The New College Latin and English Dictionary Revised and Updated* (New York: Bantam Books, 2007), s.v. "*copia.*"

Establishing Ethos with Credibility

The next piece of advice for building credibility and establishing ethos is to sell your credibility to your audience. By this I mean that you prove to the audience that you have the authority, knowledge, experience, and integrity to be speaking about the matter you are addressing. To help you understand this better, review the following example from a famous speech: In 1968 Martin Luther King Jr. was shot on the balcony of a motel. This event was symbolic of the racial division, tension, and even hatred that our country was experiencing at this time. Very soon after King was shot, Robert Kennedy, the brother of President John F. Kennedy (who had also been assassinated recently), gave a powerful speech. In this speech, he sought to calm racial tension and build a bridge to a united future in America, addressing African Americans who had been hurt and grieved by King's assassination. Here is an excerpt from it:

> For those of you who are black and are tempted to [be filled with hatred] and mistrust [because] of the injustice of such an act, against all white people, I would only say that I can also feel in my own heart the same kind of feeling. I had a member of my family killed, but he was killed by a white man.[8]

Kennedy's words effectively established ethos by demonstrating to the audience that he was not just throwing out vague platitudes in a halfhearted attempt to ease the pain. Rather, he had actually experienced the same pain recently and was learning how to move past it and embrace hope. The fact that he had only just survived a similar, horrific incident established his right to talk about such matters with the audience.

8. Robert F. Kennedy, "Remarks on the Assassination of Martin Luther King Jr.," Indianapolis, IN, April 4, 1968, http://www.americanrhetoric.com/speeches/rfkonmlkdeath.html. I recommend listening to the entire speech (Link 16-1). See also "Robert Kennedy: Delivering the News of King's Death," Echoes of 1968, April 4, 2008, http://www.npr.org/2008/04/04/89365887/robert-kennedy-delivering-news-of-kings-death.

When utilizing your own background and experience in argument, it's important to remember that appeals to ethos are not exhaustive proofs of argument. Telling people to accept your argument because of your credentials or experience has the danger of becoming one of the fallacies you've learned, such as the fallacy of *ipse dixit*. The goal of selling yourself to the audience is to make yourself believable, or credible. Keep in mind the idea of building up credit—you're making deposits of trust with your audience that you can utilize later.

There are many different ways to establish your credibility in this manner. Like Robert Kennedy, you can demonstrate that you have the experience to back what you are talking about. This can be especially important if you address a situation of extreme sensitivity and pain, as Kennedy carefully did when he spoke after his brother's death. In the 2008 presidential campaign, John McCain spoke a lot about his experience as a POW during the Vietnam War. The fact that he had survived this horrendous ordeal strengthened his ethos, especially in a country involved in a war. During that same election period, both McCain and Obama frequently stressed their efforts in Congress and the Senate to reach across party lines and work with "the other side." Whether you are demonstrating that you can sympathize with your audience or are alluding to past education and experience, building ethos can be an effective way to gain your audience's attention.

Establishing Ethos with Litotes

Another figure of speech the ancients used to establish ethos was **litotes**, which is a deliberate understatement. Now, litotes will seem like the exact opposite of "selling yourself" because when you use litotes, you actually undersell yourself. That is, you de-emphasize your credentials, often for the purpose of appearing like a normal, ordinary person. This may seem counterintuitive at first—after all, shouldn't you *want* to prove to your audience how intelligent and smart you are? Cicero, a famous ancient rhetorician, said that litotes can be extremely effective because they can make a person appear modest and humble.

The 2008 presidential elections contained a great example of this device. For example, in vice-presidential candidate Sarah Palin's speeches, she spoke at length about sitting around the kitchen table discussing things with her family and with people of the community, and she emphasized her role as a mom, and even a hockey mom, a lot. At first, this may have seemed like an odd thing to do. After all, wouldn't she want to emphasize her experience as governor? Palin undersold her credentials in this way because when she spoke about sitting around the kitchen table and about her role as a mother, it established her ethos by making her appear as though she were only a common working woman who was trying to be a good mom—a role with which many of the women of America could, and did, identify. Vice-presidential candidate Joe Biden did much the same thing when he talked about his humble, blue collar Scranton roots.[9] It is important to realize that, though audiences value education and experience, they are also drawn to people who are just like them and who come across as humble and genuine individuals, rather than as elite, political intellectuals. Perhaps the modern-day candidates took their cue from Andrew Jackson, the seventh US president, who made much of this type of litotes when he based his whole campaign on the notion that he was a nobody, just a common man. This appeared to be effective with the people of the United States, as he did eventually win the election.[10]

Since there are somewhat contradictory ways of establishing ethos, you might be wondering how you are supposed to know which one to use, and when in your speech you should go about using these different techniques. As you can probably imagine, the kind of technique you use largely depends on your audience, your environment, and, possibly, situations that are happening in the culture at that time.

For example, as previously noted, Robert Kennedy was capable of using the technique anamnesis effectively and supporting his ideas with all manner of famous quotes and passages. However, when he spoke after MLK's assassination, he did very little of this because he realized that, rather than needing someone who appeared intellectual and academic, the audience needed someone who could feel the pain they were going through—someone to give them hope. Therefore, he chose to establish his credentials by showing them that he personally had felt the pain they were feeling. From this, we can generalize that the more academic and formal your debate setting is, the more you might rely on the technique of anamnesis. This becomes clearer when we realize that in formal debates, the audience is more concerned about the quality and depth of your research than if you can feel their pain. For example, in Josh and Christy's debate, both of them should make good use of anamnesis, and it will not be as important for them to sell themselves through their experience or through humble uses of litotes.

On the other hand, as Isabel and Andrew debate about cats and dogs, their ability to convince each other of their positions might be more effective if they can put themselves in each other's shoes. For instance, Isabel might say something such as "Andrew, I can imagine that getting a dog has been a dream of yours for a long time. I mean, I think all guys dream of having a loyal dog they can go on adventures with. After all, cats are not very good adventure companions. I've actually thought this would be nice lots of times myself, and I know I would feel a lot safer going on walks in our neighborhood if I had a big dog with me. But I also know that you really care about mom and don't want to increase her workload. And I think we have to realize that getting a dog is going to make things messier for her, even if we say that we will take care of the dog." You will notice that in doing this, Isabel has demonstrated that she can see things from Andrew's perspective and that she even had had similar desires herself. This establishes her ethos with Andrew more.

Beware of *Cacozelia*

It is important to note that just as there are specific techniques you can use to build ethos, there are also techniques you can use that will damage the other side's ethos. One of the most common ways you can do this is

9. Katharine Q. Seelye, "Reaction in Scranton to Biden News" (blog), *New York Times*, August 23, 2008, http://thecaucus.blogs.nytimes.com/2008/08/23/reaction-in-scranton-pa-to-biden-news/comment-page-3/?_r=0.
10. Frank Freidel and Hugh Sidey, "The Presidents: Andrew Jackson," The White House, from *The Presidents of the United States*, The White House Historical Association, 2006, http://www.whitehouse.gov/1600/presidents/andrewjackson.

through something ancient rhetoricians called *cacozelia*. *Cacozelia* is a Latin word that means "bad taste."[11] When someone commits the stylistic error of *cacozelia*, a person uses words or phrases that are offensive or confusing to the audience in some way.[12] People commonly commit ***cacozelia*** in two ways. The first way people do this is to use a lot of foreign words to appear academic or to impress the audience. (Ironically, if you use the word "*cacozelia*" in everyday conversation, that would be an example of *cacozelia*.) The problem is, if you use many foreign or even unfamiliar English words in your speech, you will eventually alienate your audience because they will not be able to understand what you are saying. Even if you explain your words, spending lots of time to define the extravagant words you're using, instead of making good arguments, can make your audience feel you're wasting everybody's time. In this case, you are achieving the opposite effect of litotes. Instead of understating your credentials in order to relate with the common person, it is as though you are rubbing your credentials or knowledge in everyone's face. No one likes a showoff. Therefore, keep in mind that academic words and even quotes are like salt—used sparingly, they improve the flavor of the dish; applied too liberally, they destroy any possible pleasure the dish once contained.

Another common way a speaker can commit *cacozelia* is by using tasteless metaphors or examples, often with the purpose of amusing or shocking the audience, that disgust the very people he is trying to persuade. It is true that sometimes people can successfully use shocking stories or a little bit of bold humor to connect with the audience. For example, Shakespeare was a master of using subtle (and sometimes not-so-subtle) ribald humor to make a clever point. However, there is a fine line between startling your audience in a clever manner and flat out disgusting them. If you repulse your audience, you have destroyed your ethos. Therefore, if you are going to use startling and somewhat obscene humor in your speech, be *extremely* careful and follow this famous dictum: When in doubt, don't! In general, it is always wise to avoid sexual and scatological (bathroom) humor in speeches, and you should never use jokes that are sexist or racist, or that make fun of the victimization or suffering of a person or group of people. It may be true that there are some people who make a fortune off these kinds of jokes (e.g., comedians, actors), but rarely are those people considered trustworthy in debating matters of seriousness or significance.

In conclusion, when you attempt to establish ethos with an audience, you need to put yourself in their shoes and ask yourself what is likely to be the thing they want most from you. Do they want you to show them that you are learned, academic, and well researched? Do they want to know that you have experience in the area about which you are speaking? Or do they need a humble, everyday person who appears to be just like they are? Your answers to these questions should govern the techniques you choose. In a later chapter, you will learn when and how to use these techniques in your speeches. You can certainly manipulate ethos techniques to convince your audience that you are knowledgeable and benevolent without actually being so. You can even be pretty effective at doing this for a while. However, if you actually lack integrity and ethos, and rely solely on manipulating people and arguments using these techniques, the cracks in your credibility will start to show the longer someone is around you, and they will eventually see through your ruse. Eventually, what you do will reflect who you are. Therefore, to establish ethos, have ethos—be knowledgeable and benevolent.

Typically, using litotes will be most effective when your credibility in some area is undisputed, or when doing so will help you connect to your audience on a sympathetic or personal level. For instance, in his pet debate with Isabel, if Andrew had raised and trained a prizewinning dog, modestly mentioning that he has had some experience in working with animals will help his cause tremendously, as he can then casually mention his strong credential at a later time in the argument. Andrew Jackson's success in making little of himself had tremendous effect in gaining the support of poorer and more common people who, feeling unrepresented by politicians from more elite social classes, supported Jackson in droves.

11. Traupman, *Latin and English Dictionary*, s.v. "*cacozelia*."
12. Burton, *Silva Rhetoricae*, s.v. "*cacozelia*," http://rhetoric.byu.edu/.

Review Exercises

Define

Define the following words.

1. Anamnesis:

2. Litotes:

3. *Cacozelia*:

Explain

1. Why is anamnesis an effective rhetorical device?

2. How you decide when to use anamnesis or litotes?

3. Which kinds of jokes should you always avoid?

____

____

____

____

Building Copiousness

Review

Review your old quotes.

Practice

Practice saying the quotes to someone in your class, or practice writing them down on paper.

Memorize

Memorize your new quote:

It's always easier to fight for one's principles than to live up to them. —Alfred Adler[13]

Practice Evaluating Ethos

Listen

Listen to Robert F. Kennedy's speech about Martin Luther's assassination (Link 16-1).

Everyday Debate

Debate

Debate the following resolution: "Resolved: Cheaters never prosper." Use at least two common topics, one deductive argument, one ethical appeal, and one special topic or a quote from the "Building Copiousness" sections.

13. Ratcliffe, *Oxford Dictionary of Quotations*, 324.

Learning from the Masters

Observe

Watch the third set of arguments from the Intelligence Squared debate on universal health care (Link 16-2). These are the speeches presented by Art Kellermann and Michael F. Cannon. As a reminder, here is the proposition under consideration: "Resolved: Universal health care coverage should be the federal government's responsibility." Flow the arguments, and then critique these speakers' arguments and presentations by answering the following questions.

List

What are three main points made by Art Kellermann?

Explain

What is one of the common topics that Kellermann uses?

Discuss

What are some strengths and weaknesses of Kellermann's argument?

List

What are three points made by Michael F. Cannon?

Explain

What is one common topic that Cannon uses in his speech?

Discuss

Which of the speakers did a better job of developing ethos? Why do you think this?

The Big Debate: Gun Control

Discuss

How can both sides of the gun control debate develop ethos?

Develop

Decide whether you will use anamnesis or litotes to establish ethos in your gun control debate, and determine how you will accomplish this. Then, write a brief paragraph to your teacher explaining which ethical device you have chosen and how you will develop it.

Chapter 17

Internal Resources: Pathos

17

THE HEART HAS ITS REASONS WHICH REASON KNOWS NOTHING OF.
—BLAISE PASCAL[1]

Proper and Proportional Pathos

The last persuasive technique you will learn is pathos. **Pathos** is a quality that arouses feelings of sadness, sympathy, pity, or sorrow. You might be thinking to yourself, "Wait, aren't emotional appeals cheap persuasive techniques?" If you have taken a logic class, you may have already learned that emotional appeals such as appeal to pity and appeal to fear are logical fallacies. Even if you haven't taken a logic class, you probably know already that plenty of people, including crooked advertisers, salespeople, and politicians, can manipulate people's emotions to their advantage through emotional appeals. Certainly all this is true, and it must be stated up front that it is possible to use pathos in a disingenuous, underhanded manner. However, it is also important to note that it is possible to use *all* appeals, including logos and ethos, in a manipulative fashion. Human beings are not merely logic machines. Our logic is extremely important, but so is proper and proportional emotion.

Consider the following examples: When a doctor is working with a patient, he will certainly use his logic to help him in his treatment of the patient. However, he will also use his feelings of compassion and pity for a suffering patient to guide him in what he should do. There might be a particular treatment that he has been considering for a very sick patient, but his compassion and pity for the patient's pain may convince him that, ultimately, this course of action is a bad idea. Parents also experience this interplay of logic and emotion. For example, let's say parents were trying to decide which school their daughter should attend. Of course, they will look at the matter logically and attempt to figure out which school will give their daughter the best experience academically and socially. However, they will also use their emotions when they consider the type of workload their daughter can handle, how she will respond to a long versus short commute, and which school will likely allow her to make the most friends. Their compassion and sympathy for their daughter will often count just as much as their logical consideration of school factors most likely to benefit the daughter. Therefore, although people can misuse emotion in debates and discussions, pathos can be a legitimate persuasive tool.

So how can you tell the difference between legitimate and illegitimate pathos? To illustrate the difference between the two, consider the following scenarios in which a person is pulled over by a police officer for speeding.

Scenario #1 (Bob is pulled over for speeding): Officer, I just can't handle a ticket right now! This semester at school has been crazy, and my family's been going through so many money

1. Susan Ratcliffe, ed., *Oxford Dictionary of Quotations by Subject*, 2nd ed. (Oxford: Oxford University Press, 2010), 147.

Beyond the misuse of emotional appeals, emotion gets a bad reputation by being thought of as subjective and arbitrary. However, emotion is frequently relied upon as a trustworthy touchstone. Almost everyone would recognize that there are right and wrong emotional responses to a given experience or scenario. For instance, the passing of a loved one ought to be met with a response of sadness or grief. On the other hand, a person laughing at a car crash would be thought of as being monstrously callous, or perhaps as a psychopath. Not all scenarios are so clear-cut, but because there is an expected proper emotional response, or range of responses, to any given scenario, those emotions can and should be anticipated and provoked.

and health problems. To add a speeding ticket and have to pay for the insurance increase . . . I just don't know how I can deal with all of this. You've got to have mercy on me, please!

Scenario #2 (Jim is pulled over for speeding): Officer, I know I was speeding, and you have every right to give me a ticket. I did break the law. But I am asking you to please consider letting me off the hook this time. My wife was just rushed to the hospital from her work because she fell and has an extremely serious head injury. She's been in and out of consciousness, and the doctor thinks there might be something really wrong with her. I know speeding is wrong, and I fully support the law, but to be honest, officer, I'm terrified that she might not make it—I just felt like I had to speed this one time to get to my wife as quickly as possible.

Compare both scenarios. Both of them use emotion, but they use it in very different ways. In the first scenario, Bob is trying to elicit pity from the police officer by talking about his extremely stressful personal life, which would be negatively affected by a ticket. Notice, however, that Bob's excuses for speeding do not pertain at all to whether it is legitimate for the policeman to give him a ticket. He doesn't even discuss the justice of being caught for his speeding or the ticket. Alternatively, consider Jim's use of pathos in the second scenario. Jim's emotional appeal is directly related to the issues of his speeding and the possible ticket. Jim readily acknowledges that speeding is wrong, and he acknowledges that the policeman has a right to give him a ticket. However, he appeals to the pity the policeman would likely feel for a man who is concerned about his injured, hospitalized wife. In essence, Jim's emotional appeal is that it is right to suspend the law in times of extreme emergency, such as this particular time. Notice that, while he is eliciting the policeman's sympathy, his emotional appeal is directly related to whether his actions were justified. Bob, on the other hand, makes no attempt to show that his actions were valid and were conforming to a higher principle. He is merely attempting to get off the hook by making the policeman feel sad for him. Therefore, we can generalize that inappropriate appeals to emotion attempt to elicit pity and sympathy in a matter that is irrelevant to the subject at hand. Conversely, a legitimate use of emotion elicits sympathy and pity in a manner that is both relevant to the subject at hand and appeals to a higher principal such as justice.

To clarify the difference between illegitimate and legitimate emotional appeal, review the following examples, which both demonstrate lawyers who are arguing that an accused company, Masterson Pharmaceuticals, should have to pay for corporate corruption and financial dishonesty to its shareholders. Both use emotion, but one appeals illegitimately and the other does it legitimately.

Scenario #1 (Lawyer A argues that Masterson Pharmaceuticals should be penalized for corporate fraud): Masterson Pharmaceuticals deserves to pay the highest penalty. Corporate corruption is the bane of American existence and saps the livelihood and hopes of honest, hardworking American citizens. Consider the case of Mrs. Ramey. Mrs. Ramey was a dedicated employee of Masterson and a single mother, deserted by her worthless husband. She scrimped and saved her whole life so that she could pay her children's way through college, and she put a little bit aside to live on when she got older so that she would not be a burden to either her kids or society. Mrs. Ramey invested all her money in the stocks for the company she worked so hard for, and how did her company repay her? By reporting fraudulent earning and then embezzling the money that she and other good, upright people like her had so trustingly invested in the company. And Mrs. Ramey? She is left with nothing. She is sixty years old and must start from scratch. Some months, she doesn't even know how she is going to make her house payment. Dishonest companies such as Masterson Pharmaceuticals deserve to pay for all the suffering they have caused others.

Scenario #2 (Lawyer B argues that Masterson Pharmaceuticals should be penalized for corporate fraud): Ladies and gentlemen of the jury, I am asking you today to do justice and hold Masterson Pharmaceuticals responsible for the manner in which they have robbed and injured its shareholders. Throughout this trial, you have heard testimonies and seen evidence that has demonstrated that, over a period of several years, the top executives of Masterson Pharmaceuticals willingly and knowingly conspired to deceive corporate shareholders of the business's financial problems. The executives purposefully did this in order to garner the highest earnings for themselves, even though they knew that, ultimately, they were taking money from honest people who had entrusted their life's savings to Masterson Pharmaceuticals. Ladies and gentlemen, you heard recorded conversations of Masterson's top executives joking about using the retirement money of "old crones," as they called them, to fund their luxury yachts and jets. You saw memos from corporate lawyers warning these executives of the legal and ethical problems with their actions. You also saw memos from the same executives warning these lawyers to stop "being the morality police" and to do their jobs. Ladies and gentlemen of the jury, testimonies, recordings, and evidence such as this demonstrate a conscious and deliberate pattern of financial deceit, recklessness, and carelessness, the result of which has cheated thousands of hardworking people out of their entire life's savings, leaving them impoverished and anxiety-ridden in a time of their life when they should have been relaxing in peace and enjoying the fruits of their labor. Jury members, Masterson Pharmaceuticals deserves the highest penalty so that it, and greedy companies like it, will learn that America will not stand for such corporate callousness and immorality.

In these two scenarios, you will notice that both lawyers use some of the same language. They talk about the corruption of Masterson Pharmaceuticals and of the suffering of hardworking, honest Americans. However, in the first scenario, Lawyer A builds his emotional appeal around Mrs. Ramey, a single mother who invested all of her money into her company, which betrayed her by their embezzlement and fraud. This is certainly a pitiable story. However, if you examine this closely, you will observe that this story provides no evidence to actually demonstrate that Masterson was involved in corporate fraud and corruption. Additionally, this story makes a point of emphasizing that Mrs. Ramey was a single mother, deserted by her husband—which is something that, frankly, Masterson is not responsible for, and this fact does not have direct relevance to their fraudulent actions. In the second scenario, Lawyer B evokes pity about the thousands of people who should be enjoying their retirement but have been robbed of

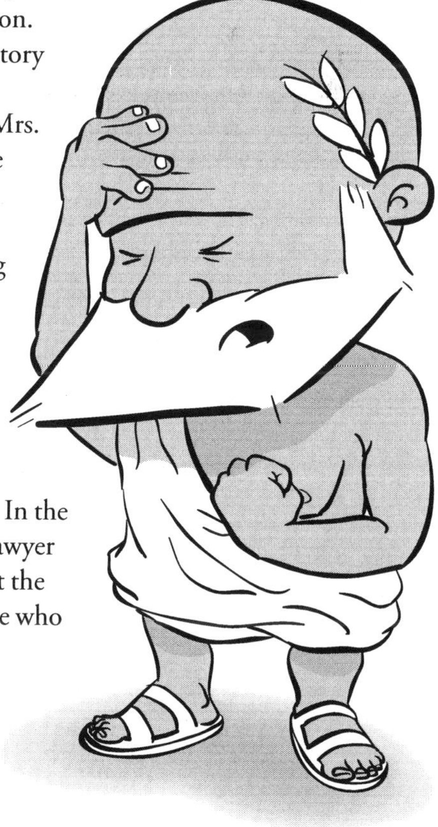

their hard-earned money, but he also makes a point to review the evidence that shows that the top executives of the company did, indeed, conspire to engage in financial fraud and take people's money to fund their luxurious lifestyles. Furthermore, Lawyer B sums up all of this evidence by reminding the members of the jury that it is just for companies such as Masterson Pharmaceuticals to pay the highest penalty so that corporations will learn that Americans, and all good people, will not tolerate such corruption. In a nutshell, when someone uses illegitimate appeals to emotion, she evokes emotion about issues irrelevant to the subject under discussion; when someone uses legitimate appeals to emotion, she evokes emotion about a relevant issue and often uses the emotion to appeal to a higher standard, such as the standard of justice.

Now that you have examined the difference between illegitimate and legitimate appeal to emotion, look at some techniques you can use to evoke legitimate emotion and avoid illegitimate appeal to emotion. First, you should know that ancient rhetoricians listed many different methods a person could use to evoke emotion. In fact, the website *Silva Rhetoricae*[2] (Latin for "Forest of Rhetoric"), which is an excellent resource for you to learn different techniques to use in your debate, lists approximately thirty techniques a person can use to stir up emotion. As you can imagine, there isn't enough space in this book to cover all of these rhetorical devices. To learn more about these in-depth, consult the *Silva Rhetoricae* website. Instead, you will look at five key methods here.

An Illustration from Shakespeare

To gain a better understanding of these five devices, review the following famous monologue from Shakespeare's play *Julius Caesar*. In this play, the senators of Rome assassinate Rome's dictator because they believe that he will gain too much power. In the play, one of the key conspirators, Brutus, makes a moving speech in which he states that he slew Caesar not because he loved Caesar less but rather because he loved Rome more. In an act of good faith, he allows Mark Antony, Caesar's protégé, to deliver a funeral oration for Caesar. At first, Antony appears to support Brutus and the conspirators. But, as his oration progresses, he very craftily and subtly uses pathos to stir the crowd's sympathy for the slain Caesar and provoke their anger against the conspirators. Read Antony's speech and then read the explanation of the different devices of pathos Shakespeare illustrates in Antony's words:

> Friends, Romans, countrymen, lend me your ears;
> I come to bury Caesar, not to praise him.
> The evil that men do lives after them;
> The good is oft interred with their bones.
> So let it be with Caesar. The noble Brutus
> Hath told you Caesar was ambitious.
> If it were so, it was a grievous fault,
> And grievously hath Caesar answer'd it.
> Here, under leave of Brutus and the rest—
> (For Brutus is an honourable man;
> So are they all, all honourable men),
> Come I to speak in Caesar's funeral.
> He was my friend, faithful and just to me;
> But Brutus says he was ambitious;
> And Brutus is an honourable man.
> He hath brought many captives home to Rome,
> Whose ransoms did the general coffers fill:
> Did this in Caesar seem ambitious?
> When that the poor have cried, Caesar hath wept:
> Ambition should be made of sterner stuff:
> Yet Brutus says he was ambitious;
> And Brutus is an honourable man.
> You all did see that on the Lupercal
> I thrice presented him a kingly crown,
> Which he did thrice refuse: was this ambition?
> Yet Brutus says he was ambitious;
> And, sure, he is an honourable man.
> I speak not to disprove what Brutus spoke,
> But here I am to speak what I do know.
> You all did love him once, not without cause:
> What cause withholds you then to mourn for him?
> O judgment! thou art fled to brutish beasts,
> And men have lost their reason. Bear with me.
> My heart is in the coffin there with Caesar,
> And I must pause till it come back to me.[3]

2. See Gideon O. Burton, *Silva Rhetoricae*, Brigham Young University, page last updated February 26, 2007, http://rhetoric.byu.edu/.

3. William Shakespeare, *Julius Caesar*, ed. Shane Weller (New York: Dover Publications, 1991), act 3, scene 2.

Take a moment to read this monologue again (preferably out loud, to someone else) so that you can catch the full effect of Shakespeare's pathos communicated through Mark Antony. When reading this speech, you probably noticed several stylistic devices Antony used to heighten the sympathetic appeal of his speech. Let's look at several of these. First, there is a particular phrase that is repeated several times throughout the whole speech: "And Brutus is an honourable man." At first, this phrase acts as a sort of "peace offering" to Brutus—it appears that Antony is going to support Brutus's judgment of Caesar. However, as the speech progresses, this repeated line starts to have the opposite effect; it serves to undermine the supposed honor of Brutus and instead becomes a subtly sarcastic taunt, for Antony describes all of Caesar's wonderful acts and then states "And, sure, Brutus is an honourable man." This phrase serves to remind the audience that the "honourable" Brutus says he killed Caesar for the supposed good of Rome, but Caesar's life was full of honorable acts. In the play, this repetition begins to stir the crowd to anger as they juxtapose the loving, noble Caesar with the supposedly honorable murderers of this great man.

Epimone

This repetition is a type of rhetorical (speaking) device called ***epimone***, which is the repetition of a phrase or question, or a plea used to evoke emotions.[4] The word *epimone* is from the Greek words *epi*, meaning "upon," and *meno*, meaning "to remain." Therefore, *epimone* literally means tarrying or delaying upon a thought. When a speaker uses *epimone*, he is, in essence, asking the hearer to tarry and delay in order to think through what the speaker is presenting her.

Note that this repeated phrase is used to cause the Romans to realize that Brutus, although he claims he is honorable, is actually *not* honorable and has slain the honorable Caesar. Another example of this is in act 3, scene 2, when Brutus gives his speech right before Antony's and attempts to justify the slaying of Caesar. He says, "Who is here so base that would be a bondman? If any, speak; for him I have offended. Who is here so rude that would not be a Roman? If any speak; for him have I offended." Notice the repetition of the question "Who here is so . . . ?" and of the phrase "for him I have offended." The recurring question evokes feelings of shame in the audience, and Brutus uses this repetition to try to convince his audience that he is on their side—that he is one of them and acted justly when he slew Caesar.

4. Burton, *Silva Rhetoricae*, s.v. "*epimone*," http://rhetoric.byu.edu/.

There are many famous examples of *epimone* in a variety of media. One well-known example is in Shakespeare's *Romeo and Juliet*. Juliet takes a sleeping potion to fake her death, and is discovered by her Nurse, who explodes into epimone: "Most lamentable day, most woeful day / That ever, ever, I did yet behold! / O day! O day! O day! O hateful day! / Never was seen so black a day as this: / O woeful day, O woeful day!"[5]

5. William Shakespeare, *Romeo and Juliet*, ed Shane Weller (New York: Dover Publications, 1993), act 4, scene 5.

Enargia

The next rhetorical device we want to examine is ***enargia***. *Enargia* is vivid description or retelling of an event. This device can be extremely effective in evoking pathos, especially when the scene or event being described is extremely tragic or brutal, or glorious and pleasant. The word *enargia* comes from the word *enarges*, which means "visible or palpable."[6] When you use *enargia*, you are making a scene so vivid to your listeners that they feel they are experiencing it, too. You will notice that Mark Antony does this throughout his speech when he describes Caesar's many noble actions: "When that the poor have cried, Caesar hath wept" and "You all did see that on the Lupercal, / I thrice presented him a kingly crown, / Which he did thrice refuse." And "He hath brought many captives home to Rome / Whose ransoms did the general coffers fill." All of these vivid descriptions invoke kindly feelings toward Caesar and anger at the assassins who killed such a wonderful man.

As another example, consider the movie *The Rainmaker*, starring Matt Damon as young lawyer Rudy Balor.[7] In the

6. Burton, *Silva Rhetoricae*, s.v. "*enargia*," http://rhetoric.byu.edu/.
7. See Michael Douglas et al., *John Grisham's The Rainmaker*, directed by Francis Ford Coppola (1997; Hollywood, CA: Paramount Home Entertainment, 2007), DVD.

film, Baylor takes on a fraudulent insurance company that made a fortune selling bogus insurance policies to poor people. Baylor acts as the defense for a woman whose son died from leukemia, who could have been treated had the insurance company honored the policy (which they did not). In Baylor's closing statement, he uses *enargia* to talk about the boy who died, what a great kid he was, and all that he missed out on because of the greed and duplicity of the insurance company. He moves the boy's family and many members of the jury to tears, and he wins the case. In fact, *enargia* is a very common device used by lawyers, especially in dramatic shows about lawyers on television. Because it helps to put the audience in someone else's shoes, *enargia* can be incredibly effective device—especially if the audience member (e.g., a juror) has also been a victim of some sort.

In another movie, *A Time to Kill*, actor Matthew McConaughey plays a lawyer who is prosecuting two men on trial for assaulting and killing a little girl.[8] In his closing statement, McConaughey uses *enargia* to describe to the jury the torment and cruelties these men inflicted on the little girl. Incidentally, both of these movies are based on books written by author John Grisham. Grisham was originally trained as a lawyer, and it is no mistake that his lawyer characters often use *enargia* to influence juries and win cases. *Enargia* can be an extremely effective tool of pathos.

In addition to *The Rainmaker* and *A Time to Kill*, the first example of Masterson Pharmaceuticals provided earlier in this chapter also utilized *enargia*. Be aware that this device can be particularly tempting to misuse, as it can be irrelevant to the real issue at hand, and it can involve imaginative speculation on details that you might not actually know or be able to confirm.

Epiplexis

The next device we are going to look at is a device called ***epiplexis***, which is the use of a question to evoke shame rather than to seek an answer. The word *epiplexis* comes from two Greek words, one of which, *epi*, you know means "upon"; the other word, *plessein*, means "to strike." You can use *epiplexis* to question the matter at hand.[9] For instance, Mark Antony did this when he asked the crowd, "Was this ambition?" This question provoked the emotion of Antony's audience because it highlighted the injustice of his murder. In Patrick Henry's famous "Give me liberty or give me death!" speech,[10] he uses *epiplexis* effectively. Henry delivered this speech to the Virginia Convention in hopes of urging them to take up arms to resist Britain. In the speech, Henry asks the men at the convention, "Why stand we here idle? What is it that gentlemen wish? What would they have? Is life so dear, or peace so sweet, as to be purchased at the price of chains and slavery?"[11] He uses these questions to rouse the men of Virginia to action. Well-worded, provocative questions such as these can do much to incite the emotion of an audience.

Apostrophe

The next device of pathos is a term you are probably familiar with from your English class: apostrophe. However, the apostrophe we are about to examine is a device of pathos, rather than the punctuation mark. **Apostrophe** occurs when someone addresses an inanimate object as though it has thoughts and emotions.[12] For instance, in Mark Antony's speech, at one point he says, "O judgment! thou are fled to brutish beasts." This is an example of apostrophe because he is addressing judgment as though it were a person. Another famous example of this can be seen in John Donne's poem "Death, Be Not Proud." Donne wrote, "Death, be not proud, though some have called thee / Mighty and dreadful, for thou are not so."[13] He addressed death as though it were a person

8. See Joel Schumacher et al., *A Time to Kill*, directed by Joel Schumacher (1996; Burbank, CA: Warner Home Video, 2009), DVD.

9. Burton, *Silva Rhetoricae*, s.v. "*epiplexis*," http://rhetoric.byu.edu/.
10. Patrick Henry, "Give Me Liberty or Give Me Death" (delivered March 23, 1775, at Henrico Parrish Church St, Richmond, Virginia, Second Virginia Convention), American Rhetoric Online Speech Bank, http://www.americanrhetoric.com/speeches/patrickhenrygivemeliberty.html.
11. Philip Gavin, "Great Speeches Collection: Patrick Henry, Liberty or Death!" The History Place, http://www.historyplace.com/speeches/henry.htm.
12. Burton, *Silva Rhetoricae*, s.v. "apostrophe," http://rhetoric.byu.edu/.
13. John Donne, "10" ("Death, Be Not Proud"), *The Norton Anthology of English Literature*, 6th ed., vol. 1. (New York: W.W. Norton, 1993), 1116.

with feelings and thoughts. Apostrophe can be a useful method to stir people's emotions because it underscores the topic in a unique way and helps the audience observe the topic from a unique angle.

Aposiopesis

The last device of pathos you'll learn in this chapter is aposiopesis. Someone uses **aposiopesis** when he is silent after speaking or when he is deliberately silent for a short time as if to meditate or quietly contemplate the matter at hand.[14] For instance, after Mark Antony says, "O judgment! thou art fled to brutish beasts," he says, "My heart is in the coffin there with Caesar, / And I must pause till it come back to me." In the play *Julius Caesar*, Shakespeare does not directly indicate that Mark Antony pauses after this line, but it seems likely that he does so, and this type of pause would certainly give the audience time to reflect on and sympathize with Mark Antony's grief. This pause emphasizes to the audience that his heart is broken and he is sorrowful over Caesar's death.

In the 2008–2009 vice-presidential debates, Senator Joe Biden demonstrated this rhetorical technique when he talked about his wife who had passed away. His voice choked with tears, and he had to pause for a minute to collect himself. This emotion was powerfully effective because it humanized him and made him seem like a regular person to the audience. Aposiopesis shows your audience that you truly care about what you are saying. Of course, some people can fake aposiopesis well and act as though they are overwhelmed with grief when they really aren't. This can be a dangerous gamble, however, because people can often tell when someone's grief is genuine or dishonest. Your best bet is to use aposiopesis honestly and naturally.

Think about these devices of pathos in conjunction with Andrew and Isabel's pet debate, as well as with Josh and Christy's capital punishment debate. Josh and Christy will certainly want to make use of these devices in their speech. The subject of capital punishment provides many opportunities for the use of legitimate pathos. On the other hand, as you can imagine, it wouldn't be natural for Andrew and Isabel to use these devices in their pet discussion. In informal debates, it is often not as necessary for you to use devices of pathos. This is because the person with whom you are having an informal debate can easily read your emotional level because she is close to you in the discussion (e.g., sitting next to you at a coffee shop, or chatting with you in your home). Therefore, there is no need to use grand devices to underscore your sorrow. Devices of pathos, when used well, can be an excellent means to connect with your audience.

The most fruitful uses of aposiopesis are rarely planned. You might have heard detailed, preplanned speeches spoken of as "canned." A canned speech's words are like vegetables, harvested long ago, stewing well beyond freshness in stale water, accumulating the metal taste of the aluminum can they rest in on the supermarket shelf until someone picks them up. Their taste is old and artificial. As you have hopefully understood from this book so far, the best speakers plan out their words, often in great detail. What can make planned words lose their luster and sound canned, however, is if they lack the emotion, energy, and context that should naturally accompany them. A dramatic, emotional pause will be interpreted as false and manipulative if there hasn't been a steady rise of believable emotion preceding it. Conversely, one of the advantages of vivid, well-chosen words is that they will not only provoke a meaningful and emotional response in an audience, but also encourage those characteristics in the speaker, producing a sincere emotion with which the audience can identify.

14. Burton, *Silva Rhetoricae*, s.v. "aposiopesis," http://rhetoric.byu.edu/.

Review Exercises

Define

Provide a definition for each of the following words.

1. *Epimone*: ____________________

____

2. *Enargia*: ____________________

____

3. *Epiplexis*: ____________________

____

4. Apostrophe: ____________________

____

5. Aposiopesis: ____________________

____

Explain

1. Explain why appeals of pathos are important in debating.

____

____

____

____

2. Explain the difference between appropriate and inappropriate appeals to emotion.

____

____

____

____

Building Copiousness

Review

Review your old quotes.

Practice

Practice saying the quotes to someone in your class, or practice writing them down on paper.

Memorize

Memorize your new quote:

> A little learning is a dangerous thing;
> Drink deep, or taste not the Pierian spring.
> —Alexander Pope[15]

Practice Evaluating Pathos

Discuss

Watch President Obama's acceptance speech on election night 2008 (Link 17-1). How does he develop ethos and pathos?

Explain

Examine the last speech of the student debating for the Harvard Debate team in *The Great Debaters* (chapter 23, "The Harvard Debate," on the DVD).[16] How do James Farmer and the student speaking for Harvard build pathos? Are these appeals to pathos legitimate? Why or why not? Which one is more effective?

____

____

____

____

____

15. Ratcliffe, *Oxford Dictionary of Quotations*, 268.
16. See Todd Black, et al, *The Great Debaters*, directed by Denzel Washington (2007; New York: Weinstein Co., 2008), DVD.

Everyday Debate

Develop

Consider the following resolution, from a quote by Edmund Burke: "Resolved: It is necessary only for the good man to do nothing for evil to triumph."[17] Develop an argument for this debate using a variety of common and special topics. In addition, use appeals to ethos and pathos to support your argument.

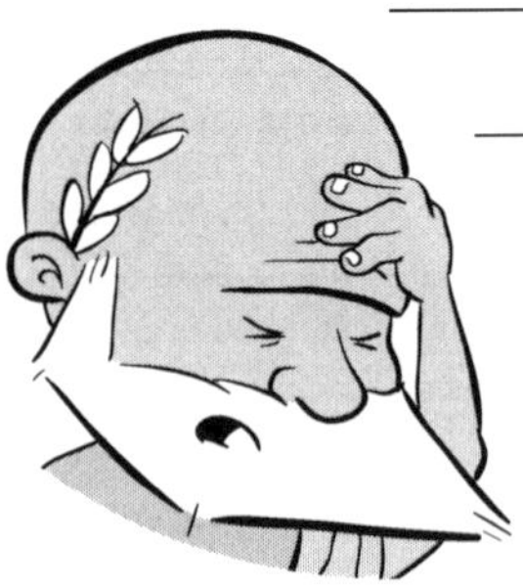

17. Ratcliffe, *Oxford Dictionary of Quotations*, 159.

Learning from the Masters

Observe

Watch the first question-and-answer session of the Intelligence Squared debate on universal health care (Link 17-2) and then answer the following question.

An audience member asked a question about whether there is a conflict between making people well and making a profit. Outline the answers from each of the respondents.

The Big Debate: Gun Control

Develop

By this point, you have read quite a bit about gun control, and about people who have had direct experiences with guns and crime. Find at least one story for each side of the issue that evokes emotion. For example, you could tell a story of someone who was shot and injured because of lax gun control, or you could tell a story about someone who was able to defend herself from a potentially violent crime with a personal firearm.

Chapter 18

Style and Rhetorical Devices

18

> CONTINUAL ELOQUENCE IS TEDIOUS.
>
> —BLAISE PASCAL[1]

Imagine that you are listening to a *terrible* speech. In your mind, what does it sound like? It probably sounds and looks like this example: The speaker has a monotone voice, doesn't make eye contact with the audience, pauses awkwardly at odd times, and can't stop repeatedly saying "um." It appears as though she is just spitting out a lot of facts merely to get the job done. You don't believe that she actually cares about you or what she is talking about. Worst of all, every sentence sounds just as dull as the last. You're not quite sure what it is about the words this speaker is using, but they are lifeless and evoke no pictures. They make you feel like you are sitting in a gray room with boring furniture and the blandest paintings on the walls. The oppressive weight of boredom squashes you down into your chair.

Throughout this chapter, you will encounter specific grammatical terms that refer to units of syntax. **Syntax** refers to the particular way that words are arranged in a sentence and the rules that govern this arrangement. Particular groups of words are called units of syntax, or syntactical units. For a quick grammar refresher, note that a clause is a unit of syntax that has both a subject and a verb (such as "I will debate you"). A phrase refers to a unit of syntax that does not have both a subject and a verb (such as the prepositional phrase "with all my might"). Sentences can contain a clause and a phrase, or multiples of both, as seen in the following example: "I will debate you (clause) with all my might (phrase) about the best kind of whale (phrase)." If you keep these different grammatical units in mind, it will help you better understand the different devices in this chapter.

Now imagine you are listening to a different speech—a *wonderful* speech. How is this different from the boring speech? In your imagination, the experience may look like the following example: The speaker looks directly at you—she makes a point to look at everyone in the room as she talks. Her voice has energy and excitement. She strolls across the stage with enthusiasm and, occasionally, moves to the front of the stage, reaching out to the audience with her hands, as if supplicating them. She fills her speech with humor and thoughtful quotes, and her words are just . . . well, they are certainly moving! You can't quite put your finger on what makes her so dynamic, but it feels as though this speaker has chosen every word and phrase carefully in order to evoke the most beautiful images and vivid sounds possible. Almost everything that comes out of her mouth inspires you, and you are almost hypnotized by her words.

Now, this contrast may seem a bit exaggerated. However, if you were to compare watching a video of a very ineffective speaker with that of an incredibly effective speaker, they would, to some degree, have this effect on you. Good speakers have all of the characteristics illustrated in the previous example—they are enthusiastic, caring, energetic, funny, and thought provoking. However, one important quality of excellent speakers that people often overlook is their purposeful arrangement and choice of words.

---

1. Susan Ratcliffe, ed., *Oxford Dictionary of Quotations by Subject*, 2nd ed. (Oxford: Oxford University Press, 2010), 448.

For instance, consider the following lines from famous speakers:

> "Ask not what your country can do for you—ask what you can do for your country."
> —John F. Kennedy[2]
>
> "Change will not come if we wait for some other person or some other time. We are the ones we've been waiting for. We are the change that we seek." —Barack Obama[3]
>
> "Give me liberty or give me death!"
> —Patrick Henry[4]
>
> "Darkness cannot drive out darkness: only light can do that. Hate cannot drive out hate: only love can do that."
> —Martin Luther King Jr.[5]

Powerful words and phrases such as these have inspired people throughout history. Certainly part of their inspiration came from the speakers who delivered them. Each of these speakers had, or has, great personal magnetism, which has encouraged and influenced listeners. Note that these presenters carefully chose effective words for their respective speeches, and this care—combined with charisma, bravery, and character—coalesced to inspire their audiences in a powerful manner.

So what is the secret to careful, effective, and eloquent word choice? Did these speakers just think of these ideas on the spot? Did their words come out beautifully arranged by chance? Is there some special formula or rule to be found and followed?

2. Ratcliffe, *Oxford Dictionary of Quotations*, 356.
3. NewsOne Staff, "Barack Obama Quotes: His Most Memorable Lines," NewsOne, September 20, 2012, http://newsone.com/2044176/barack-obama-quotes/.
4. Patrick Henry, "Give Me Liberty or Give Me Death" (delivered March 23, 1775, at Henrico Parrish Church St, Richmond, Virginia, Second Virginia Convention), American Rhetoric Online Speech Bank, http://www.americanrhetoric.com/speeches/patrickhenrygivemeliberty.html.
5. Thomas Barrabi, "Martin Luther King Quotes: 21 Memorable Sayings for MLK Day 2015," *International Business Times*, January 19, 2015, http://www.ibtimes.com/martin-luther-king-quotes-21-memorable-sayings-mlk-day-2015-1783820.

Speaking with Euphony

Although people may spontaneously think of good phrases and words with no planning, and although it is possible that speakers could deliver beautiful phrases by coincidence or on the fly, so to speak, it is more likely that these speakers were aware of some basic principles of word and sentence euphony. The word *euphony* comes from two Greek derivatives—*eu*, meaning "good" or "easily," and *phone*, meaning "voice," "cry," or "shout."[6] Therefore, when a sentence or phrase has **euphony**, it has the quality of having a pleasant, good, or sweet voice or sound.[7] It is important to understand that something that sounds beautiful to one person may not sound as beautiful to another person. As beauty is in the eye of the beholder, euphony can be in the ear of the listener. In other words, euphony certainly has a subjective element. However, there are some characteristics of sentences, such as symmetry, similarity, and balance, which—if used correctly—have a universal appeal to people. The ancient rhetoricians, as they observed and experimented with speech, became aware of these principles and developed a list of tricks or rhetorical devices that can help speakers arrange their words in a euphonic manner. These are very similar to the devices you learned about in the previous two chapters with regard to ethos and pathos. As was the case with those chapters, there isn't enough room here to cover all possible euphonic rhetorical devices; instead, for the purpose of learning techniques specific to debate, you will learn just a few of the most common and helpful devices in the lessons of this book.

Parallelism

One of the most common rhetorical devices people use to add euphony to their writing is parallelism. When someone uses **parallelism** in his writing, he repeats similarly structured words or phrases.[8] For instance, consider the following sentence that Josh could use, perhaps at the end of his debate on capital punishment: Capital punishment is vengeful; capital punishment is

6. J.T. Pring, *The Pocket Oxford Greek Dictionary* (New York: Oxford University Press, 2000), 71, 204.
7. Gideon O. Burton, *Silva Rhetoricae*, s.v. "euphony," Brigham Young University, page last updated February 26, 2007, http://rhetoric.byu.edu/.
8. Burton, *Silva Rhetoricae*, s.v. "parallelism," http://rhetoric.byu.edu/.

unjust; capital punishment is inappropriate. Notice that this sentence contains parallelism because it contains three phrases or clauses that are similar in length, structure, and content. Phrases, clauses, or sentences that have similarity in any one of these three ways (length, structure, or content) are considered to be parallel.

Using parallelism creates a sense of balance and symmetry in writing. Consider the quote from Martin Luther King Jr. above: "Darkness cannot drive out darkness: only light can do that. Hate cannot drive out hate: only love can do that." Notice the parallelism in this sentence. The first sentence talks about what darkness cannot do and what light can do. The second sentence repeats this same pattern with the words *hate* and *love*. Once again, note how the use of parallelism adds symmetry and balance to this sentence. Parallelism creates euphonic balance by repeating similarly structured phrases, clauses, and sentences.

Antithesis

The next rhetorical device is antithesis. **Antithesis** creates balance and symmetry in a sentence by juxtaposing, or placing together, two ideas that are similar in structure but opposite in meaning.[9] For example, look at the following quote that Josh created to use in his capital punishment speech: "We must forsake hatred and revenge; we must embrace forgiveness and restoration." Both of the phrases in this sentence are structured in a similar manner. They began with the phrase "we must." Then, they both contain a verb ("forsake" in the first phrase and "embrace" in the second). Lastly, they both contain a direct object of the verb. For instance, in the first phrase, "hatred" and "revenge" are the direct objects of "forsake"; in the second clause, "forgiveness" and "restoration" are the direct objects of "embrace." If you think back to Patrick Henry's quote provided earlier in this chapter—"Give me liberty or give me death!"—you will observe that it contains antithesis as well; in fact, it is one of the most famous historical examples of antithesis. It is a short but effective sentence. The first clause begins with the words "Give me" and ends with a direct object: "liberty." The second clause begins with the same words, "give me," and then it also ends with a direct object—"death"—but note that the word "death" is the opposite idea of "liberty." The JFK quote "Ask not what your country can do for you—ask what you can do for your country" is also a famous historical examples of antithesis. Antithesis is so successful because it contains the appealing use of balance and symmetry, yet its use of contrasting ideas is often startling and thought provoking.

9. Ibid., s.v. "antithesis," http://rhetoric.byu.edu/.

Alliteration

The third rhetorical device you will learn is one that you may already be familiar with from English class: alliteration. When people use **alliteration**, they juxtapose words that contain the same consonant, often at the beginning of the word.[10] For example, consider the following sentence that Christy could use in her speech: "Justice helps, heals, and harmonizes." Note the repetition of the letter *h* at the beginning of each word. This repetition is both soothing and arresting. The use of the letter *h* is especially productive in this sentence because the statement is clearly in favor of

10. Ibid., s.v. "alliteration," http://rhetoric.byu.edu/.

capital punishment, and the sound of *h* is peaceful, calm, and pleasant. The use of alliteration with the repeated, soothing sound of *h* edifies that Christy is speaking positively about her statement.

Alliteration also can be used to drive home an unpleasant, powerful, or negative feeling or thought. Consider the use of alliteration in the following sentence that Josh may use in his speech: "Capital punishment denigrates, demoralizes, and destroys." The alliterative use of the letter *d* is effective in this sentence because Josh is critiquing—lambasting, really—the idea of capital punishment, and the letter *d* has a hard, forceful sound to it. Therefore, the use of alliteration matches the message of his sentence.

Poets are exceptionally aware of how the clever use of alliteration can serve to enhance your message. For instance, in his poem "Silver," Walter de la Mare describes the moon in this way:

> Slowly, silently, now the moon
> Walks the night in her silver shoon[11]

The repetition of the letter *s* in these lines enhances our image of the moon gliding over the nighttime landscape. By the same token, Edgar Allan Poe began his well-known poem "The Raven" as follows:

> Once upon a midnight dreary, while I pondered weak and weary,
>
> Over many a quaint and curious volume of forgotten lore,
>
> While I nodded, nearly napping, suddenly there came a tapping,
>
> As of someone gently rapping, rapping at my chamber door.
>
> "'Tis some visitor," I muttered, "tapping at my chamber door—
>
> —Only this, and nothing more."
>
> Ah, distinctly I remember it was in the bleak December,
>
> And each separate dying ember wrought its ghost upon the floor.
>
> Eagerly I wished the morrow;—vainly I had sought to borrow
>
> From my books surcease of sorrow—sorrow for the lost Lenore—
>
> For the rare and radiant maiden whom the angels name Lenore—
>
> —Nameless *here* for evermore.[12]

It is interesting that in this poem, Poe uses a profusion of alliteration and assonance to underscore a variety of emotions, moods, and sounds: monotony, dreaminess, interruption of thoughts, and, eventually, urgency. If you read the rest of this poem (you can easily find this poem online by typing "Edgar Allan Poe" and "The Raven" into a search engine), you will likely notice that Poe's abundant use of alliteration throughout the rest of this poem serves to build a sense of urgency and impending doom, which leads eventually to the climax of the poem. Clever use of alliteration is extremely effective because it can enhance and complement a variety of moods and emotions.

In this chapter, we have examined the use of alliteration, which is the repetition of initial consonants at the beginning of adjacent words. There are other literary devices that also play with the repetition of certain sounds in adjacent words. For instance, **assonance** is the repetition of initial vowel sounds at the beginning of words. **Consonance** is the repetition of consonants in adjacent words, especially when these consonants are at the end of the word. In addition, there's a more specific kind of consonance called **sibilance**, which refers to the repetition of *s* sounds. If the writer and speaker are not careful with its usage, sibilance can become a rhetorical vice, due to the harsh, hissing, snake-like sound it creates.

11. Walter de la Mare, "Silver," All Poetry, http://allpoetry.com/poem/8494557-Silver-by-Walter-de-la-Mare.

12. Edgar Allen Poe, "The Raven," *Anthology of American Literature, Volume 1: Colonial Through Romantic*, ed. George McMichael, 4th ed. (New York: MacMillan, 1989), 956–957.

Anaphora

The fourth device we will look at is anaphora. Anaphora, once again, creates balance and symmetry in a sentence like parallelism and antithesis do. However, **anaphora** does this through the clever repetition of words or phrases at the beginning of successive clauses or sentences.[13] For instance, consider the following sentence: "We shall fight for human dignity; we shall cry out for those unjustly deprived of life; we shall show the way to forgiveness and peace." The repetition of the phrase "we shall" adds balance, and it also emphasizes the mood of protest and moral urgency that this sentence contains. Here is another example of anaphora from Barack Obama's "Audacity of Hope" speech:

> It's *the hope of* slaves sitting around a fire singing freedom songs; *the hope of* immigrants setting out for distant shores; *the hope of* a young naval lieutenant bravely patrolling the Mekong Delta; *the hope of* a millworker's son who dares to defy the odds; *the hope of* a skinny kid with a funny name who believes that America has a place for him, too.[14]

The anaphora in these sentences, which occurs with the phrase "the hope of," is extremely effective because the repetition of the word *hope* builds a feeling of excitement and optimism. It also provides a common link between widely different kinds of people and circumstances: slaves, immigrants, soldiers. Being able to connect things the audience might not expect through anaphora can be a powerful tool. Anaphora is also especially effective when the speaker chooses an especially provocative or inspiring word to repeat. The repetition of meaningful words in anaphora both focuses the reader and balances the sentence.

Anadiplosis

The last rhetorical device is **anadiplosis**, which occurs when a word at the end of one phrase or clause is repeated at the beginning of the next phrase or clause.[15] Anadiplosis, in some ways, is a combination of parallelism and anaphora. That is, when a speaker uses anadiplosis, he certainly uses similarly structured phrases or words, and he also uses repetition, but he does it in a very unique way. Consider the following example: "Capital punishment restores the balance, balances rights, and rights horrible wrongs." Notice that the word *balance* is at the end of the first phrase and then repeated at the beginning of the next. Then, the word *rights*, which is at the end of the second phrase, is repeated at the beginning of the third. Also, notice that all of these phrases are structured in a similar manner—there is a noun at the beginning of the clause or phrase, followed by a verb or direct object. Another example can be found in the following quote which I created: "Our goal is peace, and peace is our work." In both of these examples, the word used both at the end of one clause and the beginning of the next serves as a focus, a balance, and an emphasis, which is the benefit of utilizing anadiplosis.

How to Avoid Overusing Rhetorical Devices

There are several important factors to keep in mind when using rhetorical devices. First, it's important to remember that rhetorical devices can be overused. The salt metaphor is helpful here: Salt, when applied sparingly to food, enhances its flavor; when applied too liberally, it certainly ruins the taste. In the same way, rhetorical devices applied wisely enhance the meaning and the beauty of words. However, used lavishly and carelessly, these rhetorical devices can become distracting and even laughable. Therefore, use them sparingly and thoughtfully.

Second, it may help you to know that most people feel as though their words sound contrived when they begin to use these rhetorical devices. This is because people do not usually speak in rhetorical devices. Indeed, they are a formula invented to achieve a purpose. Think of these devices, in terms of their connection to speaking, in the same manner as one would consider a basketball play in relation to the game and its players: A basketball play is a

13. Burton, *Silva Rhetoricae*, s.v. "anaphora," http://rhetoric.byu.edu/.
14. Barack Obama, "2004 Democratic National Convention Keynote Address" (delivered July 27, 2004, Fleet Center, Boston), American Rhetoric Online Speech Bank, http://www.americanrhetoric.com/speeches/convention2004/barackobama2004dnc.htm; italics added.
15. Burton, *Silva Rhetoricae*, s.v. "anadiplosis," http://rhetoric.byu.edu/.

formula—a strategy—used to achieve a specific purpose. It isn't necessarily what players would do naturally if they were all just dribbling on their own with no set agenda. Just as basketball plays are used by team members at certain times and for particular purposes in a given game, you also use rhetorical devices purposefully to achieve certain goals in the construct of debate and speech.

Lastly, consider that whether you use rhetorical devices largely depends on the kind of speech you are delivering. Ancient rhetoricians recognized low, middle, and high style. **Low style** is used when you just want to deliver basic facts and get the job done as quickly as possible. You might use this type of speech if you wanted to teach someone. **Middle style** is used when you need to deliver a lot of facts and your main purpose is to persuade. **High style** is used when you want to pull out all the stops—that is, you want to not only persuade but also charm your audience and move them.[16] You will rarely use rhetorical devices in low style. They can be an effective way to underscore and emphasize ideas in middle style, but you should still use them somewhat sparingly. You will use them most commonly, and with the greatest impact, in high style.[17]

Regardless of the kind of style or occasion, aptly styled sentences or phrases can be a sign that you have not only thought about the content or argument, but also are comfortable and confident enough with those things to package them well. Using a rhetorical device in communicating your central point or points, for instance, is a good challenge for you to set. Even if you decide not to use the end result, you'll spend quality time clarifying the idea in your mind, trying several different ways to phrase it that might illuminate an aspect of the idea or argument that you didn't see earlier.

When considering the use of rhetorical devices, always remember to use them thoughtfully, give yourself time to become familiar with their use, and bear in mind the style of your particular speech.

16. Edward P. J. Corbett and Robert J. Connors, *Classical Rhetoric for the Modern Student*, 4th ed. (New York: Oxford University Press, 1999), 21.

17. Cicero, *Rhetorica ad Herennium*, trans. Harry Caplan (Cambridge, MA: Harvard University Pres, 1954), 253.

Josh and Christy definitely could use rhetorical devices effectively in their speeches. Formal debates are a cross between middle and high style, and, depending on the type of debate, might actually move into the realm of high style quite a bit. In an informal debate or discussion, however, which is low style, people will rarely, if ever, use rhetorical devices. In fact, if someone were to use rhetorical devices, such as the ones we have been discussing, in an informal debate or discussion, he may appear pompous and ridiculous. Occasionally, however, in informal debates a person can use a quote (either original or borrowed from someone else) for a humorous effect or emphasis. For example, consider this use of antithesis that could apply to Andrew and Isabella's pet debate: "Dogs live to serve you; cats think you live to serve them." Andrew could use this type of quote effectively in discussing his ideas because it is short and humorous. Wit is almost always used best in low style. The point is that rhetorical devices are almost always helpful in formal debates, but they are not as helpful in informal debates and discussion, which are conducted in low style, unless used briefly for the purpose of humor or emphasis.

Review Exercises

Define

Provide a definition for each of the following words:

1. Euphony: ______________________________
____

2. Parallelism: ______________________________
____

3. Antithesis: ______________________________
____

4. Alliteration: ______________________________
____

5. Anaphora: ______________________________
____

6. Anadiplosis: ______________________________
____

Building Copiousness

Review

Review your old quotes.

Practice

Practice saying the quotes to someone in your class, or practice writing them down on paper.

Memorize

Memorize your new quote:

For what should a man live, if not for the pleasures of discourse? —Plato[18]

Practice Evaluating Rhetorical Devices

List

Read Martin Luther King Jr.'s "I Have a Dream" speech. Locate and list at least three rhetorical devices King uses in his speech (Link 18-1).

18. Ratcliffe, *Oxford Dictionary of Quotations*, 98.

Practicing Rhetorical Devices

Develop

Write three sentences containing rhetorical devices about past topics from the "Everyday Debate" sections at the end of previous chapters. You can write either three sentences on three different topics or three sentences on the same topic.

____

____

____

____

Everyday Debate

Debate

Hold a debate on the following resolution: "Resolved: Silence is golden." Practice a variety of strategies to develop your argument. See the appendix, "Arguments and Appeals Chart," for a list of the various techniques you have learned.

Learning from the Masters

Observe

Watch the second question-and-answer session of the Intelligence Squared debate on universal health care and then answer the following question (Link 18-2).

Please note: This session is a continuation of the previous session, so the debaters are still responding to the question about whether there is a conflict between making people well and making a profit.

Explain

An audience member says that health care is rationed in the United States just as in other countries—there aren't enough services for everyone. The difference is that other nations ration by lottery, but we ration by price. How do the debaters respond to this suggestion?

The Big Debate: Gun Control

Develop

Write a statement containing a rhetorical device for each side of the gun control debate.

Chapter 19

Humor

> HUMOUR VERY OFTEN CUTS THE KNOT OF SERIOUS QUESTIONS MORE TRENCHANTLY AND SUCCESSFULLY THAN SEVERITY.
>
> —HORACE[1]

In the last chapter, you learned that while rhetorical devices aren't usually used in low style, everyday discussion, or informal debate, they can be used effectively if they are humorous. In fact, humor, when used appropriately, can be a great contribution in many debate and discussion situations. There are several reasons for this. When we laugh with someone, we feel connected to them and open to what they want to tell us. This might be because when we feel comfortable enough to laugh with someone, we have begun to trust them. In this way, using humor can be a fruitful way to build ethos because it helps our audience to trust us, open up to us, and to be favorably disposed to what we have to say. In addition, the clever use of humor is certainly quite a skill. Therefore, someone who uses it well can impress people with their panache and cleverness. This also builds their credibility.

Why do we connect humor to ethos? After all, the class clown isn't always the most trustworthy person in the room. And, as discussed briefly later in this chapter, many of the most famous comedians or comic actors make names for themselves by being the most provocative or outrageous in their field, which are character traits that we don't always equate with trustworthiness. So how, then, can humor build trust? It seems that the skill of humor relies on being able to perceive reality accurately. That is, humor relies on being able to have true insight on some aspect of reality. Most jokes rely on keen insight into some kind of incongruity, or lack of harmony: things that don't normally fit or go together are matched up. Therefore, it seems a good sense of humor requires a certain kind of intelligence and wisdom. When people demonstrate intelligence and wisdom and insight about life, we tend to trust them more.

Many people feel a little (or a lot) intimidated by the use of humor—it can be tough to be funny on command. And not very many of us are so gifted with wit that we constantly and spontaneously crack jokes that keep everyone around us in stitches. It may relieve you to know that even if you don't feel like a naturally funny person, you can still use humor successfully in your speeches—don't be afraid to try! One way to accomplish this and build confidence in using humor is to memorize a few jokes or funny quotes that can work in a variety of situations. For example, one day when Andrew was researching quotes and facts about cats for his debate, he found the following amusing quote by Montaigne: "When I play with my cat, who knows whether she isn't amusing herself with me more than I am with her."[2]

This quote is funny because it cleverly illustrates a "lordly" and "aloof" side of cats that most of us have witnessed and with which we can identify. With cats, we aren't really sure who the master of the household actually is. When he shared this quote with Isabel, they had a good

1. Susan Ratcliffe, *Oxford Dictionary of Quotations by Subject*, 2nd ed. (Oxford: Oxford University Press, 2010), 239.
2. Ratcliffe, *Oxford Dictionary of Quotations*, 65.

Not all jokes have to be concise and end with an obvious punch line. For example, Andrew's quote doesn't have an obvious punchline, but it humorously points to a feeling many people have that our cats are really the ones in charge. In your search for effective comic strategies, don't limit yourself to only one type of comedy!

laugh, and Isabel decided to see what humor she could find about cats. At a website dedicated to cat quotes, she found the following:

> "I have studied many philosophers and many cats. The wisdom of cats is infinitely superior." —Hippolyte Taine
>
> "Everything I know I learned from my cat: When you're hungry, eat. When you're tired, nap in a sunbeam. When you go to the vet's, pee on your owner." —Gary Smith
>
> "After scolding one's cat one looks into its face and is seized by the ugly suspicion that it understood every word. And has filed it for reference." —Charlotte Gray[3]

Self-Deprecating Humor

These quotes are effective for Isabel as well because, although they do show the lordly, or occasionally annoying, side of cats in a humorous way, they also highlight the intelligence and wisdom of cats (except for the part about cats peeing on their owners, of course). What is interesting is that even though these quotes are somewhat self-deprecating about cats, they nevertheless give a positive view of cats as well. Interestingly, sometimes **self-deprecating humor**, or even humor directed toward the speaker's topic, can actually serve to build the speaker's credibility. This is probably because it communicates that the speaker is humble and confident enough to poke fun at herself. Humor is very effective in informal discussions, and it can also be very helpful in a variety of speeches.

It can be a little tricky to use humor appropriately when debating more serious issues, such as capital punishment. After all, murder and death are no laughing matter, and using humor at the wrong time or in the wrong manner in such a discussion can alienate people, rather than forge a connection with them. Consider a joke such as the following in light of the capital punishment case:

> Once there was a woman who was called to serve for jury duty. However, the woman had strong beliefs about capital punishment, and so she thought it was only right to ask to be excused from jury duty if the case was a case involving capital punishment. When she expressed her concern to one of the lawyers involved, he said, "Oh, don't worry, ma'am. This isn't that kind of case. It involves a woman bringing a lawsuit against her husband because he used money that they had saved to remodel the kitchen for gambling." Upon hearing what the case was about, the woman said thoughtfully, "Well, I guess I can serve. It seems I do believe in capital punishment after all."[4]

Note that both Josh and Christy could use this mildly humorous joke, or one similar to it. Josh could use it to illustrate that, for many people, their desire to enact capital punishment is often due to a desire for personal vengeance, rather than for just retribution. Christy could use it to explain that, although we have all desired vengeance at times, capital punishment can help us make sure that we apply the death penalty in a just, rather than an arbitrary, manner. Although vengeance and retribution are certainly serious issues, a story like this, with a sweet older lady as its subject, can make a point without being threatening. This story illustrates that it can be possible to use humor with a subject as serious and grave as capital punishment.

Comic Relief

Imagine, for example, that Christy decides to use this joke in her speech. You can imagine that because

3. All three quotes are taken from Australian Media Pty Ltd., "Cat Quotes," on CatQuotes website, http://www.catquotes.com/catquotes1.htm.

4. "Jury Duty Joke" in "Archive for Wife Jokes," Great Clean Jokes, 2015, http://www.greatcleanjokes.com/jokes/marriage-humor/wife-jokes/.

Christy is arguing in favor of the death penalty, she is going to have to share a lot of very serious, and likely even disturbing, facts and stories about murder in order to demonstrate that the death penalty, as severe a penalty as it is, is necessary in some situations. She might need to share upsetting stories about specific murders, and some of these stories could be overwhelming to an audience. In such a situation, one tool speakers can use is to tell appropriate and gentle jokes as a form of **comic relief**. Shakespeare used this technique of inserting lightness or humor into otherwise serious situations frequently in his tragedies. After a specifically tragic or grave scene, he would often include a scene with some silly character, to provide the audience some relief from all of the sadness and heaviness of the former scene. This illustrates an important point about humans—we can only handle so much seriousness at once. Therefore, a well-timed bit of humor can serve as an effective mental pause that allows us to regroup and face the tragedy again.

What Not to Joke About

This leads us to the last item you will learn in this chapter about wit: what *not* to do when using humor. First, it's important to note that there are certain kinds of jokes you should never, ever use with an audience. Sexual, sexist, racist, and scatological (bathroom, or gross) humor are so offensive to a common audience that using these types of jokes in a speech is always a very bad idea. It is true that some movie stars and comedians make a career out of starring in movies filled with this type of humor (and make quite a bit of money doing so). However, it's important to note that when people go to a movie of this nature, they choose to do so, and they attend already knowing that the movie will showcase this type of humor. This is very different from someone listening to a speech or debate, because people will not necessarily choose to hear your speech, and even if they do, they are most likely not expecting to hear this type of humor. Being verbally "assaulted" with crude humor when you didn't choose to hear a speech, or weren't expecting to hear such humor, can be extremely offensive. Using humor of this nature will almost always alienate your audience.

Former president Jimmy Carter learned this lesson the hard way. Once, during a trip to Mexico, he made a reference to having "a case of Montezuma's revenge" to describe the traveler's intestinal distress he was experiencing. Not only was this scatological reference distasteful to most viewers, but the people of Mexico generally considered this colloquial term ("Montezuma's revenge") a racial slur. Needless to say, Carter, who normally was considered a very kind and civil president, unintentionally alienated Mexican officials and people with this one-two punch of a slur.[5] Always keep in mind that while humor can be an effective speech device, jokes that involve offensive subject matter are almost universally a bad idea.

Not only are sexual, sexist, racist, and scatological jokes inappropriate, but jokes that make fun of people or groups who are weaker or disadvantaged in some way are also considered to be in extremely poor taste. For example, President Obama, who generally

5. Walter LaFeber, *Inevitable Revolutions: The United States in Central America*, 2nd ed. (New York: W.W. Norton, 1993), 213.

demonstrates himself to be a considerate, thoughtful man, made a joking reference early in his presidency to the Special Olympics, a sports organization that works with people with intellectual disabilities. Many people who heard his speech were offended, even though they were generally supportive of him. Soon after, Obama made a public apology for his words.[6] The fact that people are often offended by this type of humor is probably based on traditions of chivalry or noblesse oblige, both of which have had a strong influence on our culture. With both of these ideas, the notion is that those who are stronger should look after those who are weaker. Those who have many advantages should care for, or be protective of, those who suffer from many disadvantages. Whenever we make fun of people who are weak or disadvantaged, it reverses this idea, and we then take the role of the bully: the tougher, bigger kid who makes fun of the weaker, smaller kid. Just as no one wants to be bullied, no one should want to be a bully. Always avoid humor that makes fun of weak or disadvantaged people.

Humor, when used well, is usually a beneficial speaking device. However, if you use inappropriate material for a joke or make fun of disadvantaged people, you will alienate rather than connect with your audience.

It would only be fitting to end this chapter with a famous joke:

> Two men were in the woods hunting when one of them suddenly fell to the ground unconscious. In a panic, his friend called 911 and said, "My friend just fell to the ground, and I think he's dead. I don't know what to do!" The operator said, "Stay calm, Sir. First, make sure he is dead." The operator, waiting for the man to reply, suddenly heard a gunshot in the background. The man got back on the phone and said, "Yep, he's dead. What next?"[7]

A 2002 study by British psychologist Dr. Richard Wiseman found that this was the funniest joke in the world. Individuals worldwide voted on a list of jokes they thought to be particularly funny, from which this was selected as the funniest. Though other jokes were found to be funnier by some, this joke was found consistently funny by a wide-ranging group of people. Why do you think that is? And given what was said earlier about the need to avoid jokes that are potentially insensitive or offensive, why might so many people find a joke about death funny?

This man's error consisted of misapplying good advice. Learn from this example. It's good advice to use humor in speeches. But don't misapply humor. Make sure that you use appropriate material at the right time, and that you use gentle jokes as comic relief in serious speeches.

6. CTV.ca News Staff, "Obama Apologizes for Special Olympics Gaffe," CTV News, March 20, 2009, http://www.ctvnews.ca/obama-apologizes-for-special-olympics-gaffe-1.381398.
7. Alva Noe, "What Is the Funniest Joke in the World?" NPR Cosmos & Culture, March 7, 2014, http://www.npr.org/sections/13.7/2014/03/07/287250640/what-is-the-funniest-joke-in-the-world.

Review Exercises

Explain

Explain what self-deprecating humor is.

List

What kinds of humor should never be used in a speech?

Explain

How can a speaker incorporate humor into his speech if he is not naturally humorous?

Discuss

What benefits can a speaker gain by incorporating humor into his speech?

Building Copiousness

Review

Review your old quotes.

Practice

Practice saying the quotes to someone in your class, or practice writing them down on paper.

Memorize

Memorize your new quote:

Natural abilities are like natural plants, that need pruning by study. —Francis Bacon[8]

Practicing Humor

Develop

It takes some practice to tell jokes effectively, so the purpose of this exercise is to provide some joke-telling practice for you. Find two jokes that are clean and funny in your opinion. Tell them to a friend. Which joke seems to be more humorous, and why? Does it seem as though one joke reveals a keener insight or greater wisdom regarding the world than the other one? Which do you think would be more effective in a speech or debate?

____

____

____

____

____

8. Ratcliffe, *Oxford Dictionary of Quotations*, 1.

Discuss

Watch the last speech at Harvard in the movie *The Great Debaters* (chapter 23, "The Harvard Debate," on the DVD).[9] Which side used humor more effectively? Defend your answer.

Everyday Debate

Debate

Consider this adage: "To have friends, you must be a friend." It is a common quote. Develop an argument on this topic. Make sure to use a variety of proof and stylistic devices. See the appendix, "Arguments and Appeals Chart," for a list of the various argument strategies you have studied.

Learning from Masters

Observe

Watch the closing arguments of the Intelligence Squared debate on universal health care and then answer the following question (Link 19-2).

Discuss

Which closing arguments did you find the most helpful? Why?

9. Todd Black, et al, *The Great Debaters*, directed by Denzel Washington (2007; New York: Weinstein Co., 2008), DVD.

The Big Debate: Gun Control

Develop

Find a joke about gun control or a related topic and write it here or on another piece of paper. Will this joke be effective for a debate? Why or why not? (Hint: In order to find jokes, try typing the following phrases in your Internet search engine: "guns and jokes," "crime and jokes," and "firearms and jokes.").

Chapter 20

Arrangement: Affirmative

> POOH BEGAN TO FEEL A LITTLE MORE COMFORTABLE, BECAUSE WHEN YOU ARE A BEAR OF VERY LITTLE BRAIN, AND YOU THINK OF THINGS, YOU FIND SOMETIMES THAT A THING WHICH SEEMED VERY THINGISH INSIDE YOU IS QUITE DIFFERENT WHEN IT GETS OUT INTO THE OPEN AND HAS OTHER PEOPLE LOOKING AT IT.
>
> —A.A. MILNE[1]

You have now learned all of the different ways that you can develop proof when you prepare for a debate. Now you'll discover how to properly arrange your debate. A debate's organization depends on which debate style is chosen. In an informal debate, how you put together your points will depend on what kind of informal discussion you are having. The arrangement of a formal debate, too, hinges on which kind of formal speech or discussion you are doing.

Certainly, however, informal and formal debates should be approached differently. Because informal debates can take place in almost any situation, you will need to gauge your particular situation to know what kind of format you should use. Unless it is some kind of public event, you and the person with whom you are having the discussion likely will just go back and forth, with no particular format in mind, sharing your ideas. In addition, you'll probably ask your opponent questions to clarify why she believes what she does, as well as to, possibly, expose what you consider to be weaknesses of the argument. If you are in a formal debate, as you have learned, the most basic format for this is as follows: affirmative arguments, negative arguments, affirmative rebuttals, and negative rebuttals. Depending on which type of debate you perform, the affirmative and the negative may have two presentation times, and there also may be a cross-examination time in which people can ask their opponent (or opponents) questions to clarify ideas and undermine the credibility of their arguments. In both informal and formal debates, both sides share and critique ideas, and sometimes they also ask each other questions to clarify ideas. The order and organization in which they do this, however, will vary.

Organizing Your Debate Speech

Because formal debates are more regulated than their informal counterparts, we will first focus on a simple way that you can organize a basic debate. Then you will learn to relate some of these general strategies to informal debate too. Just as there are methods for developing logos, ethos, and pathos, ancient rhetoricians also developed clever ways to handle the organization of speeches. When these

1. Susan Ratcliffe, ed., *Oxford Dictionary of Quotations by Subject*, 2nd ed. (Oxford: Oxford University Press, 2010), 475.

ancient rhetoricians desired to persuade their audience of something (which is precisely what we wish to do in our debates), they used the following common format in delivering their speeches: ***exordium***, or the introduction to the speech. Your goal, as the speaker, is to catch the audience's attention and preview what your speech is about. The most common way to do this is with an arresting quote or story. Always make sure that you explain how your quote or story relates to your subject. It may seem obvious to you, but it won't necessarily be obvious to your audience. Lastly, make sure that you give the audience a glimpse of what your speech will be about, and remember to clearly state your thesis; in other words, what is the purpose—the persuasive goal—of your speech?

Narratio is the statement of the key facts, definition, and history of the speech. This will help your audience understand what the speech is about. The most common items people include here are definitions of key terms, pertinent history, and facts about how this subject is important for everyday life. Since the purpose of *narratio* is to provide the relevant context for the issue and argument at hand, a good guiding question to ask is, what does the audience need to know in order to understand my arguments? Is there essential background information that I can put succinctly before the audience?

Partitio: In this section, explain the basic breakdown of what you will discuss in the upcoming speech. As many pastors do at the beginning of their sermons, use this brief section to outline your points.

> In addition to outlining their points or offering what debaters often call a "roadmap," some speakers use the *partitio* to explain where their own position differs from their opponent's, and where they share common ground. For example, a speaker arguing against the death penalty might say, for example, "My opponent will argue that society needs strong deterrents against violent crime, and that violent crime merits serious retribution inherently. I agree with both of these points, but I maintain that the death penalty is not the answer. I will argue that capital punishment is unjust for the following three reasons . . ."

Confirmatio is the part of the speech in which you prove your case. The most effective way to do this is to state arguments in order of importance, from the least to the most significant. This is where you use all of the arguments of logic, ethos, and pathos that you have learned.

Refutatio: At this point of the speech, you have the opportunity to discredit the opposition's key arguments. This can be done by attacking their points one by one, or by attacking the credibility of the opposing speaker or viewpoint. Most powerfully, this can involve anticipating objections to your *confirmatio* arguments and being prepared to deal with them before the opposition has the chance to. In a debate, this is typically done in a rebuttal.

Peroratio: This is when you wrap up your arguments, reemphasize important points, and leave the audience with a strong, concluding idea. An arresting quote or story, or even a call to action, are usually the best choices for a solid conclusion. In a debate, this usually comes at the end of the main argumentation section. Some debate formats actually have a specified conclusion time, and, in those instances, the conclusion would occur at that time. Make sure that you remind the audience of key points of the debate—your own key arguments, aspects in which the opposition's stance or arguments were weak, and so forth. Don't forget to take time to appeal to your audience directly, and not merely provide a summary. Using powerful imagery, emphasize what's at stake in the arguments and issues, and you'll create a stirring finish.

Christy's Speech

To help you understand how an argument might flow, take a look at Christy's speech, and pay close attention to how she organized it:

> (*Exordium*) I want to tell you a story. I should warn you—it's not a happy story, and it doesn't have a happy ending, but it's a story that must be told. One night, four burglars broke into Ned Alday's trailer while he was with his father. They shot and killed both Ned and his father and continued to burglarize the house. Next, Ned's brother Jimmy arrived at the trailer to visit his brother. They grabbed Jimmy and shot him,

too—execution style. Sadly, the bloodshed didn't end there. Soon after, Ned's wife, his uncle, and his other brother arrived home. They shot the uncle and brother in the head and killed them. Then, they grabbed the wife and drove out in the woods, where they assaulted her for several hours. Finally, they shot and killed her too. The entire Alday family was slaughtered that night.[2]

I wish I could stop there, but I have to tell another story. Timothy McVeigh was a former military man with a lot of anger. He thought our country had betrayed its people, and he had a major grudge against the government. So one day, McVeigh parked a truck in front of a federal building in Oklahoma City. He got out and walked away as fast as he could, sticking ear plugs into his ears. A short time later, the truck blew up. The impact was so intense that people walking on the sidewalks yards away from the building were knocked off their feet by the impact. The blast also destroyed its target, the Oklahoma City Federal Building, killing 168 people, 19 of whom were children, and 3 of which were pregnant women.[3]

I don't like telling these stories. I wish with all my heart that evils like the Oklahoma City bombing did not exist in the world. But they do, and because they do, we cannot forget their victims, and we must judge what the proper response is to their killers. People kill for many different reasons. Some people do it in self-defense. Some people do it accidentally. Some people do it in the heat of the moment and are eaten up with remorse afterward. I do not mean to lump all murderers into one class, because they are certainly different and do not all deserve the same penalty. However, there are murderers, such as Timothy McVeigh, who coldly calculate and plan their murders for maximum impact, horror, loss, and pain. There are murderers that systematically assault their victims day after day, fully aware of what they are doing, with no concern for the agony of their victims. There are murderers, such as those who killed the Alday family, who choose to wipe out a whole family in cold blood, torturing for fun. Their only regret is that they are caught. Murderers such as these are certainly in a class by themselves, and they deserve a penalty that is in a class all by itself: the death penalty. Although the death penalty should be used cautiously and thoughtfully, it is certainly a legitimate punishment. Capital punishment is the only just retribution in some cases. It deters at least some crime and incapacitates the killer from ever killing again; in so doing, it saves lives. Therefore, capital punishment as it is practiced in the United States is ethical.

> Aristotle, among other rhetoricians, recommended that you begin with your *second* best argument, in order to better hook the audience and highlight the significance of your argument. Then, he recommended that you give your weakest argument and proceed with stronger and stronger points until you end with your strongest, *best*, proof.

(*Narratio*) First, before we begin to explore the justness and deterrent effect of capital punishment, we need to understand what capital punishment is. In the United States, people can only receive the death penalty for murder, or for actions such as robbery, rape, or kidnapping that result in someone's death. Furthermore, for a person to receive the death penalty, there must be an aggravating circumstance. Typical aggravating circumstances are factors such as premeditation, cruelty, or violence against the government. This would be the case if someone murdered someone such as a police officer, judge, or witness in a case. People

2. Hugo Bedau and Paul Cassel, eds., *Debating the Death Penalty: Should America Have Capital Punishment? The Experts on Both Sides Make Their Case* (New York: Oxford University Press, 2004), 3.
3. Ibid.

who are found guilty of murder actually have a separate trial to decide whether they deserve the death penalty, and it is a jury that decides this. People who receive the death penalty have many options to appeal the case and ask for different sentences, such as life without parole in prison. Because of this appeals process, it is typically ten to twelve years before someone who receives the death penalty is actually put to death. People who are put to death in the United States are executed by the gas chamber, the electric chair, or by lethal injection. Today, lethal injection is the most common execution method. Thirty-one of the fifty states in the United States allow capital punishment; nineteen states have abolished it.[4] I have taken pains to explain what capital punishment is and why we use it because it is a serious penalty. Therefore, I want to be clear about what exactly the penalty is that I am advocating. Now I want to discuss why I advocate capital punishment as a just punishment in at least some cases involving murder.

(*Partitio*) In the following speech, I will first explain three reasons why I advocate the death penalty. First, it allows for retributive justice. Second, capital punishment saves lives. Third, we are using the death penalty appropriately in the United States.

(*Confirmatio*) The first reason that I advocate the death penalty is because it is the only just form of retribution in some cases. The idea of retributive justice is based on three foundational ideas: "All the guilty deserved to be punished. Only the guilty deserve to be punished. The guilty deserved to be punished in proportion to the severity of their crime."[5] Retributive justice enacts punishment, not out of a delight on inflicting pain back on the person who has inflicted it, but rather out of a desire to restore a balance that has been lost. To understand this better, it is helpful to review a foundational principle of our government: the social contract. US culture is founded on the notion that people in society give up certain rights to the government in exchange for government protection and order in society. For example, the government provides law enforcement to make sure that people do not steal our possessions. If someone does steal, the law finds them (or at least tries to), returns our possessions, and punishes the wrongdoer. In exchange for this protection, we give up the privilege of being allowed to steal things for ourselves, or being permitted to hunt down and punish a person who would steal our possessions. This system certainly isn't perfect, but it is arranged to bring about a high degree of fairness, social order, and justice in a world where life without law can be "nasty, brutish, and short" as Thomas Hobbes said.[6]

The point is, when someone commits a crime, such as murder, they have disrupted this social contract. They have upset the balance, and in order for the balance to be restored, they must be caught, and they must either pay back in proportion to what they have taken or be punished in proportion to their crime, when no actual payback is possible. If this does not occur, the social contract will begin to fail, for people will no longer believe that anyone is truly trying to protect their possessions and their livelihood. People will no longer believe that they are treated with justice.

4. "States With and Without the Death Penalty," *Death Penalty Information Center*, 2014, http://www.deathpenaltyinfo.org/states-and-without-death-penalty. The number of states abolishing or allowing capital punishment changes from year to year, based on new state legislation.

5. Louis P. Pojman, "A Defense of the Death Penalty," *Contemporary Debates in Applied Ethics*, ed. Andrew I. Cohen and Christopher Heath Wellman (Chichester, UK: Wiley Blackwell, 2014), 160.
6. Thomas Hobbes, "Leviathan," in *Ethics: History, Theory, and Contemporary Problems*, ed. Steven M. Cahn and Peter Markie (New York: Oxford University Press: 2012), 240.

People will no longer believe that good is rewarded and evil is punished. Therefore, they may begin to take matters into their own hands—and social order would break down. Retributive justice is necessary for the maintenance of an ordered society.

It is important to distinguish retribution from revenge. To illustrate this, I'd like to tell you a little story. This one does have a happy, or at least a humorous, ending.

Once there was a woman who was called to serve for jury duty. However, the woman had strong beliefs about capital punishment, and so she thought it was only right to ask to be excused from jury duty if the case was a case involving capital punishment. When she expressed her concern to one of the lawyers involved, he said, "Oh, don't worry, ma'am. This is isn't that kind of case. It involves a woman bringing a lawsuit against her husband because he used money that they had saved to remodel the kitchen for gambling." Upon hearing what the case was about, the woman said thoughtfully, "Well, I guess I can serve. It seems I do believe in capital punishment after all."[7]

This humorous story illustrates a common characteristic of human beings. We often react more severely than the situation warrants. When someone hurts us, or hurts those we love, it is a natural human tendency to want to hurt them back—to make them feel pain for what they have done so they will regret it. This, we believe, restores some type of balance. However, humans are famous for acting on our emotions and anger, and we are notoriously bad at judging objectively (especially in cases close to us) whether our punishment is just or proportional. We are much more likely to punish too severely, rather than too leniently. This is why cycles of violence start, such as those seen in American gang wars and in Palestine. Someone, or a group of people, commits a crime. Another group retaliates, but the retaliation is motivated by rage and is too severe. Then, the other group retaliates out of rage. A vicious cycle has begun. It is important to understand that vengeance and retribution are very different. While revenge seeks to inflict pain and suffering (often without regard to justice), retribution seeks to restore balance and uphold social order—in fact, retributive justice can be enacted without any type of personal feeling toward the offender. The key emotion motivating retributive justice is a strong desire for social order.

I maintain that the death penalty is the only appropriate form of retributive justice possible in some cases. When society faces crimes such as those of the four men who killed the Alday family and tortured Mrs. Alday, a sentence of life in prison does not restore the balance. When society faces the cold, calculated killing of people, such as during the Oklahoma City bombing incident when Timothy McVeigh perpetrated a violent act against the government—which resulted in the loss of 168 people, 19 of whom were children, and 3 of whom were pregnant women—the instrument that maintains our social order, life in prison, does not restore the balance.

A criminal who faces life in prison, even one sentenced to life without parole, knows that there is always a chance his sentence could be commuted through some technicality or through a shortage of prison space. A criminal who faces life in prison knows there is always the chance to escape. A criminal who faces life in prison knows he has a hard life of violence and cruelty ahead of him—but he also knows he has a bed, three meals a day, and the chance to be involved in all sorts of recreational activities. Plus, he has a whole jail full of captives upon whom he can perpetrate new crimes. The worst that could ever happen

7. "Jury Duty Joke" in "Archive for Wife Jokes," Great Clean Jokes, 2015, http://www.greatcleanjokes.com/jokes/marriage-humor/wife-jokes/.

is that he'll get life in prison. Oh, wait . . . he's already there for life in prison. So it can't get any worse, can it? What does he have to lose? No matter how hard jail time becomes, the prisoner in jail for life always has hope (even if it is a sick and twisted hope). He always has choices. He always has new possibilities and opportunities. The death penalty removes all hope, choices, possibilities, and opportunities once and for all. This is an act that greatly, though not perfectly, restores balance.

In fact, for someone who has tortured, battered, and killed innocent people in such a cold, calculated manner, just as these men in these stories did, the death penalty is actually quite merciful. Absolute retributive justice might actually demand that we torture and batter them before we kill them, and that we kill them in horrible ways such as blowing them up, strangling them, or shooting them in the face at close range; mercy and civility demand that we refrain from such atrocities. Therefore, the death penalty is the most humane and merciful manner through which we can exact retributive justice in these situations. It is crucial that our government be just in order to maintain social order. In some situations, the death penalty is the only just response.

Next, I would like to maintain that capital punishment is necessary because it saves innocent lives. I think it is obvious that a person's most valuable possession is his life. After all, if a person does not have his life, none of his other possessions matter. Therefore, in a society based on the abdication of some rights in exchange for protection and civil order, one of the utmost concerns of government should be the protection of people's lives. In addition, governments should be willing and eager to use any humane and just method that protects people's lives. Capital punishment is a humane and just method that protects people's lives. Therefore, the government should be willing to use capital punishment.

So does capital punishment really deter crime? I think that common sense and actual testimonies from criminals can give us some important answers to this question. First, we have already established that most people value their lives above all their other possessions. The flip side of this is that the possession people fear losing the most is their life. People will do whatever they can to avoid what they fear the most. Therefore, people will do whatever they can to avoid death. If this is true, and logic tells us it is, this would mean that most people would avoid committing murder if they knew it would lead to their death. Interestingly, we do not have to rely merely on logic to answer this question. People have actually interviewed criminals on this issue, or they have spoken out themselves. Therefore, we can look at whether criminals think the death penalty deters crime. First, let's look at the words of John Wojtowicz. He and some of his buddies held up a bank and took hostages in a state where was no death penalty. Wojtowicz reportedly said to his hostages, "I'll shoot everyone in the bank. The Supreme Court will let me get away with this. There's no death penalty. It's ridiculous. I can shoot everyone here, then throw my gun down and walk out, and they can't put me in the electric chair. You have to have the death penalty, otherwise this can happen every day."[8]

It is interesting that the words of a convicted criminal and would-be murderer confirms what we have already been talking about. Retributive justice—justice that restores the balance and people's relationship to each other—is necessary to maintain social order. And in some cases, the death penalty is the only way to do this.

In addition, in the years 1949 to 1953, the British Royal Commission on Capital Punishment actually interviewed criminals to determine the motivation behind their

8. Bedau and Cassel, *Debating the Death Penalty*, 183.

crimes and learned some very interesting things. Some interviewed criminals stated that they had purposefully refrained from carrying a weapon while committing a crime because they were afraid they would have killed someone and would have received the death penalty.[9] Other criminals said that they had refrained from killing their would-be captors, even though they might have escaped if they had killed those people. When asked why they had made this choice, the criminals said it was because they didn't want to get the death penalty if they were caught.[10] And lastly, some criminals who had killed their victims stated that they purposefully moved their victims from a state with the death penalty to a state without the death penalty because they wanted to be able to kill without fear of the death penalty.[11] At least some criminals say that they do, indeed, make conscious decisions based on a desire to avoid the death penalty.

Does the threat of the death penalty deter every single murderer? Well, obviously not. If this were the case, then in every state that has the death penalty we would have no murder. This is certainly not the case. Therefore, while the death penalty, by their own confession, does deter some would-be murderers, the death penalty does not deter every single murderer. And this really should not surprise us. For example, while the fear of getting a speeding ticket does deter quite a few people from speeding, and thereby decrease accidents, it doesn't deter everyone from speeding. There are some drivers who are drunk or high and, therefore, speed because their inhibitions are lowered and their decision-making processes are impaired. There are some drivers who think they won't get caught speeding because they use radar detectors or are full of hubris. There are some drivers who are in despair over a personal tragedy while they are driving, and so they speed unconsciously. We know that these people often are not deterred by the threat of a speeding ticket; yet we still employ police to catch people who speed and to give them tickets because we know that this practice deters at least some people and, therefore, saves lives. In the same way, there are murderers who are not deterred by the death penalty because they are intoxicated, arrogant, or, for whatever reason, uninhibited. Yet it is logical that some are deterred by the death penalty (just as they are by a speeding ticket), and, if this is so, then the threat of the death penalty will save some, and possibly many, lives. We should use the death penalty when appropriate because it does, indeed, save innocent people by deterring some murderers, and any method that preserves innocent lives in a just manner is a worthy method to employ.

Not only does capital punishment save lives by deterring some would-be killers from murdering, it also incapacitates murderers from killing again. Once again, this is logical. If a murderer is killed, he cannot kill anymore because he cannot be released from jail to kill again, and he cannot kill anyone while he is in prison. If a murderer is truly imprisoned for the rest of his life and is never paroled (and assuming he doesn't escape), then he cannot murder anyone outside of the prison. But what about people on the inside of the prison? As mentioned before, a murderer who is serving life in prison for murder has little to lose if he has the opportunity and desire to kill his inmates or prison guards. After all, what's the worst that could happen—more of the same? Executing a murderer who has been imprisoned for life will certainly incapacitate him from murdering any people inside the prison. However, we must also realize that many murderers, even very

9. Pojman, "A Defense of the Death Penalty," 165.
10. Ibid.
11. Ibid.

violent murderers, are released from prison because of legal technicalities, prison space shortages, and supposed good behavior (which may or may not be an indication of true rehabilitation). The word *recidivist* is an important term to understand for this argument. A recidivist criminal is one who, upon being released from jail, commits the same crime he committed before.

To illustrate the danger of recidivism, I must tell another tragic story. In 1966 Kenneth Allen McDuff kidnapped two boys and one girl. He shot the boys at close range and then assaulted, tortured, raped, and killed the girl. He was sentenced to death but his sentence was later commuted to life in prison. Eventually, because of prison overcrowding, he was released in 1989. In the early 1990s, McDuff went on to rape, torture, and murder nine known women in Texas. After he was captured, he was on record as saying, "Killing a woman's like killing a chicken. . . . They both squawk."[12] McDuff certainly met the criteria for the death penalty. Not only did he murder, but he murdered numerous people and his cruel torture of his victims was certainly an aggravating circumstance. Had McDuff received retributive justice through the death penalty, the lives of at least nine innocent women would have been saved. Once again, because our lives are our most valuable possession, and because it is the government's job to protect our possessions, they should be willing to employ the death penalty in situations such as the McDuff case because it is a just method of preserving innocent lives.

Lastly, I would like to emphasize that because the death penalty is the gravest of punishments, it certainly deserves the most serious consideration when it is about to be implemented. The death penalty should only be enacted after many different people have scrutinized every aspect of a case in an objective and impartial manner. After all, this is the only way we can be sure we are enacting retributive justice rather than revenge. Revenge will only perpetuate the cycle of violence; retribution will repair the balance of civil society. We see this careful scrutiny taking place in the United States. I would like to quote from Louis Pojman's essay "Why the Death Penalty Is Morally Permissible" in Bedau and Cassel's book *Debating the Death Penalty*. Pojman writes, "In 1993, there were 24,526 cases of murder and nonnegligent manslaughter and only 56 executions; and in 1994, there were 23,305 cases of murder and nonnegligent manslaughter and only 31 executions."[13]

These statistics demonstrate that Americans, in general, are not applying the death penalty willy-nilly or in an attitude of vengeance. Instead, it is a tool of retributive justice that saves lives and is undertaken with the gravest and most careful of considerations. This is how it should be. Capital punishment as it is practiced in the United States is ethical and it deters crime. We should keep capital punishment as a legitimate governmental method of upholding social order.[14]

(*Peroratio*) In conclusion, we must continue the practice of capital punishment. We live in a world where heinous and violent crimes still occur, and often capital punishment is the only way that we can respond appropriately to these crimes. Capital punishment is a necessary societal practice because it allows for retributive justice and it saves lives. In addition, research shows that we are using the death penalty justly and appropriately in the United States. Capital punishment allows us to honor lives that have been violently and unjustly ended, and it allows us to bring peace and closure where it is needed in these situations.

12. Bedau and Cassel, *Debating the Death Penalty*, 184–185.

13. Ibid., 64.

14. Note that Christy's example speech does not include refutation. That is because her *refutatio* section will come later in her rebuttal, which is discussed in chapter 23.

In Christy's speech, note that she did not deal with any arguments against the opposition in her main arguments. Although debaters occasionally critique some of the strongest opposing arguments during their main argument time, it is more common for them to use all of their presentation time to build their case and save critique for the rebuttals. You can probably imagine why this is so. A debate speech in which the speaker states all the reasons why her side is correct is much stronger than a debate speech in which the speaker states all the reasons why the opposition's side is not correct. Therefore, since the main argument time is limited, it is wise for the arguer to build his case and save critique for later. Furthermore, a speaker never knows which cases the opposition will bring up. When you debate, if the opposition has researched the case well, it will certainly bring up some important points that you need to critique. You can do this in the rebuttal. You can, however, anticipate responses to your points, rather than directly attack the other side.

Christy should know, for instance, that some of the individuals she brought up in her examples could be perceived as mentally insane, and therefore may not be considered deserving of the death penalty. If she can address either why such individuals do deserve capital punishment, or how a just and ethical system of capital punishment will not execute impaired individuals, then she can strip away a powerful weapon from the hands of her opponents. Although it is a good strategy to remove this powerful weapon from her opponent, there is the risk of bringing up a subject that she may not have time to deal with effectively, or that her opponents would not have thought of in the first place. Using discernment to figure out the appropriate strategy in a given circumstance is key, and this can only be developed with experience with debating. In conclusion, depending on the debate format with which you are involved, you may need to follow a very specific debate format. But for basic speech organization, a good foundation to use is *exordium*, *narratio*, *partitio*, *confirmatio*, *refutatio* (do this in the rebuttal), and *peroratio*.

Review Exercises

Define

Define each of the following words.

1. *Exordium*: ______________________________

____

____

2. *Narratio*: ______________________________

____

____

3. *Partitio*: ______________________________

____

____

4. *Confirmatio*: ______________________________

____

____

5. *Refutatio*: ______________________________

____

____

6. *Peroratio*: ______________________________

____

____

Building Copiousness

Review

Review your old quotes.

Practice

Practice saying the quotes to someone in your class, or practice writing them down on paper.

Memorize

Memorize your new quote:

Wit is the salt of conversation, not the food. —William Hazlitt[15]

Evaluating Christy's Argument

List

Read Christy's speech and find at least ten different argument strategies she used. A list of the argument types and strategies we have used in this book is provided. Identify and provide at least one kind of argument for each of the following categories (some categories will have more arguments than others): common topics, special topics, deductive arguments, ethos, pathos, humor, and rhetorical devices.

Common Topics:

____

____

____

____

____

____

____

15. Ratcliffe, *Oxford Dictionary of Quotations*, 511.

Special Topics:

Deductive Arguments:

Ethos:

Pathos:

Humor:

Rhetorical Devices:

Explain

Which part of Christy's speech did you find particularly convincing? Which parts did you find less convincing? Why?

Everyday Debate

Debate

Hold a debate on the following proposition: "Resolved: There is no such thing as ghosts." As you develop your argument for your side, use as many of the different argument types as possible that you have studied in this book. If you need to, consult the argument strategies chart in the appendix.

Learning from the Masters

Explain

Socrates was a master at finding weaknesses and problems in people's reasoning. Because of this, his dialogues are excellent literature to help you learn how to analyze people's arguments. Read *Crito* by Plato (Link 20-1) and answer the following questions.

1. What does Crito try to persuade Socrates to do?

2. Why does Crito mention the opinions of other people to try to convince Socrates to escape?

3. Explain the gymnastics argument that Socrates uses to combat Crito's argument.

4. Socrates and Crito then explore whether it is right for Socrates to leave (and break Athenian law) because he has been given an unjust sentence. How does Socrates demonstrate that it is not right for him to do this?

The Big Debate: Gun Control

Develop

You have completed your research for your argument about gun control. Now, it's time for you to prepare your speech. Read Christy's argument again so that you can get a sense of how an argument flows. For your debate speech, you will only need to outline the introduction and narration (the *exordium* and *narratio*) for the argument. (You will write the other parts of the speech at a later time.) If your debate team is very small or you are the only person debating one side of a resolution, your introduction and narration will need to be a little longer because the body of your speech will be longer and will cover more topics. If you have a lot of people on your debate team, your introduction and narration will be shorter.

Chapter 21

Arrangement: Negative

21

> HE COULD MAKE MEN WEEP OR TREMBLE BY HIS VARIED UTTERANCES OF THE WORD, 'MESOPOTAMIA.'
> —DAVID GARRICK[1]

When you are on the negative, rather than the affirmative, side of a debate, you will usually speak second. Just like the affirmative speaker, you should state all of the strongest arguments that support your negative view of the case. Presenting second may give you a slight advantage because you have heard the affirmative arguments already. Therefore, if you can think on your feet, you can insert phrases, or emphasize certain points, in your speech that critique the opposition when the arguments you are explaining disprove something that your opponent has previously stated. As you will see, Josh does this in his negative arguments. Also note that the negative speaker can organize his speech in the same manner as the affirmative side: *exordium*, *narratio*, *partitio*, *confirmatio*, *refutatio*, and *peroratio*. To illustrate how a negative argument is organized, read Josh's negative speech for the capital punishment debate:

Josh's Speech

(Exordium) Sadly, we live in a world in which murderous violence is commonplace. At any given minute of the day, conflicts are going on all over the globe in which innocents are murdered. Individuals murder for every reason imaginable: from the petty desire to steal someone's running shoes to the desire for redress for some past wrong. In fact, murder has become so common today that people actually engage in it for entertainment. We watch movies that idealize brutal violence, and our children gleefully play video game versions of killing sprees, all in the name of good, clean fun. Tragically, we are beginning to imitate the brutal aspects of our predecessors, the ancient Romans—a group of people who enacted barbaric forms of capital punishment such as crucifixion, and who entertained themselves in the Coliseum by watching enslaved gladiators battle to a bloody death or by throwing hapless prisoners to the wild beasts, only to watch them be torn to shreds. At their lowest point, the Romans exhibited a distinct lack of value for human life. Today, we may put a more glossy veneer on our barbarisms, but when we engage in behavior such as capital punishment, we exhibit a similar lack of humanity. The United States should abolish capital punishment because capital punishment is unethical, and it does not deter crime. Capital punishment is not only unethical and a failure in its efforts to deter murder, but also unnecessary and purposeless, and it unintentionally encourages more murder.

1. Susan Ratcliffe, ed., *Oxford Dictionary of Quotations by Subject*, 2nd ed. (Oxford: Oxford University Press, 2010), 447.

(Narratio) My opponent has very carefully and thoroughly gone about defining capital punishment, and I don't think anything more needs to be said about what capital punishment is except for this: Whether you justify capital punishment as a type of justice or not, capital punishment is, at the bottom line, the taking of a human life. It is also important to clearly state something that seems obvious: Once a human life is taken, that's it. There is no chance for redemption. There is no chance for further restitution. There is no chance for rehabilitation. Death is final and irrevocable.

Furthermore, I would like to emphasize something about the history of capital punishment that my opponent failed to mention. Capital punishment has been practiced in virtually every society in the world since civilization began. Many of you are probably aware that, for much of history, capital punishment was nothing less than thinly veiled bloodlust and vengeance. In the past, people seem to have taken delight in developing the most brutal punishments imaginable for people. In the name of capital punishment, people have been burned to death, drawn and quartered, and boiled alive.[2] I know this is gruesome, and I won't share any more for fear of entertaining rather than horrifying my audience with these stories. Sadly, a tragic characteristic of human nature is that we sometimes (perhaps more often than we'd like to admit) are entertained by people's pain—especially when we hate someone or feel they have done us an irredeemable wrong. This is partially the reason why public executions used to be such popular spectacles. Hundreds of people would gather to watch a "criminal" be hung or executed in some other manner.

Throughout history, various people recognized this base aspect of human nature as well as its accompanying abuses in the form of the death penalty. Over time, the practice of capital punishment was curtailed and slowly abolished in many places. In the 1700s, English law cited over 200 offenses that were deserving of the death penalty.[3] But in 1965, England completely abolished the death penalty.[4] Many other European countries followed suit, if they had not already abolished it. In 1998, Canada abolished the death penalty.[5] After the 1980s, most European countries had either outlawed or stopped using capital punishment.[6] This is an interesting situation. How is it that so many people in the United States are so convinced of the effectiveness of the death penalty when so many people in other developed nations are convinced of its ineffectiveness? It may be that people in the United States see this issue more clearly than people in other countries. After all, the majority has been known to be wrong before. However, the fact that so many countries, which we normally consider our allies in the fight for human dignity, oppose the death penalty should give us at least a little bit of pause. In fact, there are many reasons people should be skeptical and adversarial to the death penalty.

(Partitio) In the following speech, I will explain why I believe the death penalty is immoral and ineffective. First, I will explain why the death penalty often does not deter people from committing murder. Second, I will explain how the death penalty can actually increase instances of murder

2. Death Penalty Information Center (hereafter cited as DPIC), "Introduction to the Death Penalty," in "Part I: History of the Death Penalty," http://www.deathpenaltyinfo.org/part-i-history-death-penalty.

3. Ibid.
4. Rebecca Cafe, "Does the Public Want the Death Penalty Brought Back?" BBC News, August 4, 2011, http://www.bbc.com/news/uk-14402195.
5. DPIC, "Countries That Have Abolished the Death Penalty Since 1976," in "Abolitionist and Retentionist Countries," http://www.deathpenaltyinfo.org/abolitionist-and-retentionist-countries.
6. DPIC, "Recent Developments in Capital Punishment," in "Part II: History of the Death Penalty," http://www.deathpenaltyinfo.org/part-ii-history-death-penalty.

through something called the *brutalization effect*. Lastly, I will argue that although the death penalty can be used as a form of retributive justice, there are better and more humane ways of responding to the terrible tragedy of murder.

(Confirmatio) First, we must examine the issue of deterrence. I think my opponent is right that the threat of capital punishment does deter some criminals. This is certainly logical. However, I must reemphasize that many people who commit murder do so because they are chemically intoxicated, because they are insane or sociopaths, because they are mentally disabled, or because they lash out in a fit of rage. All of these states of mind inhibit impulse control and delayed-gratification skills. In order for someone to stop and consider the consequences of her actions, such as whether her actions will lead to capital punishment, she must be able to control her impulses and delay gratification. If both of these skills are severely limited in many murderers, which common sense tells us they are, then many criminals will not be deterred by the death penalty.

The death penalty might still be worth it for the lives it did save if there were no other negative consequences of the death penalty. However, what many people don't realize is that the death penalty, inadvertently, likely causes additional murders. This certainly seems counterintuitive, but it may make more sense if we compare it to another scenario with which we are more familiar. For years, people have been decrying violence on TV and in video games because it appears that this type of virtual violence perpetrates more physical violence. Obviously, not everyone who views violent movies and video games will go out and be violent, but it appears that some of them will act violently. We know this because many people who commit violent acts often cite violent games, movies, songs, or people as the inspiration for their crimes. This is such common knowledge that there have been lawsuits against the purveyors of these violent media for their culpability in crimes. Because of all of the media attention surrounding death penalty cases, it is logical to deduce that a certain portion of the populace will be affected in a similar way—that is, they will be made more violent by their exposure to these instances of (government-sanctioned) violence in the media.

In fact, studies seem to indicate that this is so; sociologists refer to this phenomenon of increasing violence as the *brutalization effect*. A study on the issue showed that after every capital punishment case from 1907 to 1963 in New York State, murders increased by two more than the average in the month after the execution.[7] This may seem like an isolated phenomenon, but a September 2000 *New York Times* survey "found that during the last 20 years, the homicide rate in states with the death penalty has been 48 to 101 percent higher than in states without the death penalty."[8] Indeed, "10 of the 12 states without capital punishment have homicide rates below the national average, Federal Bureau of Investigation data shows, while half the states with the death penalty have homicide rates above the national average."[9] While it might be easy to explain away the so-called brutalization effect in one or two instances, it is hard to do it for a study such as this, which spans twenty years and covers every single state in the United States. This pattern cannot be easily ignored. It appears that capital punishment might inadvertently lead to more deaths.

7. "Politics, Courage and Death," Opinion column, *New York Times*, May 18, 1982, http://www.nytimes.com/1982/05/18/opinion/politics-courage-and-death.html.
8. Raymond Bonner and Ford Fessenden, "Absence of Executions: A Special Report; States With No Death Penalty Share Lower Homicide Rates," *New York Times*, September 22, 2000, http://www.nytimes.com/2000/09/22/us/absence-executions-special-report-states-with-no-death-penalty-share-lower.html.
9. Ibid.

Capital punishment appears not only to have a brutalization effect, but also to drain money from programs that actively prevent murders. According to figures from 2010, "the median cost for defense representation in a death case that went to trial was $465,602, including $101,592 for experts. If the authorized case was settled by a plea, the median cost was $200,933, still far greater than the median cost of a death-eligible case in which the death penalty was *not* sought—$44,809." [10] This is usually because the appeals process is so long and time-consuming for many lawyers in an average death penalty case. If you are going to have the death penalty, then I think this legal process is crucial and necessary. As my opponent mentioned, this legal scrutiny and the process of appeals is necessary to make sure that justice is indeed being done, and that the people being sentenced to death are indeed guilty and deserving of the death penalty. However, it is common knowledge that the death penalty, for this very reason, is considerably more costly than the average life in prison case.

Consider the following: If spending more money were the only negative side effect of the death penalty, we might decide that it was worth it. However, not only is it more expensive, but it actually takes money from programs that deter murder. For instance, in a study of randomly selected judges and policemen, the people who work most with murderers and their victims, the majority said that the death penalty, by itself, was the least effective method for deterring murder. Other more effective methods were increasing police surveillance and developing drug and alcohol programs and antigang efforts, which remedied some of common causes of violence such as drug abuse and family violence.[11] The experts in fighting crime cited these programs as a much more effective method of fighting crime than capital punishment. If these methods are more effective for preventing crime, and if each death penalty case drains money that could be spent on these programs, then we can logically assume that each death penalty case contributes to the probability of more murders occurring. When we consider the murders that could have been prevented by investing money in communities, along with the brutalization effect, it appears that we may be losers rather than winners in the deterrence game when we use capital punishment.

Of course, we live in an imperfect world, which means that sometimes there is no perfect solution and the only choice available is either a greater evil or a lesser evil. In the case of murder, if retributive justice were the only means of justice available to us, we would be wise to choose an imperfect form of justice over no justice at all. After all, justice is important. Justice must be preserved and maintained. If we ignore justice, then we pave the way for perpetrators of injustice to wreak havoc on our society. However, there are better alternatives to retributive justice. We are all familiar with the Old Testament saying "an eye for an eye, and a tooth for a tooth." Interestingly, some theologians have noted that while people often interpret this verse as a command, it is actually a concession.[12] That is, this verse is not commanding that we must take an eye for an eye when we punish; rather, it is commanding that we take no more than an eye for an eye when we punish. Jesus, who claimed in the biblical New Testament that he came to fulfill the law, said,

> You have heard that it was said, "An eye for an eye, and a tooth for a tooth." But I say to you, do not resist an evil person; but whoever slaps you on your

10. DPIC, "New Resources: Cost of Representation in Federal Death Penalty Cases," in "News," http://www.deathpenaltyinfo.org/news/past/16/2010.
11. DPIC, "Law Enforcement and the Death Penalty," in "Law Enforcement Views of Deterrence," http://www.deathpenaltyinfo.org/law-enforcement-views-deterrence#lawenforcement4.
12. "Benson Commentary," in Bible Hub's commentaries on Matthew 5:38, http://biblehub.com/commentaries/matthew/5-38.htm.

> right cheek, turn the other to him also. If anyone wants to sue you and take your shirt, let him have your coat also. Whoever forces you to go one mile, go with him two. Give to him who asks of you, and do not turn away from him who wants to borrow from you. You have heard that it was said, "You shall love your neighbor and hate your enemy." But I say to you, love your enemies and pray for those who persecute you.[13]

We have to be careful when applying this verse to the context of capital punishment. After all, neither Jesus nor any moral teacher would advocate allowing a killer to go on his merry way and murder as many people as he could. Rather, this verse seems to indicate that while "an eye for an eye" is a common principle to live by (and is perhaps even permissible), a greater principle is "love, forgiveness, and prayer."

Is this pie-in-the-sky, rose-colored glasses thinking? It is certainly a different way of thinking, but a closer look may reveal that this type of response to crime is more just, humane, and ultimately effective in healing the victims of crime and preventing recidivism than the death penalty. One method that embodies these principles that many countries and prison systems are starting to use is something called *restorative justice*. Before I explain restorative justice, I must state, unequivocally, that there are some criminals who are beyond any kind of rehabilitation. They are either morally warped, or perhaps mentally disabled, to the extent that they are permanently damaged and beyond reach. For example, one famous murder case involved a man who killed a young housewife. It was found that this criminal had an IQ far below a normal level. Furthermore, upon investigating this man's life, they discovered that as a child, his mother had severely abused him and, for most of his childhood, she had locked him in a closet and forced him to live in beast-like conditions. We should not be surprised that criminals such as this are so damaged and warped that almost nothing can repair the harm that has been done to them. We should feel sorry for these people and lock them away for life, and we should amend the justice system so that there is no way that these people can be let out. Criminals such as this, thankfully, are not extremely common, and they are fairly easy to identify.

It is important to note that restorative justice is never mandatory; it is always voluntary, for both victims and offenders. Obviously, in a murder case, the "victims" who are involved with restorative justice will be the family and friends of the victim, rather than the deceased victim himself. In a murder case, a mediator would meet with a victim and an offender who have both voluntarily accepted the offer to meet with the mediator. Restorative justice humanizes crime to the offenders who, by meeting face to face with their victims, can understand the impact their crime has had on the victim and his or her family. Mediators who work with restorative justice often comment that "victims commonly report a new peace of mind, even when the answers to their questions were worse than they had feared."[14] It is also common, in restorative justice, for the offenders and the victims to work out an agreement in which the offender does something to atone for his crime. This doesn't mean that the criminal is released from jail. It means that he has an opportunity to engage in an atonement that is somehow meaningful for the victim. Although this type of justice is contrary to the common method of handling criminals, it has surprising results. Marty Price, an attorney and founder and director of the Victim-Offender Reconciliation Program Information and Resource Center, reported that

13. Matthew 5:38–44 (NASB).

14. Marty Price, "Personalizing Crime: Mediation Produces Restorative Justice for Victims and Offenders," *Dispute Resolution Magazine,* Fall 2001, Victim-Offender Reconciliation Project Information and Resource Center, http://www.vorp.com/articles/justice.html.

> more than 95 percent of the cases mediated resulted in a written restitution agreement. More than 90 percent of those restitution agreements are completed within one year. In contrast, the rate of payment of court-ordered restitution is typically only from 20 to 30 percent. Recent research has shown that juvenile offenders who participate . . . subsequently commit fewer and less serious offenses than their counterparts in the traditional juvenile justice system.[15]

James Bonta, a leading researcher in restorative justice, has noted that restorative justice may actually bring better closure than retributive justice, and may also decrease crime recidivism rates.[16] Restorative justice may bring better balance and closure to both victims and offenders than retributive justice.

Once again, the practice of restorative justice is so different from typical methods for dealing with criminals that at first we may not grasp the underlying logic of it. However, restorative justice is based upon some principles which we normally advocate. First, we all value forgiveness and understand its importance. While victims need to be recompensed for their loss, they also have a need to understand and forgive their offender. People who harbor hatred and fear long term may actually end up harming themselves. Restorative justice allows forgiveness and understanding. Second, victims need to restore a sense of control to their lives. Restorative justice gives them the opportunity to understand why the crime happened, and it provides them some influence in establishing appropriate restitution and restoration. Third, people want to believe that good can come out of the bad situations in their lives. Restorative justice allows people to see this good. They see this because they are able to forgive, to decide how their offender can work to restore what has been lost, and, in some cases, decide the rehabilitation of the offender.[17]

(Peroratio) In conclusion, capital punishment is unethical. It is unethical because although it may deter some criminals from committing murder, it actually encourages murder through the brutalization effect. Furthermore, it encourages murder because it drains money away from programs that actually are effective in deterring murder. In addition, capital punishment isn't the only possible form of just punishment. Life in prison is a just punishment because it protects the public from these murderers and it "takes the life" of a prisoner. Very few would argue that life in prison is a meaningful life. Lastly, life in prison allows for the possibility of restorative justice, which is more likely to bring healing to victims and less likely to lead to offender recidivism than retributive justice. In conclusion, capital punishment is unethical because it actually encourages crime rather than decreases it. There are much better ways to deal with murder than this.

---

15. Ibid.
16. See, for example, James Bonta, "Retributive Justice and Recidivism," vol. 8, no. 1, January 2003, http://www.publicsafety.gc.ca/cnt/rsrcs/pblctns/jstc-rcdvs/jstc-rcdvs-eng.pdf.
17. Note that Josh's example speech does not include refutation. That is because his *refutatio* section will come later in his rebuttal, which is discussed in chapter 23.

Review Exercises

List

List the five common topics.

1. ______________________________
2. ______________________________
3. ______________________________
4. ______________________________
5. ______________________________

List

Review the special topics by listing the three unique types of discourse when you would use these topics. In addition, list the specific special topics for each type of discourse category.

____

____

____

____

____

____

____

____

Define

Define each of the following terms.

1. Deductive logic: ______________________________

____

2. Ethical appeals: ______________________________

____

3. Appeals to pathos: ______________________________

____

4. Rhetorical devices: ______________________________

____

Explain

Describe the parts of a speech.

Building Copiousness

Review

Review your old quotes.

Practice

Practice saying the quotes to someone in your class, or practice writing them down on paper.

Memorize

Memorize your new quote:

> He that overvalues himself will undervalue others, and he that undervalues others will oppress them.
>
> —Samuel Johnson[18]

Evaluating Josh's Argument

List

Read Josh's speech and find at least ten different argument strategies or rhetorical devices that he used. A list of the argument types and strategies you've learned in this book is provided. Identify and provide at least one kind of argument for each of the following categories (some categories will have more arguments than others): common topics,

18. Ratcliffe, *Oxford Dictionary of Quotations*, 426.

special topics, deductive arguments, ethos, pathos, humor, and rhetorical devices. Note that Josh did not use one of the categories—identify which one.

Common Topics:

Special Topics:

Deductive Arguments:

Ethos:

Pathos:

Humor:

Rhetorical Devices:

Everyday Debate

Debate

Hold a debate on the following proposition, from a quote by Epicurus: "If thou wilt make a man happy, add not unto his riches but take away from his desires."[19]

As you develop your argument for your side, use as many of the different argument types as possible that you have studied in this book. If you need to, consult the arguments and appeals chart in the appendix.

Learning from the Masters

Observe

Watch the first two speakers of the Intelligence Squared debate on illegal immigration: Heather MacDonald and Daniel T. Griswold (Link 21-1). They are debating this motion: "Resolved: Let's stop welcoming undocumented immigrants." Since immigration can have a significant effect on our economy and national security, the issues of illegal or undocumented immigration are matters of great concern to our country. The speakers in this debate argue about how specifically we should respond to the issue of undocumented immigrants. Discuss the appeals the speakers make to ethos, pathos, and logos. Flow the arguments, and then critique these speakers' arguments and presentations by answering the questions that follow.

19. Ratcliffe, *Oxford Dictionary of Quotations*, 200.

List

What are two arguments that MacDonald makes?

Explain

1. Explain one strength of MacDonald's arguments.

2. Explain one weakness of MacDonald's arguments.

List

What are three arguments Griswold makes?

Explain

1. What is one strength of Griswold's arguments?

2. Explain one weakness of Griswold's arguments.

The Big Debate: Gun Control

List

On a separate piece of paper, list three common arguments against your side of the gun control debate. How can you critique them?

Chapter 22

Arrangement: Cross-Examination

> YOU WILL FIND IT A VERY GOOD PRACTICE ALWAYS TO VERIFY YOUR REFERENCES, SIR!
> —MARTIN JOSEPH ROUTH[1]

Many debate formats have a cross-examination time after the main presentation. This time provides an opportunity to understand more clearly, as well as expose, the weaknesses of your opponent's arguments.

Tips for Cross-Examination Time

Keep in mind that one of the most important parts of cross-examination is to help you clarify any facts, statistics, or evidence that you didn't hear correctly or comprehend. After all, the only way you can build a case against the opposition is to make sure that you have heard them correctly. During cross-examination, be sure to ask about points that you did not hear properly—this will help you be prepared for the main purpose of cross-examination, which is to expose weaknesses in your opponent's reasoning. Sometimes the best thing you can do in a conversation or debate is ask a good question. In this way, you require a person to back up his evidence or explain his argument. Many times, as a person begins to respond, it becomes evident that he does not have true evidence or a well-considered argument. And when a person exposes his own poor evidence or reasoning, this can be even more effective than you exposing it.

The following are common types of mistakes people regularly make in informal and formal debate that you can challenge with thoughtful questions. Here are eight basic strategies for cross-examination:

1. Challenge *unsupported claims*: Ask your opponent about the basis of any claim for which she does not quote a specific source. Ask, "Could you please explain the evidence upon which you are basing that claim?"

2. Challenge *vague statistics*: If your opponent presents a vague statistical study, ask him to clarify the legitimacy of his study—for instance, who conducted the study, and what the sample size was. Ask, "What group or person formulated that statistic?" or "How was that statistic constructed?"

3. Challenge *hasty generalizations*: Ask your opponent to provide further examples to support a claim when she cites only one or two cases to back an argument. Ask, "Do you have any other examples to support that generalization?"

4. Challenge *questionable causal relationships*: Challenge causal relationships when it appears that there could be factors other than the one mentioned causing a given effect. Ask, "Is it also possible

1. Susan Ratcliffe, ed., *Oxford Dictionary of Quotations by Subject*, 2nd ed. (Oxford: Oxford University Press, 2010), 250.

that another factor could be involved, such as . . . (if possible, provide an alternative factor)?"

5. Challenge *poor comparisons*: Question your opponent about possible weaknesses in his analogies. Ask, "Isn't it true that the two things you are comparing are different because . . . (be sure to specify the difference)?"
6. Challenge *questionable authorities*: If it is not clear why a person who was cited to support an argument has authority in that matter, question this. Ask, "What are the credentials of the authority you cited in your argument about . . . (name the argument in question)?"
7. Challenge *with opposing evidence*: If you know about a study or piece of evidence that directly contradicts a "fact" stated by the opposition, present this fact or statistic to your opponent, and then ask her to explain. Ask, "I have a study that demonstrates . . . (name what your study proves, specifically). How do you reconcile the two?"
8. Challenge *contradictory claims*: If you notice a contradiction in claims, present these ideas to your opponent and ask him how he explains the contradiction. Ask, "At the beginning of your speech you said . . . (name the first idea), but later in your speech you said . . . (name the second idea, which contradicts the first). How do you reconcile the two?"

First, you should learn how to identify and respond to the first four mistakes people regularly make in debate: unsupported claims, vague statistics, hasty generalizations, and questionable causal relationships.

Challenge Unsupported Claims

Consider when you should challenge unsupported claims. One of the most common mistakes people make in debate or conversation is making claims without backing them with research. Sometimes people do this by mistake—perhaps they are rushing at the last minute and forget to mention or don't have time to include the information. However, sometimes your opponent doesn't actually have any legitimate evidence to support his claims. This is important to remember because, unfortunately, we do this a lot in life. We will make a claim that sounds right or cite a statistic that seems correct, but there really isn't any evidence to prove or reinforce it. You may have heard the following witty saying about statistics: "Over 85 percent of all statistics are made up on the spot." (Of course, this statistic is made up as well.) Interestingly, making up or abusing statistics (as well as other types of evidence) is more common than you may think. Therefore, always ask about unsupported claims.

Challenge Vague Statistics

On a related note, you should also challenge vague statistics. Someone may cite a statistic to back a claim, but it may be unclear who formed the statistic and the method by which the person or organization derived the information. You might remember from chapter 11 that it is very easy to lie with statistics. In fact, if your sample size is small enough, you can make a statistic to prove just about anything. Therefore, the best statistics are constructed from randomly chosen large sample sizes. Furthermore, they are constructed by people who know how to form accurate, reliable statistical studies. If an opponent's provided statistic is not based on a large or random sample, you should question it.

Challenge Hasty Generalizations

Not only statistics but also common generalizations should involve a large sample size. Remember from chapter 13 that a common fallacy of inductive argumentation is hasty generalization—this occurs when someone generalizes from too small a sample size, or too few examples. This is sometimes referred to as the "person who" fallacy because people have a tendency to support an argument with a story of only one person who did something that supposedly supports the arguer's point. For example, this fallacy would be committed if a person decided to argue that people who own guns are more naturally violent and, to support her point, she said the following: "For example, I know this guy who is a strong gun-ownership proponent, and the police had to put him in jail for a couple of days once for threatening a neighbor with a gun." The point is that one person or example may illustrate a point, but it never proves it. The example about the story of the guy with the gun *illustrates* what the woman meant to say when she claimed that gun owners are more naturally violent, but one story certainly doesn't *prove* her point. Therefore, if your opponent appears to support an argument with one example or story, be sure to challenge this in the cross-examination time by asking her if she has any other examples to support this **induction**.

Challenge Causal Relationships

Always challenge questionable causal relationships. Statistical studies often attempt to demonstrate a causal relationship between two factors. For example, someone might try to prove a causal connection between the death penalty and low homicide rates, or between gun possession and high homicide rates. Often these statistics make it appear that a given causal relationship is obvious. However, as you can imagine, societal factors such as crime have many possible causes, and it is rarely possible to attribute one factor as the primary, or sole, cause of the rise and fall of such a complex factor. Keep in mind that if an argument claims an obvious causal connection between two complex social factors, it is likely not as obvious as it seems. That is, there are probably more factors involved. It is always a good idea to challenge this type of claim. During an opponent's presentation, always be on the lookout for unsupported claims, vague statistics, hasty generalizations, and questionable causal relationships. Make sure to challenge these during the cross-examination.

Four other mistakes you need to be able to pinpoint and challenge, if possible, are poor comparisons, questionable authorities, opposing evidence, and contradictory claims.

Identify Poor Comparisons

First, learn to identify poor comparisons. You will remember from chapter 10 that a good analogy must compare two items that are similar but not too similar for the purpose of drawing a generalization. A common dictum about analogies is this: "At some point, every analogy breaks down." There is no way that two different things can be similar in every respect, and so every analogy has a weak point—a point at which the two things being compared are very dissimilar. A good cross-examiner looks for major dissimilarities between **analogues** (i.e., compared items) and challenges these. Don't challenge petty, irrelevant dissimilarities between analogues. If you do this, your opponent will likely respond, "Well, of course, no analogy is perfect, but that difference is irrelevant." Instead, challenge analogies that are dissimilar in important respects that pertain to the argument. As an example, some people who address the possibility of executing innocent people when practicing the death penalty use the following analogy: "Well, innocent people die every day. For instance, innocent people die all the time in car wrecks, but we don't ban cars." The glaring weakness in this analogy is that innocent people choose to drive, though they know the risk involved; they do not choose to receive the death penalty. Therefore, be ready to challenge glaring, relevant dissimilarities in weak analogies.

A key set of terms to keep in mind is **causation** and **correlation**. Causation implies a relationship where thing X makes thing Y happen. An allergy to lactose in dairy, for instance, will cause a variety of bad reactions, such as stomachaches and intestinal distress. If a person has lactose intolerance and consumes dairy products (which contain lactose), then that person will likely develop a stomachache and intestinal distress. The lactose intolerance causes the intestinal distress and discomfort—the connection is clear and direct. However, causal relationships are notoriously difficult to prove. Far more common are relationships of correlation, where two things occur or develop together, but one does not necessarily cause the other. For example, many people who smoke tobacco also drink alcohol. However, tobacco smoking does not cause alcohol consumption—they are merely correlated. When evaluating statistical claims, whether they are yours or another person's, look carefully to discern whether a causal relationship is being proposed and is justified by the evidence, or if the relationship is merely correlative.

Identify Questionable Authorities

In addition to being ready to challenge glaring weak analogies, also be ready to challenge questionable weak and illegitimate appeals to authorities. Remember that the mark of a valid authority is that she has credentials or expertise in the area in which she is being called to testify. One of the most common ways a person can commit an appeal to an illegitimate authority is to cite someone who has a PhD—but not a PhD related to the field in which she is testifying. For example, someone who has a doctorate in literature is certainly an expert in many aspects of literature but is not an expert in scientific matters, and vice versa. Someone who has a doctorate in biology is not an expert in French literature. Therefore, if the credentials of a cited authority are unclear, make sure to challenge this and ask your opponent to state the authority's credentials.

Identify Shaky Evidence (and Oppose It)

You should be prepared to challenge with opposing evidence. It is likely in a debate, especially one about a popular controversial idea, that your opponent will state a strong statistical study for which you have an equally strong opposing statistical study. One of the best things you can do is present them with the study and ask the opponent how he would reconcile the two studies. An opponent may not be aware of the study or be able to reconcile the discrepancy, and this can strengthen your case. The strategy of presenting opposing evidence is one of the most useful strategies you can use as a debater. Sometimes when you are debating with someone, that person will present a statistical study that sounds conclusive and irrefutable. If someone presents a study like this, don't panic. For almost any study that presents a conclusion that sounds convincing, you can find another study that presents opposing evidence in an equally convincing light. Any issues in the world that we study are going to be complex because the world is complex. People can arrive at very different conclusions about issues depending on the questions they ask concerning the issues or the particular view from which they study them. The fact that there is opposing evidence does not entail that there is no right view about the matter and that every view is equally correct; it merely entails that each subject is complex and deserves to be considered carefully from multiple perspectives.

Identify Contradictory Claims

Lastly, be ready to challenge contradictory claims. Often during the course of a speech, a speaker will state multiple ideas that are blatantly contradictory or that have contradictory implications. This happens because people often fail to think through all of the implications of their arguments. Be ready to challenge these contradictions—but be civil and charitable. It is wise to assume that your opponent is a reasonable, intelligent, and thoughtful person. If you approach your opponent in the debate in this manner as you challenge contradictory claims, it will create a hospitable space in the debate in which it is possible for one of two positive outcomes to occur: One way your opponent might respond is that she might demonstrate how the claims which seem to be contradictory actually aren't contradictory at all. If this outcome occurs, it will help you learn more about the issue. Another way your opponent might respond is that she might realize that the contradictory claims cannot be resolved or explained in any way. In this case, she might end up changing her view, and she will have learned more about the issues. Both of these possible outcomes for a debate are positive outcomes.

In conclusion, as your opponent is arguing, be on the lookout for (in addition to unsupported claims, vague statistics, hasty generalizations, and questionable causal relationships) poor comparisons, questionable authorities, opposing evidence you know of, and contradictory claims. During cross-examination time, ask about these weaknesses and ask your opponent to reconcile, explain, or justify them.

After Josh and Christy gave their main arguments in their capital punishment debate, they asked each other the following questions during the cross-examination period.

Josh Challenges Christy:

- "Christy, you claim that retributive justice is based on a desire to restore social balance rather than to act out of revenge. Would you say that no anger is involved in juries or judges who sentence criminals to death, especially in the case of violent murder or violent sexual assault?" (Josh is challenging a contradictory implication in Christy's speech. Christy emphasized that retributive justice is superior to vengeance because retributive justice is administered according to rational and objective standards, rather than being administered in the heat of emotion. However, common sense dictates that judges and juries often feel anger, hatred, and vengeance for the people they sentence to death. Therefore, this question highlights a contradictory implication in Christy's argument.)
- "You say that you have some statistical studies that indicate capital punishment deters crime. Can you name any of these?" (Josh is challenging a vague and unsupported claim that Christy made. If Christy cannot produce an example statistic, it may appear that no such statistics exist.)
- "You mentioned a claim that every time the death penalty is enacted, eight murders are deterred. Where is this statistic coming from?" (Josh is challenging another unsupported claim.)

Christy Challenges Josh:

- "Josh, you made the comment that 'many criminals will not be deterred by the death penalty.' Upon which study are you basing this claim?" (Christy is challenging an unsupported claim made by Josh.)
- "You mentioned one study that seems to indicate the brutalization effect of capital punishment. Are there any other studies which support this theory?" (Christy is challenging a possible hasty generalization.)
- "Josh, you stated that people may respond to capital punishment in anger with more violence and killing, and that this is one reason why capital punishment should be abolished. What if a rebellious son responds out of anger because of his parents' legitimate punishment? Should the parents stop punishing their son?" (Christy is using an analogy to challenge a contradictory implication.)

What should you do after an opponent is unable to answer your question, or if he exposes a weakness in his argument in response to your questions? You may pursue several strategies. You may choose to be aggressive and uncompromising. If your opponent, for instance, is unable to tell you what the academic degree is for their source, you may choose to either chide him for not thoroughly researching the evidence presented or directly question the validity of the evidence. This approach relies on being consistent and ensuring that your arguments and evidence meet the same standard that you expect from your opponent.

You may choose a more moderate approach and indirectly express doubt about the credibility of the evidence's source. For example, you could say, "This evidence, presented by, well, apparently some kind of doctor . . ." You may also choose to, having made an inconsistency or gap apparent through your questioning, let those admissions stand on their own, perhaps only making reference to a lack of thorough sourcing or substantiation by the opposition in your closing argument. In choosing these options, remember that while subtlety has its merits, clarity is the most important characteristic to ensure a powerful closing in a debate.

- "You mentioned that capital punishment cases are very expensive. Are you aware that this is because of the endless string of appeals made by offenders and lawyers? Couldn't we cut costs and enact justice by waiving the right to appeal in obvious murder cases?" (Christy is challenging a possible weak or contradictory argument.)

So far, you have examined how to question your opponent during a debate's cross-examination period, but you also need to examine how to prepare for, and respond to, your opponent during cross-examination. First, although it may seem as though your opponent could ask you any one of a number of infinitely possible questions, this is actually not the case. Your opponent will most certainly question you using one or all of the challenging strategies listed in this chapter. Therefore, as you prepare your debate, you should practice cross-examining yourself with these challenges in mind. For instance, the following are great questions to ask yourself

In preparing for both the planned and unscripted parts of a debate, do not be too proud, afraid, or tardy to seek out the opinions of peers, friends, or family to help evaluate your arguments and evidence. Sometimes, the amount of work you have put into your research and arguments can bias your vision and make you less able to see the flaws or gaps in it. Ask for advice from others concerning your work! Explaining your ideas in many different practice contexts and situations will help you articulate them well during the actual formal and informal moments of the debate.

as you assemble your arguments: "Do I have any vague or unsupported claims?"; "Do I have any weak statistical studies?"; "Do I make any hasty generalizations?"; and so on until you work through the list of the most common types of challenges. It is important to note that we often have problems seeing the flaws in our own reasoning. Therefore, another good strategy is to practice by explaining your arguments to several people, then ask them to tell you if they observed any of these possible weaknesses. In addition, once you become familiar with the opponent's arguments, you will likely know the types of arguments he may bring against you. This knowledge can help you to have a ready answer when he inevitably asks you about opposing arguments or statistical studies. If you are aware of the most probable arguments ahead of time—and if you prepare a possible critique of, or response to, those arguments—you'll be able to think on your feet more easily. Thorough research and practicing your arguments in advance with friends can greatly prepare you for cross-examination.

You may think that cross-examination is not as important in an informal debate but it actually can be a very important part of the discussion. Certainly in an informal debate, as you have learned, you will not have a specific cross-examination time. However, it is still important for you to sharpen and challenge your opponent's thinking through the use of skillful questioning. This is actually a kind action, because this helps a person make sure that she has good, valid reasons for believing what she believes. It sharpens and deepens her thinking. Of course, if you were to ask your opponent questions in a snobby or condescending manner, this would not help and would probably produce more rancor than enlightenment in your conversation. You should, instead, consider yourself as a coseeker of the truth, just as Socrates did in the dialogues you have read.

In summary, the purpose of cross-examination is to ask questions that will clarify ideas in your mind so that you know exactly how to rebut. It is also a time in which you can expose any weaknesses of your opponent's arguments. Avoid the desire to argue and make statements in this time. That is the purpose of the rebuttal, which you will examine in the next chapter.

Review Exercises

Explain

Explain what cross-examination is.

List

What are five different ways you can challenge someone during cross-examination?

Building Copiousness

Review

Review your old quotes.

Practice

Practice saying the quotes to someone in your class, or practice writing them down on paper.

Memorize

Memorize your new quote:

> Patience is a bitter thing, but its fruit is sweet. —Sadi[2]

Everyday Debate

Debate

Debate the following proposition: "Resolved: Fast food restaurants should be sued like cigarette companies." As you develop your argument for your side, use as many of the different argument types as possible that we have studied in this book. If you need to, consult the arguments and appeals chart in the appendix.

Learning from the Masters

Explain

Watch chapter 3, "The Hot Spot," in *The Great Debaters*, in which Melvin Tolson challenges Samantha Booke's arguments. What techniques does he use to challenge her?

____

____

____

2. Ratcliffe, *Oxford Dictionary of Quotations*, 354.

Observe

Watch the next two speakers on the Intelligence Squared debate on illegal immigration: Vernon M. Briggs Jr. and Enrique Morones (Link 22-1). Flow the arguments, and then answer the following questions.

Explain

At the beginning of his speech, Briggs called attention to the real proposition under debate. Why was this clarification an important move on his part?

Explain

How does Briggs's argument about the labor force evoke pity? Is it relevant?

List

Which common topic is used in the argument about erosion of the rule of law?

Explain

Did Briggs's failure to end his speech on time have a negative effect on his presentation? Explain your answer.

Discuss

1. How did Morones's greeting the audience in several languages build ethos?
2. How did Morones's speech build pathos? Was it relevant to the topic at hand?

The Big Debate: Gun Control

Develop

Your teacher will assign you to a partner in your class. Take turns telling each other one argument for or against gun control (one of you should argue for it, and the other should argue against it). Then, take some time to think about how you can cross-examine your partner on this issue. Write down at least three questions you can use to challenge his argument. After you have spent a few minutes thinking about this, cross-examine each other and listen to one another's responses. This exercise will help you practice for your debate.

Chapter 23

Arrangement: Rebuttal

23

> THE REASON WHY WE HAVE TWO EARS AND ONLY ONE MOUTH IS THAT WE MAY LISTEN THE MORE AND TALK THE LESS.
>
> —ZENO[1]

The rebuttal time is your opportunity to state arguments that critique the arguments of your opposition. To be effective at rebuttal, you need to think on your feet a bit. This may seem difficult at first, but the ability to think and react quickly is a matter of being a good listener, becoming familiar with your material, and remembering your opponent's various reasoning flaws. Always take notes during your opponent's presentation time, as well as the cross-examination time. Tracking the flow of the argument[2] will help you spot weaknesses in reasoning or evidence.

It is important to note how the rebuttal time is connected to the rest of the debate. During the time that your opponent presents her main argument, listen for and identify potential weaknesses. You will use the cross-examination strategies you studied in the previous chapter to question your opponent about these possible weaknesses. When you cross-examine your opponent, sometimes she will have an adequate response that addresses your concerns, but sometimes she will not, and it will become apparent that the weaknesses you detected in the main argument are actually weaknesses. It is in the rebuttal time that you will specifically argue against your opponent's thesis by discussing the various weaknesses of her argument that your cross-examination revealed.

Using Rebuttal Strategies to Challenge Your Opponent's Argument

To organize your rebuttal, make sure that you draw on the cross-examination strategies discussed in the last chapter. Consider which of the following problems with your opponent's argument you would discuss in the rebuttal: unsupported claims, vague statistics, hasty generalizations, questionable causal relationships, poor comparisons, questionable authorities, opposing evidence, or contradictory claims. Sometimes your opponent's argument might contain several of these problems, but sometimes it might have just one or two. You don't need to worry about whether you have detected all of these possible problems in your opponent's arguments; you only need to address the potentially weak parts of your opponent's argument that you have identified while listening to the main argument and conducting your cross-examination.

1. Susan Ratcliffe, ed., *Oxford Dictionary of Quotations by Subject*, 2nd ed. (Oxford: Oxford University Press, 2010), 448.
2. Remember, when you track the flow of an argument (i.e., flow an argument), you just make an outline of the key points and supporting evidence.

Sometimes, however, after you listen to your opponent's argument and conduct a cross-examination, you may discover that her argument is strong and that you can't find any glaring weaknesses in it. If you find yourself in this predicament, don't panic. There are a still a couple of good rebuttal techniques you can practice to rebut a strong argument.

First, keep in mind that no matter how strong an argument is, there is some issue or aspect of an issue that it has not touched on, simply because debate issues are extremely complex and debaters have a limited amount of time in which to address these complexities. As you gain practice in debating, you will start to gain a sense for the aspects of an issue that your opponent hasn't addressed that might possibly shed a different light on the topic. It is always good to ask questions about these unexplored areas in your rebuttal time. In addition, realize that even if someone's evidence for a particular point sounds like strong evidence, it is often possible to draw different conclusions from any given evidence. Therefore, as you are listening to an argument, try to get into habit of asking yourself what different conclusions could be gained from the evidence being presented. Sometimes you may even find that while the conclusions drawn from a particular piece of evidence seem to be possible or likely conclusions, there are other conclusions that are stronger and more complete conclusions in that they take more evidence into consideration. It makes sense, then, to keep in mind that even if a particular argument sounds strong, there are almost always questions that the argument leaves unexplored or different conclusions that can be drawn from the evidence, and the rebuttal time is a great place to mention these unexplored questions or other possible conclusions.

Rebuttals may seem difficult to pull off, but as long as you listen carefully to your opponent's speech, you will likely find at least one or two strategies you can use to organize your rebuttal. After all, it is difficult to construct an absolutely perfect speech. Furthermore, the more you research and think about your topic, the more you will be able to present information that is superior to your opponent in at least some respects. For example, here are a couple of points Christy made against Josh's argument in the rebuttal section of their debate:

Christy's Rebuttal

Christy: Josh, you have said that capital punishment doesn't seem to deter many criminals, but you have stated during cross-examination that you aren't sure how many it does or does not deter. Common sense suggests many people will be deterred by capital punishment. A simple syllogism will show us the wisdom of this:

> All people avoid things that result in what they fear the most.
> People fear death the most.
> Therefore, people will do things to avoid that which results in death.

This syllogism demonstrates that the death penalty logically deters some, and, possibly, many people, which is corroborated by the testimony of many would-be murderers.

You have also claimed that murderers will not be deterred by capital punishment because they are in a rage, or possibly drunk or high. Therefore, they cannot think through the consequences of their actions. It is certainly true that the reflexes and thought processes of drunk, high, or enraged people are impaired, but there is no reason to believe that none of them could still think or react in such a way as to avoid murdering people. Many people still retain a clear picture of right and wrong even when they are in these conditions, and they can control themselves to a significant degree. The fact that we don't have more murders on college campuses is a clear example of this. We know that a great deal of drinking and illegal drug activity occurs on these campuses, and—with the pressures of college—there are undoubtedly people in various states of rage. However, even though some murders do happen on campus, it's not extremely common. This shows us that many people can still control themselves despite being intoxicated, high, or in an emotional state of extreme rage.

You also mentioned the brutalization effect, noting one study that suggested that capital punishment brutalizes people and desensitizes them to violence. Therefore, as you state, it increases violence. However, you only cited one statistic to prove this, and it seems, quite frankly, that this hypothesis is a little fishy. After all, just look at how violent regular television programming and the news are today. People see murders on television shows or hear about them on the news regularly. It's hard to believe that one death penalty case is going to desensitize them so much more than all of these other murders they see. But let's say, hypothetically, that the brutalization effect does occur with capital punishment cases. It must also be true, then, that reports of death in war also brutalizes people. In fact, we could even argue that this would brutalize people more than the report of a death penalty murder. After all, war kills innocent people in more horrible, gruesome, and needless ways than the death penalty does. However, few people would say that we should stop going to war, even if it were shown to have a brutalization effect. This is because we know that war is, regrettably, our only alternative sometimes. This is the same with capital punishment. We don't like capital punishment, but sometimes, regrettably, it is the only solution. Sometimes life in prison just won't work. Criminals can escape from jail. Criminals can kill in jail, and criminals, even those in prison for life, often get out because of overcrowding or legal loopholes. Especially in the case of violent recidivist murders and recidivist violent sexual murders, life in prison is never an acceptable option. Only the death penalty will suffice.

Throughout Christy's argument, she has directly addressed her opponent, Josh, as she makes her arguments. During less formal debates, cross-examination, and strategic moments in other sections, this is a good choice. However, be careful not to overuse direct address. First, doing so personalizes the debate in a way that can be harmful to the dialogue—you want to make sure that your focus is on the issue under question and the arguments that your opponent makes, rather than the person. Second, spending too much time addressing your opponent directly takes your focus away from addressing the judges or audience who may be present, who will ultimately be the ones who determine success in a formal debate. Phrases such as "my opponent has said" or "she/he/they argued that" clearly refer the issues under question to your opponent, but such phrases do not address them directly.

Josh's Rebuttal

The following are few arguments that Josh used to rebut Christy's arguments:

Josh: Christy, your main reason for believing that death penalty deters murder is because of the testimony of criminals and supposed common sense. However, it is by no means certain that criminals are reliable sources of information, even when they testify about their own motivations. Many criminals like to boast and brag about their crimes and will say anything to get attention. And if a criminal is in prison, I imagine he would do and say quite a lot to get interviewed by people. It makes his dreadful life exciting and brings him a certain amount of notoriety. Furthermore, many of the testimonies of criminals that you relied upon to build your argument gave those testimonies when they were in prison. People in prison are not exactly free agents, able to do and say what they please.

It is very possible that the person conducting the interviews with prisoners asked them leading questions or placed undue pressure on them to answer questions in a certain way. For both of these reasons, I would say we should be highly skeptical about claims made by imprisoned criminals.

Furthermore, you say common sense tells us that people fear death and will do anything to avoid it. Well, I would say that this is true. However, common sense tells us that many criminals are impetuous and egocentric, and they don't believe they will get caught. They think they will be able to outsmart the system; otherwise, they wouldn't have murdered in the first place. Therefore, the fear of the death penalty doesn't deter many murderers from killing because they don't believe they will get caught. We see similar reasoning in people who do crazy, dangerous stunts with fire, racing cars or motorcycles, or extreme rock climbing. I'm sure these people fear death. However, they don't think they will die. Therefore, the fear of death does not deter them from their activities. In the same way, many murderers don't think they are going to get caught, and, therefore, they don't fear the death penalty because they have no fear of ever receiving it. If you are going to claim common sense as a basis for your argument, then you need to look at all of what common sense tells us.

You also place a lot of emphasis on the fact that killers can escape from jail, kill people in jail, and get out again and kill other people. First, it's important to realize that prison escapes are so rare as to be virtually nonexistent. They may have been more common in the previous low-tech era, but today with the technological advancements, security systems, and monitoring devices we have, it is virtually impossible for a prisoner to escape from prison. Furthermore, when guards take jobs at a prison, they know that it's dangerous and that they could be attacked or killed. No one is making them choose to be guards. You brought up the analogy of war earlier. It is an appropriate analogy here. When soldiers go to war, they know they could die. However, we believe that their mission is worth the risk of life. Prison guards are like soldiers. They risk their lives, but the mission is worth it—the mission is protecting and preserving lives, even if it costs them their own. In addition, the murder of prison guards is highly unlikely.

Furthermore, I want to point out something that you mentioned in your own speech. Murderers have a low recidivism rate—only 1 percent as you have mentioned. This means that, even if they do manage to get out of prison, it is unlikely that they will kill again. Also, it's important to note that when someone who was in jail for murder becomes a recidivist, this doesn't automatically mean that the person has committed a murder. A murderer who is a recidivist can go back to jail for other reasons, such as violating parole or for committing another "lesser" crime. In addition, regarding your concern that violent murderers will be let out of jail because of a legal loophole, if a murderer is an especially violent offender such a serial killer, it is very easy to make laws that keep this type of egregious criminal in jail.

What you are saying, Christy, is that you want to continue an inhumane, unnecessary, highly ineffective, and often incorrectly applied practice in order to prevent a highly unlikely scenario—for example, a violent murderer escaping from jail or being let out because of a legal loophole. This just doesn't make sense.

Strategies Christy and Josh Used

Hopefully, you noticed that both Christy and Josh made use of several key strategies in their rebuttals. Christy challenged contradictory claims Josh seemed to make about whether capital punishment does or does not deter murder. She also challenged with opposing evidence Josh's claim that murderers are too drunk or high to be deterred by capital punishment because they actually can't think through the consequences of what they are doing. She pointed out that if people who are angry, drunk, and high could not reason properly, there would be a lot more murders on college campuses, since there tends to be a lot of drinking and drug use on college campuses. She also challenged questionable causal claims that people are brutalized by hearing about murders on the news. She noted that if this was the case, given the news we hear about wars (where death and murder happens) and given the number of television shows involving murder that we see, it seems that our murder rates would be much higher if the brutalization effect was true.

When Josh rebutted Christy's speech, he also used a number of techniques we discussed in this chapter. He challenged questionable authorities when he questioned the testimonies from criminals testifying about whether or not they were deterred by the death penalty. He challenged with opposing evidence when he suggested that although people fear death, as Christy pointed out, many or even most criminals don't think they are going to get caught. Therefore, they don't really think they will ever have to worry about capital punishment. Josh also challenged with opposing evidence when he suggested that the notion that murderers are going to escape from jail just isn't realistic today, given the high-tech security systems prisons use today. Lastly, Josh suggested other conclusions that could be drawn from the evidence Christy was presenting when he argued that while 1 percent of murderers released from jail are recidivist, this doesn't necessarily mean they are murdering more people, because some murderers become recidivist for violating parole or committing other crimes not related to murder.

As noted previously, in most informal debates, you will not have a formal rebuttal time; however, a healthy informal discussion is one in which people are able to challenge each other's ideas and pose counterarguments. We should all remember to treat debate as Socrates did—choose to make the search for truth the primary goal of your conversation. It can feel uncomfortable to have people challenge your cherished viewpoints, but realize that this process will make you a stronger, clearer, and more effective thinker.

Andrew and Isabel's Informal Rebuttal Time

As an informal debate example, review the following discussion that Andrew and Isabel had one afternoon, after both of them had spent a lot of time thinking about their cat and dog debate. They are finally able to come to an agreement on the family pet. Watch how their rebuttal process helped them come to this decision:

Isabel: OK, Andrew. I think we should sit down and discuss the conclusions we've reached about which pet we should own. I really want to get a pet this summer so that we can spend a lot of time getting to know it and training it before we have to go back to school in the fall. And so we need to figure out what we think and tell Mom and Dad.

Andrew: Well, you know what I think. I want a dog.

Isabel: Why don't you tell me your arguments, and then I will tell you mine. But remember, we are not debating about what pet *we* want, necessarily. We both decided that we need to figure out what pet is most practical for our *family*.

Andrew: You are right, good point. I think that a dog is the most practical pet for our family for several reasons. First, he can guard our house. With some of the robberies we've had in our neighborhood lately, I just think it would be a good idea to have a guard dog that could help protect us or warn us of intruders. I also don't think it's practical to have a pet that you invest a lot of time and money into but then doesn't really do a whole lot. I mean, you do have to invest money in cats for food and vaccinations and other health issues, but they don't really *do* very much. They can't do tricks, and a lot of cats ignore their owners. Dogs almost always love their owners and, besides guarding the house, they can learn a lot of fun tricks. Plus, dogs are more practical because you can take them on vacations. You can't take a cat on a vacation. If we get a dog, we could take it on our vacation to Oregon! But if we get a cat, we will need to ask someone to look after it. That's not very practical.

Isabel: Interesting—I hadn't thought about the vacation argument. I have to say, though, I don't think that the fact that dogs learn tricks is a good example of them being more practical. I just think that's something you particularly like about dogs.

Andrew: Touché. OK, now you tell me why you think a cat is more practical.

Isabel: I still think a cat is more practical for several reasons. If you really want to get a dog to protect us and guard our house, then you are going to have to get a big dog. And the bigger the dog, the more mess he is likely to make, and the more exercise he will need. In fairness to Mom, she does not have time to clean up any more messes. She has to work too much as it is. And, quite frankly, you are really busy with basketball and mock trial team, and I don't think you are going to have time to walk the dog regularly, even if you want to do it. So that means that either Mom, Dad, or I are going to have to walk the dog a lot, and it's just not practical to make us do that all the time. If we get a cat, it won't make messes—at least not big ones—and it will not need walks, but we will still have a pet to play with, and I actually do think you can teach cats a few tricks.

Andrew: Those are reasonable arguments, but if you are going to be strict with my use of the word *practical*, then I'm going to be strict with your usage of it as well. The fact that you may walk the dog more than I would isn't a matter of practicality. It's a matter of fairness.

Isabel: Very true, but I could have worded it this way: It is not practical to choose a pet that you cannot adequately take care of, and I don't think you—or any of us, to be honest—will be able to adequately take care of a dog—at least not a big one.

Andrew: All right—that's honest. I still think I would walk the dog, but let's get back to that in a moment. I have a question for you. It sounds like your main objection to a dog is that it will make a big mess and that you will have to walk it all the time. Is that correct?

Isabel: Hmm. I guess that's true.

Andrew: So, hypothetically speaking, let's say that you had a dog that didn't make big messes and that you didn't have to walk all the time. Would you like a dog like this just as much as you would a cat?

Isabel: I guess so. I do love cats, but I think I could like a dog, maybe, if it didn't make messes and if I didn't have the sole responsibility of walking it.

Andrew: OK, then I have a proposal for you. What if we got a smaller dog—say, a beagle, or some breed of dog like that. A smaller dog isn't going to make very many messes. Plus, if we get the dog before the summer, I will have a lot of time to train it so that it will learn not to make messes.

Isabel: But what about taking it on walks?

Andrew: Well, I have another proposal. What if we worked out a system so that you and I alternated walking the dog? In fact, I would even make a deal with you where I promise to walk it four or five days a week, and you only have to walk it two or three days weekly. I have to run for basketball training several days a week anyhow, so I could take the dog with me when I run.

Isabel: You say this now, but what if we get the dog and you don't follow through on your arrangement—that is, what if you don't walk it according to the schedule, and then I'm stuck doing it?

Andrew: That's a fair question, and I have a solution. How about I line up some substitute dog walkers this summer? I have friends who wouldn't mind walking the dog for me—in fact, they'd probably love it. So that way, if I am in a bind, I could just call one of them and they can walk the dog for us. Or, if you decide you want to take over my walking duties for a day or two, I will pay you some of my allowance. Also, it's not going to hurt the dog if we don't walk it for a day or two, as long as it never became a habit.

Isabel: I suppose that sounds pretty reasonable. Will you clean up after the dog in the backyard, too?

Andrew: If we had a cat, you would have to clean its litter box. It seems only fair that you clean up after the dog sometimes, too. Besides, a smaller dog won't be as hard to clean up after.

Isabel: That makes sense. I've always liked small dogs, actually. I just think I wasn't too excited about the prospect of having a big dog, but I think a cute, small dog could be fun for the family. I also think everyone would enjoy taking a dog on vacations. You know what, Andrew? I think we have a deal!

Andrew: Really? Cool! Let's tell Mom and Dad.

As you can see, in this informal debate, Andrew and Isabel's arguments, cross-examinations, and rebuttals all overlapped. However, the process of presenting and critiquing arguments helped them create a workable solution to their pet dilemma. I want to emphasize to you that even if you never participate in any kind of formal debate, you can use the skills that you have learned in this debate to help you in any kind of informal debate you have. Using the skills of logical argumentation and critique will provide an invaluable aid to you as you seek the truth and attempt to find resolutions to questions and dilemmas in your own life.

Review Exercises

List

List the cross-examination strategies you learned in chapter 22, as these are the strategies you will draw from to organize your rebuttal.

____

____

____

____

____

____

____

____

Building Copiousness

Review

Review your old quotes.

Practice

Practice saying the quotes to someone in your class, or practice writing them down on paper.

Memorize

Memorize your new quote:

The best is the enemy of the good. —Voltaire[3]

Everyday Debate

Debate

Debate the following proposition: "Reading is more valuable than watching television." As you develop your argument for your side, use as many of the different argument types as possible that we have studied in this book. If you need to, consult the arguments and appeals chart in the appendix. See if you can use humor and/or some of the copiousness quotes you've memorized in your speech during this debate.

Learning from the Masters

Observe

Watch the last two speakers on the Intelligence Squared debate on illegal immigration: Mark Krikorian and Karen K. Narasaki (Link 23-1). Flow the arguments, and then answer the following questions.

3. Ratcliffe, *Oxford Dictionary of Quotations*, 161.

List

What are two arguments Krikorian makes?

Discuss

Discuss at least two argument techniques that Krikorian used.

Explain

1. Explain one strength of Krikorian's arguments.

2. Explain one weakness of Krikorian's arguments.

List

What are two arguments Narasaki makes?

Discuss

Discuss at least two argument techniques Narasaki uses.

Explain

1. Explain one strength of Narasaki's arguments.

2. Explain one weakness of Narasaki's arguments.

The Big Debate: Gun Control

Develop

In the last chapter, you practiced cross-examination with a partner in class. Now, write a rebuttal to your partner's cross-examination to your argument. It should be a short paragraph that directly responds to each critique your partner made of your argument. Use at least two of the rebuttal strategies discussed in this chapter.

Chapter 24
Memory

> THE TRUE ART OF MEMORY
> IS THE ART OF ATTENTION.
> —SAMUEL JOHNSON[1]

How good is your memory? Can you remember important information quickly and easily, or do crucial facts seem to slip through your mind like sand through a sieve? For many people, remembering important information for tests or even for everyday life can be quite a challenge. With all of our modern conveniences such as cell phones, computers, calculators, and even books, memory has been made, for the most part, an obsolete necessity. After all, as some people might reason, why bother to remember phone numbers when you can just store them in a computerized phone list? Why memorize the capital of Oregon when you can look it up on the Internet with a few clicks? Why memorize multiplication tables when you can figure out any equation on a calculator?

Unfortunately, today's technology has made us a bit lazy; however, throughout history, memorization has been an integral aspect of people's education and life. Consider these amazing feats of memory:

- Greek bards, or traveling poets, may have recited complete epic poems, such as the *Iliad* and the *Odyssey* from memory. Simplicius, a friend of the philosopher, theologian, and rhetorician Augustine, was able to recite Virgil's poetry backward.[2] Today, books containing these poems are hundreds of pages long. When is the last time you met someone—anyone—who could recite an entire novel or tale, hundreds of pages in length, from memory?
- It has been said that Roman rhetorician Seneca the Elder could recite two thousand names from memory, in the exact order in which he had originally heard them. If this wasn't impressive enough, he also once had a class of two hundred students, each one of whom he told to each recite a line of poetry to him. He then amazed all of the students by perfectly reciting all of their lines back to them—in reverse order![3]
- The current World Memory Champion, Dominic O'Brien, earned this title when he was able to recite, in order, every card he had seen from a deck of 54 cards. The total number of cards he recited, from memory, in perfect order was an astonishing 2,808 cards.[4]

How have people throughout history, and even today, been able to accomplish such amazing feats of memory? Is it magic? Believe it or not, many people who have been and are able to remember seemingly impossible amounts of information rely on a memory device that has been around for centuries: the method of *loci*.

---

1. Susan Ratcliffe, ed., *Oxford Dictionary of Quotations by Subject*, 2nd ed. (Oxford: Oxford University Press, 2010), 311.
2. Frances Yates, *The Art of Memory* (Chicago: University Chicago Press, 1966), 16.
3. Ibid.
4. Luciano Passuello, "Develop Perfect Memory with the Memory Palace Technique," Litemind, http://litemind.com/memory-palace/.

The Method of *Loci*—Its History

To understand this method, it will help you to learn about a bit of interesting history. Once there was a famous Greek orator named Simonides of Ceos.[5] Simonides's recitations were so famous that a certain Greek nobleman paid Simonides to come to a banquet and recite a panegyric—a poem in praise of the nobleman himself.[6] Simonides, indeed, recited a beautiful panegyric, but part of the account included a story about two Greek gods, Castor and Pollux. The nobleman loved the part of the panegyric that praised him, but he wasn't too happy about sharing the limelight with Castor and Pollux. Therefore, when Simonides came to collect his fee, the nobleman sarcastically told Simonides that he would only receive half of his fee, and he could collect the other half from Castor and Pollux, who had also received half of the praise in the poem. Simonides was disheartened but stayed for the rest of the banquet.[7] Unexpectedly, a servant came and told him that there was someone waiting for him outside the banquet hall with a message. However, when Simonides left the banquet hall to find the messenger, he could find no one. As Simonides was searching for this supposed "someone" in the banquet atrium, the roof of the banquet hall suddenly collapsed, crushing everyone inside. Only Simonides and those in the atrium escaped. It appeared that Castor and Pollux had honored Simonides for praising them by sparing his life!

Sadly, the bodies of the banquet guests were so horrifically mangled that even the families of the victims were unable to identify their loved ones when they came to claim them for burial.[8] Simonides realized he could (and then did) identify all of the victims because he could remember where everyone was sitting. With this thought, Simonides understood that memory was tied to organization and place.[9] With this moment of clarity and awareness, ancient rhetoricians said that Simonides invented the art of memory. He invented what came to be known as the **method of *loci***, also known as the "method of place."[10] The word *loci* is the Latin plural of the word *locus*, which means "place."[11] The method of *loci* is a memory strategy which uses association between objects and place as a memory device.

The Method of *Loci*—How It Works

Before you learn the method of *loci*, which is a little complex, you must first learn one of the underlying skills upon which it rests. One of these underlying skills is picture association. When you use picture association with a vocabulary word you need to remember, you consider what the vocabulary word sounds like. Take the word "egregious," for example. You don't need to know what the word "egregious" means yet. Instead, think about how it sounds when spoken. Say it out loud. What does it sound like to you? Or what does it look like to you, in terms of the written term? You may have noticed that the letters *g-r-e-g*, which look like the name Greg, are in this word. That is probably something that stood out to you. Now, just to let you know, the word "egregious" means "flagrantly bad" or "offensive."[12] For instance, someone who has an egregious fashion sense wears completely horrible, tasteless clothing combinations. Someone who makes egregious insults says absolutely terrible, inappropriate comments to people.

Now that we know what egregious means, and we know that the word reminds us of the name Greg, we need to combine the two concepts—this is where picture association is involved. To do this, picture a guy named Greg in your mind—make the picture very specific. For instance, maybe he has unruly carrot-orange hair and is six feet five inches tall (the more vivid or bizarre the image is, the better you will remember it). Now, imagine that our incredibly tall, orange-haired Greg has egregious fashion sense. What does that look like, specifically? Remember, it has to be flagrantly horrible and bad. Try this: Visualize Greg dressed in brown plaid golf pants with bell-bottoms, a purple polyester '70s shirt with really broad, pointy collars, a neon-yellow bow tie, and a formal tuxedo coat—with tails. Picture this (rather

5. Yates, *Art of Memory*, 1–2.
6. Ibid., 1.
7. Ibid., 1–2.
8. Ibid., 2.
9. Ibid.
10. Ibid., 7.
11. Cicero, *Rhetorica ad Herennium*, trans. Harry Caplan (Cambridge, MA: Harvard University Press, 1954), 207–209.
12. *Webster's Ninth New Collegiate Dictionary*, s.v. "egregious."

jarring) image clearly in your mind, or feel free to create an equally awful outfit for Greg. Carefully go through the following process in your mind: Think of the word "egregious." Note that egregious reminds you of Greg. Picture Greg in your mind sporting his flagrantly bad fashion statement. Picture how truly dreadful this outfit looks. Make this image really clear in your mind. Now close your eyes and count to ten, and then read the next sentence. What does "egregious" mean? Did you remember the meaning of the word? It means "flagrantly bad" or "offensive." By making these visual connections in your mind, you were able to recall the word's meaning. Now that you understand how picture association works, you are prepared to learn how the method of *loci* works.

In order to use the method of *loci* to remember something, you need to go through several important steps, just as you did for picture association. First, you need to think of a building you are very familiar with. It could be a house, a church, or a shopping mall. Whichever building you use, it needs to have many rooms or areas within it (i.e., rooms, closets, entry areas, hallways, etc.), and you need to be so familiar with this building that you can easily picture each of the rooms vividly in your mind. Next, take any speech that you need or want to memorize, such as your debate speech, and divide it into logical parts. The parts of the speech might be the introduction, the harms, the advantages, and so forth. However, you will probably need to divide each of these parts further into two or three sections. For instance, you could divide the introduction into three sections—maybe you have a quote, then an explanation, and then a thesis statement.

Once you have divided the speech into several parts, think of a vivid image that symbolizes each section of the part you are memorizing. The more odd and unique these symbols are, the better. Next, place each of these symbols in a specific place in the house in your mind. For example, you could place the first symbol in the entryway of your house. Then, if the living room is the first room you'd encounter after the entryway, place the next symbol there. If the kitchen is the next room in the house after the living room, place the next symbol there. The point is, go through the rooms of your house (or whatever building you are using) in your mind in a logical order, that is, a manner in which you would normally go through the house if you were giving first-time guests a tour of the space. As you go through the building in your mind, place the symbols (which stand for particular parts of your speech) in the rooms of your house in a logical order.

In order for this method to work, you must review it frequently as you develop it. For instance, after you create the first two symbols and place them in their appropriate rooms, develop the third symbol and place it in the next room. Then, to review, go back (mentally "walk" back through the rooms) and remind yourself about the first two symbols, what they stand for, and which rooms they are in. After every couple of symbols that you place, pause and go back to review the old ones. This will keep the symbols and their meanings fresh in your mind. If you have difficulty remembering what a symbol signifies, create a different symbol for that point or section. Remember, when it comes to creating these symbols, the more bizarre the better. (In the "Review Exercises" section at the end of the chapter, there is an activity that will help you practice the method of *loci* with

a poem or vocabulary words. Feel free to conduct this exercise now if you want immediate practice using this method.)

Granted, using this method will seem extremely odd, foreign, and time-consuming at first, and you might be tempted to wonder if it actually works and if anyone ever truly uses such a device. Believe it or not, this device was extremely common in the ancient world. Ancient Romans were said to have used the method of *loci* with the signs of the zodiac in order to remember speeches and other important facts.[13] Medieval monks built complex memory gardens, the different spaces of which they used to memorize long passages of scripture or Latin.[14] Monks also used cathedrals for this same purpose (they would place symbols for various scriptures in the rooms of the cathedral in their minds to aid their memory). In the Middle Ages, Italian philosopher Giulio "Delminio" Camillo built something he called his theater of memory. This theater of memory was a small replica of a house, which had all sorts of boxes people could open with levers. These boxes contained symbols that could help people remember facts considered very important in the Middle Ages, such as list of the seven vices and virtues and key passages of scripture.[15] Camillo's theater was extremely popular for some time and attracted lots of visitors. An Italian man going to see the contraption told a friend he had heard that it was "a work of wonderful skill, into which whoever is admitted as spectator will be able to discourse on any subject no less fluently than Cicero."[16]

I have used both picture association and the method of *loci* to teach vocabulary words, history facts, and poems, and have found that most students who invest some time and concentration into this method solve most of their memorization problems for tests and other memory assignments. Because the method of *loci* connects important information to vivid symbols in our mind and organizes them in a familiar pattern (i.e., the rooms of a house), it can be a very effective memorization tool.

13. John Michal Greer, "The Art of Memory," *Renaissance Magazine*, 1997, http://www.renaissancemagazine.com/backissues/memory.html.
14. Ibid.
15. Ibid.
16. Ibid.

Other Memory Aid Techniques

The method of *loci* is certainly not the only tool for memorizing information. A student attempting to learn a speech can use something I call the look, write, say method. This method is just what it seems to be. To use this method, divide a speech into small chunks such as one or two sentences. Look at these sentences, practice writing them, and then practice saying them out loud. Repeat this process several times until you have the small section of the speech memorized. Then, move on to the next small chunk and repeat the process. Make sure you also review the old section you first memorized. Repeat this process for the whole speech, learning new sections and reviewing old ones—until you have the entire speech memorized.

Another memory device that may be helpful to you is creating **mnemonic devices**. Mnemosyne was the Titan goddess of memory,[17] and a memory device is one that specifically helps you remember something.

A common mnemonic device is an **acrostic**. An acrostic is a list of items to remember, each line of which has a first letter or first word that makes a new word that acts as the memory device. For instance, in the Renaissance, Sir John Davies wrote a book of poems called the *Hymns of Astraea*. The first letter of the first word of every single line in each poem in this book spelled out the name "ELISABETH A REGINA"—of course, because Elizabeth I was queen at this time.[18] While Davies wasn't necessarily creating these poems as a memory device, they are an interesting example of how acrostics can function.

Other people have created commonly used acrostics, such as Roy G. Biv (ROYGBIV) to remember the order of the colors of the rainbow (*R* for red, *O* for orange, *Y* for yellow, *G* for green, *B* for blue, *I* for indigo, and *V* for violet). Another example is the phrase "Kings Play Chess On Funny Green Spaces" (KPCOFGS), which is used to remember the scientific classification of living organisms: *K* for kingdom, *P* for phylum, *C* for class, *O* for order, *F* for family, *G* for genus, and *S* for species. These

17. Atsma, *The Theoi Project*, s.v. "Mnemosyne," http://www.theoi.com/.
18. Sir John Davies, "Hymn I: Of Astraea," Luminarium: Anthology of English Literature, last updated February 13, 2012, http://www.luminarium.org/renlit/astraea1.htm.

same devices could be used to memorize speeches. For example, to create a memory acrostic for your speech, you would need, once again, to divide your speech into parts—five to ten parts is probably adequate. For each part, think of a word that represents the information in that section (i.e., that acts as a tip-off). Then, put the first letters of each word together to see what kind of acrostic you have created (this one would be formatted as a string of letters, e.g., ROYGBIV). It may be memorable just as it is (e.g., ROYGBIV can be remembered as Roy G. Biv), or you may need to reconsider which words you use for the different parts to try different acrostic letter combinations until you find one that works well for you. As another option, you could just use the letters of the words to create a *sentence* acrostic, just as "Kings Play Chess On Funny Green Spaces" was developed from the letter string of KPCOFGS (which was created from the words, or parts, of the scientific classification system for life). Once again, you may need to experiment with and adjust the words as needed to find an acrostic that works well for you. After all, you are the one who will need to remember the meaning of the acrostic, so it is important that the acrostic makes sense to *you*, and is easily recalled.

In closing, consider another story that Plato once told through Socrates in the famous dialogue *Phaedrus*. This story is about an old Egyptian god named Theuth, who is the inventor of writing. Theuth went to Thamus to show him his great discovery. Theuth thought that Thamus would be delighted with his discovery because it seemed to Theuth that in learning writing, the Egyptians would become wise and more knowledgeable, and that writing would improve their memory. Thamus, however, was wary of Theuth's discovery. He argued that writing would actually cause the Egyptians to practice the art of memory less and, if they practiced memory less, they would actually become more forgetful and therefore less wise.[19]

Consider that even though our advanced technology can often be a tremendous help in many areas in life, sometimes it prevents us from recalling or maintaining knowledge because it decreases our memory power. Sharpening your memory through practice exercises such as the ones mentioned in this chapter will help you not only memorize your speeches effectively but also store important information in your brain so you can use it whenever you need it.

19. Plato, *Phaedrus*, trans. Alexander Nehemas and Paul Woodruff (Indianapolis, IN: Hackett Publishing, 1995), 79–80.

Review Exercises

Explain

1. Explain the method of *loci*.

2. Explain two other techniques you can use to remember or memorize concepts or facts.

Building Copiousness

Review

Review your old quotes.

Practice

Practice saying the quotes to someone in your class, or practice writing them down on paper.

Memorize

Memorize your new quote:

> I know nothing except the fact of my ignorance. —Socrates[20]

Practicing Memory

Memorize

Choose a short poem, a list of ten vocabulary words, or some other list and memorize it using some of the devices mentioned in this chapter. Your teacher will present options from which you can choose.

Everyday Debate

Debate

Debate the following proposition: "Resolved: We should never say something about someone behind her back that we wouldn't say to her face." As you develop your argument for your side, use as many of the different argument types as possible that we have studied in this book. If you need to, consult the arguments and appeals chart in the appendix. When you are done, use one of the memory devices discussed in this chapter to memorize your speech. You will deliver this speech using no notes.

20. Ratcliffe, *Oxford Dictionary of Quotations*, 268.

Learning from the Masters

Observe

Watch the first question-and-answer section on the Intelligence Squared debate on illegal immigration and then answer the questions below (Link 24-3).

Moderator John Hockenberry asked the speakers the following questions: "To those supporting the proposition, how would you define success? How many fewer illegal immigrants should be in the country for our policies to be considered successful? To those against the proposition, how many of the 12 million illegal immigrants should be allowed to stay?"

Explain

What was Heather MacDonald's response to John Hockenberry's question above? (She is for the proposition.)

____

____

____

____

____

____

Discuss

Use the rebuttal techniques discussed in chapter 23 to discuss possible weaknesses with MacDonald's answer.

Explain

What was Enrique Morones's response to John Hockenberry's question above? (He is against the proposition.)

____

____

____

____

____

Discuss

Use the rebuttal techniques discussed in chapter 23 to discuss possible weaknesses with Morones's answer.

Explain

1. Audience member Jerry Orstrom asked, "Heather, given my blind luck in being born American, how can I deny this privilege to others?" How did MacDonald respond to Orstrom?

____

____

____

____

2. Explain one possible weakness of MacDonald's response.

____

____

____

____

3. How did Mark Krikorian respond to Orstrom?

____

____

____

____

4. How did Morones respond to Orstrom?

____

____

____

____

Discuss

What is one possible weakness of Morones's argument?

The Big Debate: Gun Control

Practice

Build your confidence by practicing the presentation of your argument on this topic to a friend or your debate team members. Make sure you do so without using notes. Talk to your friend (or team members) the way you would if you were explaining your ideas over coffee or in your living room at home. In situations like these, you don't worry initially very much about how you sound or whether or not you are remembering every part of the argument. Rather, you concentrate on communicating your ideas as clearly and coherently as possible so that your friend understands what you are talking about. If you practice explaining your speech in this way several times, you will become much more comfortable about the logic and the organization of your argument. When you eventually present your argument in a formal debate, it will be far less threatening because you will have already rehearsed it several times and will be familiar with the different parts of your argument.

Chapter 25

25

Delivery: Keys to Effective Presentation

> I HAVE DISCOVERED A UNIVERSAL RULE WHICH SEEMS TO APPLY MORE THAN ANY OTHER IN ALL HUMAN ACTIONS OR WORDS: NAMELY, TO STEER AWAY FROM AFFECTATION AT ALL COSTS, AS IF IT WERE A ROUGH AND DANGEROUS REEF, AND (TO USE PERHAPS A NOVEL WORD FOR IT) TO PRACTISE IN ALL THINGS A CERTAIN NONCHALANCE WHICH CONCEALS ALL ARTISTRY AND MAKES WHATEVER ONE SAYS OR DOES SEEM UNCONTRIVED AND EFFORTLESS.
> —BALDESAR CASTIGLIONE,
> *THE BOOK OF THE COURTIER*[1]

For hundreds of years, people have tried to learn (and teach others) the art of being—or at least appearing to be—confident, easy, and natural in their speeches and interactions with others. In fact, the quote at the beginning of this chapter comes from *The Book of the Courtier*, which was written by a sixteenth-century author named Baldesar Castiglione. The purpose of the book was to do this very thing: to teach people how to act with grace and confidence.[2] People today still wonder about how to build confidence, or at least how to make others believe they have confidence, especially when they are giving speeches in front of people. Now, in one sense, there is no special magic trick that will make you instantly graceful and nonchalant in front of people. It is true that, as with many things, grace and ease come with much practice. However, there are a few tricks you can learn to help you appear and feel more at ease; there are also a few things you should avoid that could make you feel and appear less confident. When speakers try to increase their confidence, grace, and poise on stage, they generally focus on several key areas: eye contact, voice projection and articulation, posture, dress, and gestures. You will examine each of these areas in turn.

The Audience Is on Your Side

First, before you look at different aspects of a strong speaking presence, you should examine the concept of confidence in general. Let's address a fact of which you are likely already aware: Most people fear public speaking. If we were to ask most people why they fear speaking so much, many people would say that this fear stems from a common cause—they fear looking foolish in front of others. This is an understandable fear, but it's one that people can learn to overcome if they focus on a few important facts concerning public speaking.

1. Baldesar Castiglione, *The Book of the Courtier* (London: Penguin Group, 1976), 67.

2. Ibid.

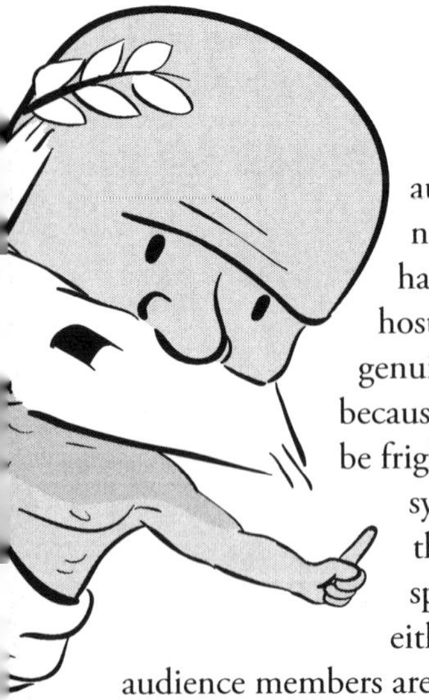

You should know that most audiences want you to succeed, not fail. Very few people ever have to give speeches in front of hostile audiences. In general, people genuinely want speakers to succeed because audience members know it can be frightening to give speeches, and they sympathize with the speaker. Since they would not want to fail giving a speech, they don't want a speaker to, either. In addition, realize that most audience members are more concerned about themselves than they are about the people around them. Sometimes we get the idea that everyone is looking at us and thinking bad things about us. But in actuality, though people think of us occasionally, most people are thinking more about themselves, their lives, and their problems. How many times have you listened to a speaker and your mind has wandered to things concerning your own life and responsibilities? This is the same of all people in an audience; they won't be nitpicking everything you say or do because they aren't focused on you alone. Therefore, speakers shouldn't worry that everyone in an audience is thinking about them and all their faults and how they will fail. This just isn't realistic.

In addition, a lot of people worry about whether they sound interesting or whether their ideas are worthwhile. Of course, there are some speakers who may be more knowledgeable and skilled than others. However, it's important to realize that every person, because of his personality and life situations, has a unique outlook on life and people. Therefore, everyone has an idea to share that is truly unique. Furthermore, if you act like yourself, your personality and ideas are going to be attractive to other people who have similar interests and ideas. If you stay true to who you are, you will feel more comfortable sharing a point that is interesting and unique to your interests, personality, and/or ideals, and people—especially those like you—will be interested in hearing about it. Gaining confidence is often a matter of recognizing that most people are more worried about themselves than you, and realizing that you, indeed, have something worthwhile and meaningful to say. Just relax and be yourself.

Memorization

Speaking confidently mirrors and encourages your own personal confidence, so building this will certainly help you. Another really important method for growing your speaking confidence is establishing familiarity with your material. Except for in a few special situations, it is not necessary for you to memorize your speech word for word. What is necessary is that you become very knowledgeable about the different parts of your speech. That is, each part of your speech has a specific idea or argument it is trying to communicate. You need to gain a strong familiarity with the basic concepts of each part of your speech and the order in which these ideas flow. One way you can do this is to use the memorization techniques you learned in the last chapter.

Another method for gaining familiarity is to practice telling people about the arguments in your speech. For example, if Christy wanted to build confidence for presenting her speech about capital punishment, she should first organize her speech. Then she could practice explaining her arguments to her parents, her sibling, and a few of her friends during the week before her speech. At this point, Christy will have done a lot of research for her speech, and she will have a general idea of her key arguments. If she practices simply explaining these arguments to her friends, with or without notes, she will grow even more familiar with her arguments, and she'll feel increasingly more comfortable reciting them. In fact, it will go a long way toward helping her memorize her arguments. If you think about it, this type of practice makes sense because we all do this every day. For instance, when someone asks us why we like a particular movie, we don't worry about whether or not we sound organized or impressive. We just tell them our opinion. If someone asks you about a more serious topic, such as whether you think video games are good for teenagers, you should be able to generally explain your ideas because you are just having a normal, everyday conversation. Practicing explaining your arguments in everyday conversational settings will help you gain more confidence.

Eye Contact

Once you have built your own personal confidence and become familiar with your topic, one of the first presentation aspects you need to work on is eye contact. Have you ever listened to a speaker who read from his notes throughout the whole speech and rarely ever looked at the audience? I don't know about you, but when a speaker reads from his notes and fails to make consistent eye contact, I don't feel as though he is actually talking to me. It appears as though he is having his own little monologue up there on the stage, and I just happen to be present in the room. When this happens, it's very easy for the audience to get bored and distracted. Therefore, after you build your own confidence and become familiar with your material, you need to work on your eye contact. After all, you don't want to bore your audience, do you? There is an old dictum that states that one way you can keep calm while giving a speech is to look just above your audience members' heads. This tip may help you remain composed if you have not practiced your speech a lot and are struggling with nervousness; however, it's actually much better to make a point to look at all of your audience members in the eye. This is because your audience can often tell the difference between when you are looking at them and when you are looking over them. Work on becoming very comfortable and familiar with your speech, and then practice making eye contact with each member of your audience. This will help them to feel more connected to you and will draw them into your speech.

Developing engaging eye contact is one of the more difficult skills of effective presentation. Strong eye contact means sustained, meaningful contact. But it is often best to build yourself slowly up to this, if eye contact is difficult for you. You can start by looking in the direction of individual audience members, before you build up to engaging them in direct eye contact. You can quickly scan the room to make contact with more individuals before you build up to making eye contact for one or two seconds at a time with each audience member. You can start by looking up from your prepared writing or notes every third sentence, then every other sentence, then for half of a given sentence. Remember, quick eye contact looks like nervous eye contact—if your habit of eye contact is to flit your gaze across the room like a hummingbird, your audience will feel less comfortable with you. On the other hand, most speakers naturally tend to make continual eye contact with several audience members who, for whatever reason, stand out; avoid anchoring your gaze to only a few key members—be sure to share your gaze with the rest of the audience as well.

Voice Articulation

Another important part of your speech presentation is articulation. It's important to remember that speaking on stage is not the same as speaking to someone in a conversation. In a conversation, you can speak softly and mumble your words or run them together, and the person you are speaking to will likely still understand. In a speech, the physical distance between you and an audience creates a barrier, and this barrier makes it extra difficult to interpret soft, mumbled words. Therefore, volume and articulation become especially important. The best way to improve in this area is to practice your speech several times before an audience and to ask them if they both heard and understood you.

There are several tips you can keep in mind to help you out. First, you need to speak slowly enough that you can articulate all of the sounds in the words you speak—consonants are especially important because they are the sounds by which we most commonly identify words, and if you hit all your consonants, you will likely punctuate the vowels as well. Be sure, then, to speak slowly enough that all of your consonants are clear.

Next, work on developing a full, rich voice. A lot of us speak from our chests, but if you speak from your diaphragm, you will have a much fuller voice.[3] Your diaphragm is the muscle that separates your lungs from your stomach area—your gut. So when you speak, project your voice in such a way that your gut pushes out a little bit, as though it was forcing your words out. To hone a richer speaking voice, practice reciting your speech to a person sitting across the room, or speak in wide outdoor spaces, where you are forced to project clearly and forcefully.

3. Those of you who have sung in choirs may have been instructed to sing from your diaphragm. The goal here is the same: you are trying to project your voice with strength.

Gestures

Lastly, as you become more comfortable with eye contact, articulation, and volume, consider incorporating hand gestures, which, if used thoughtfully, can enhance your speech just as rhetorical devices do. To help you consider how to use hand gestures effectively, recognize that there are different reasons we use hand gestures. One reason is to emphasize an important point in your speech. Sometimes a speaker will emphasize a specific point by pounding or tapping her podium, or making an emphatic arm gesture in the air. Another reason that you could choose to use a hand gesture is to point out someone in the room you are talking about. For instance, if you are referring to your opponent, you might indicate her by sweeping your hand in her direction. You can also use hand gestures to help describe an idea. For example, if you are discussing something that appears at a distance, you might use a gesture that illustrates this. You could point off toward the horizon to help your audience picture something that is far away. Sometimes as I am teaching a class, I will refer to something outdoors to illustrate a point. It is very natural for me to gesture toward the window, as though as I am directing the students' attention outside. Keep in mind that gestures should be used sparingly and judiciously (similar to using salt to season food) in order to add a little extra emphasis to your speech. If you use hand gestures too frequently, you may start to look cartoonish or overly dramatic, which could result in the audience not taking you seriously.

In the last chapter you memorized a poem, a quote, or vocabulary to practice the memory techniques you learned. Deliver as a speech what you memorized, using one or more of the types of gestures discussed in this chapter. It is not necessary to use a gesture if it doesn't feel natural and comfortable as you speak. Rather, you want to try to find places in your speech where a gesture naturally seems to fit and also could lend some emphasis.

Notice the gestures that others use when they speak. Periodically, try adopting others' movements and see how they feel. Even if these movements do not feel natural at first, don't be afraid to expand beyond your comfort zone and add different motions to your speaking style.

In conclusion, here are some general rules about behaviors you should avoid when speaking: Don't shift on your feet while you are speaking. Plant your feet firmly on the ground about shoulder-width apart to give you balance—be sure to gently bend your knees so that you don't lock them and pass out or fall. Avoid clasping your hands behind or in front of you, as this can look strained, uncomfortable, or too stiff. A more natural pose is to place your arms at your sides or rest them on a podium. Lastly, avoid common speech distractions such as rustling your papers, flipping your hair (especially if you have long hair), or frequently clearing your voice. These are some of the most common distractions people unconsciously engage in when presenting a speech; being aware of them can help you avoid them. After all, you can't fix a problem if you aren't aware it exists.

We are rarely conscious of our delivery habits. As you practice a speech or delivery of an argument, ask someone to sit down and write down every distracting or repetitive thing you do (or, if you have the ability to do so, record yourself practicing). How many of those behaviors were you aware of as you gave the speech? Were there any behavioral patterns you did that you never noticed about yourself before? Being conscious of those tendencies can help you avoid redundancy, little by little, as you become more and more effective as a speaker. Think about ways to break these distracting habits in the future.

Review Exercises

List

List three aspects of your physical presentation that you should be aware of when you give a speech.

Explain

1. How can you improve eye contact?

2. Explain the general rule to remember for using hand gestures.

List

List three things you should not do when you give a speech.

____

____

____

____

____

____

____

Building Copiousness

Review

Review your old quotes.

Practice

Practice saying the quotes to someone in your class, or practice writing them down on paper.

Memorize

Memorize your new quote:

The unexamined life is not worth living. —Socrates[4]

4. Susan Ratcliffe, ed., *Oxford Dictionary of Quotations by Subject*, 2nd ed. (Oxford: Oxford University Press, 2010), 361.

Everyday Debate

Debate

Hold a debate on the following proposition: "Resolved: Dogmatism is dangerous."

As you develop your argument for your side, use as many of the different argument types as you can that we have studied in this book. If you need to, consult the arguments and appeals chart in the appendix. Deliver your argument from memory, and pay special attention to your eye contact, articulation, and gestures.

Learning from the Masters

Observe

Watch the second question-and-answer section in the Intelligence Squared debate on illegal immigration, then answer the questions that follow (Link 25-1).

> Moderator John Hockenberry asked Enrique Morones and Karen Narasaki, "Do you believe that everyone should be able to come here to America?"

Discuss

1. What were the responses to this question?
2. Are these good responses to the question? Why or why not?

List

John Hockenberry then asked Griswold and Morones, "Is there any enforcement of immigration that you think is good?" List at least two responses to this question.

Discuss

Discuss the strengths and weaknesses of these responses.

Observe

Watch three different versions of Shakespeare's famous "To be or not to be . . ." speech from *Hamlet*.[5]

The Big Debate: Gun Control

Observe

One of the best ways to improve your speechmaking skills is to watch yourself delivering a speech. Make a recording of yourself speaking (or have somebody else do the recording for you) with a cell phone, computer, video camera, or other device. (If you aren't sure whether or not your phone or computer has these features, ask a friend or family member to help you.) Once the recording is finished, watch it and critique yourself. Look for any potentially distracting speaking habits. For instance, you might notice yourself frequently saying "um," playing with your hair, or looking away from the camera off into the distance. Most people have some type of speaking idiosyncrasy of which they are unaware. Watching a recording of yourself speaking helps you become aware of these distracting habits so that you can fix them before you speak in front of an actual audience.

5. The idea of comparing the versions of *Hamlet* was suggested to me by Ralph Janikowsky, upper school principal, teacher, and debate coach at Rockbridge Academy, Millersville, MD, in a discussion with me during the summer of 2009.

Chapter 26

Other Types of Debates

> FACTS DO NOT CEASE TO EXIST BECAUSE THEY ARE IGNORED.
> —ALDOUS HUXLEY[1]

Now that you understand basic debate structure, it may interest you to know that there are several different types of debates common in the United States. Each kind of debate can help you develop different skills or varied styles of speaking. In this chapter, I will be focusing on team policy debate, Lincoln-Douglas debates, public forum debates, and congressional debates. These are the four most common debates that you will participate in if you are involved in high school debate tournaments.[2] By developing an understanding of what these debate structures are like, as well as knowledge of some of the most well-known debate associations, you will have some basic tools at your disposal if you and your teachers are interested in starting a high school debate team.

Team Policy Debate

Probably the most historically common type of tournament debate is the **team policy debate**, which is debate that centers on a specific policy that the government should or should not adopt.[3] For example, here are several resolutions someone in team policy might debate:

> Resolved: The federal government should adopt a comprehensive, long-term agricultural policy in the United States.[4]
>
> Resolved: The federal government of the United States should establish a foreign policy that significantly limits the use of weapons of mass destruction.[5]
>
> Resolved: The US federal government should substantially increase social services for persons living in poverty in the United States.[6]

You may have noticed that these resolutions are general and wide open for broad discussion. This is one of the interesting things about team policy debate. The leaders of a team policy tournament or league pick the topic at the beginning of the year, and this is the debate topic for the entire year. When students go to a tournament to participate in a team policy debate, they don't know which side of the resolution they

1. Susan Ratcliffe, ed., *Oxford Dictionary of Quotations by Subject*, 2nd ed. (Oxford: Oxford University Press, 2010), 167.
2. David Arnett (director of debate at the University of Kentucky, Lexington, KY), telephone interview with the author, February 3, 2015.
3. Arnett interview.
4. Taken directly from Glen Whitman, "Team Policy Debate," *Debate*, page last modified September 5, 2000, http://www.csun.edu/~dgw61315/debformats.html#policy.
5. Taken directly from "Past Policy Topics, 2001-2002" in "About Speech and Debate," National Speech and Debate Association, http://www.speechanddebate.org/pastpolicytopics.
6. Taken directly from "2009–2010 National High School Debate Topic: Poverty," Economic Thinking: Understanding and Creating Prosperity, http://www.economicthinking.org/poverty/index.html.

will be on. Furthermore, they don't know which aspect of the topic the other team is going to argue for.[7] As you can imagine, with a broad topic such as the second resolution provided (regarding America's policy toward weapons of mass destruction), there are many possible aspects of this topic about which someone could argue. Therefore, in order to prepare for team policy debate, participants must do exhaustive research on *all* of the possible cases or issues that could be argued under that specific topic.[8]

The other interesting characteristic of modern team policy debate is that speakers sometimes speak extremely fast and use very specific jargon.[9] Over the years, some team policy debaters have developed some unique terms that refer to key concepts or aspects of team policy debate. This jargon acts as a type of verbal shorthand in team policy debates. That is, using these particular words or jargon allows people presenting a speech to communicate a range of ideas in one word or phrase. The problem is that the jargon used by some team policy debaters is not familiar to the everyday, average person on the street.[10] Team policy debate emphasizes good research and organizational abilities, but some people in the debate community started to feel that this format had become too technical and removed from the everyday person. They thought that the emphasis on exhaustive research deemphasized the skills of improvisational persuasive reasoning, as well as ethical and philosophical reasoning.[11]

Lincoln-Douglas Debate

Because some within the debate community grew disenchanted with team policy debate, a format was developed called **Lincoln-Douglas debates**. Lincoln-Douglas debates focus on values such as justice and morality, rather than on policies.[12] Because of this, they are also sometimes called value debates. Here are some examples of resolutions people might propose for a Lincoln-Douglas debate:

> Resolved: In the United States, private ownership of handguns ought to be banned.
>
> Resolved: In the United States criminal justice system, jury nullification ought to be used in the face of perceived injustice.
>
> Resolved: Adolescents ought to have the right to make autonomous medical choices.[13]

As you can see, because a Lincoln-Douglas debate pertains to values, rather than policy, people participating in this type of debate will have to use logic and philosophy more than facts alone to prove their points, as you can't prove the justice or morality of something through facts alone. A person could certainly use facts to help explain debate details, but the emphasis is placed more heavily on logic. Because Lincoln-Douglas debates developed as a reaction to the fast-speaking, jargon-laden format of team policy debates, speakers in Lincoln-Douglas debates usually talk at a slower, more conversational rate than team policy debaters. Interestingly, however, over the last few years, Lincoln-Douglas debates have started to become more jargon-laden and fast-paced like team policy debate. As a result, other debate formats have become more popular in reaction to this.[14]

Public Forum Debate

A new type of debate that is becoming increasingly popular is **public forum debate**, which focuses on current topics. Two of the goals of public forum debate are that not only should an average, everyday person be able to easily understand what the debate is about, but she should also be able to judge the debate.[15] Because of the audience-friendly, practical goals of this debate format, the people who form the resolutions for these debates try to form them as though they were based on current events.[16] For instance, the National Speech and Debate Association has debated the following resolutions:

7. Arnett interview.
8. Ibid.
9. Diane Lockman (classical educator, author of several books, and debate coach), telephone interview with author, June 2009.
10. Arnett interview.
11. Lockman interview.
12. Ibid.
13. All three sample debate topics are taken directly from "Past Lincoln-Douglas Debate Topics, 2015–2016," in "About Speech and Debate," National Speech and Debate Association, http://www.speechanddebate.org/pastlincolndouglastopics.
14. Lockman interview.
15. Arnett interview.
16. bid.

Resolved: On balance, economic sanctions are reducing the threat Russia poses to Western interests.

Resolved: On balance, standardized testing is beneficial to K-12 education in the United States.

Resolved: In response to the current crisis, a government should prioritize the humanitarian needs of refugees over its national interests.[17]

Public forum debate will be attractive to many students because of its practical, everyman appeal.

Congressional Debate

A fourth common tournament debate style is **congressional debate**. Congressional debate tournament events simulate a session of congress. Just as members of congress do, students develop and propose bills, and then the students in the congress debate these proposed bills. A congressional debate in a debate tournament will look a lot like a meeting of congress in our government.[18] This style of debate can be very attractive to students who wish both to gain experience in speaking and debate and who also wish to gain a deeper understanding of how our government works.

If you become involved in debate in high school and enjoy it, it may help you to know that many local colleges have debate teams. College debate teams can be helpful to high school debate teams in two ways. First, students who enjoy debate in high school should know that their debating career does not need to end when they graduate from high school. Some colleges and universities offer partial or even full scholarships for debate. In addition, many college debate teams are willing to visit local high schools and offer debating strategies and tips, and even hold mock debates to show students how debate works. One such college debate organization that may be able to work with high schools is the National Educational Debate Association (NEDA).[19] NEDA's website home page states that they are especially interested in debate styles that "reflect the stylistic and analytical skills that would be rewarded in typical public forums (i.e., courts, congress, the classroom, civic gatherings, etc.)."[20] NEDA is a debate association for colleges and college students, but if their debate vision appeals to you as a high school student, you can contact them to gain more information about their debate format and about middle and high school debate tournaments that practice a similar type of debate.[21]

Depending on what type of debate format is used, the order of presentations will differ considerably. For some of these debates, there is only one person on a team. For others, there are two people on a team. All of these formats have times for affirmative and negative presentations, as well as rebuttal. Some of them, however, also have a second presentation time when both the affirmative and negative teams elaborate, clarify, and strengthen their positions. In addition, while most of them have cross-examination times, some of may include secondary cross-examination times.

Keep in mind that if you have enjoyed learning about and practicing debate, then you might be a good candidate for formal debate. And, depending on the particular aspects of debate you enjoy, certain types of debate might be better suited to you. If you like exhaustive research and an intense competitive atmosphere, team policy debate might be the right fit for you. If you like the more logical and philosophical aspects of debate, Lincoln-Douglas might be for you. If you appreciate the logical and persuasive sides of debate, and if you care a lot about exploring issues pertinent to society and politics, then public forum and congressional

17. All three sample debate topics are taken directly from "Past Public Forum Topics, 2015–2016," in "About Speech and Debate," National Speech and Debate Association, http://www.speechanddebate.org/pastpublicforumtopics.
18. Arnett interview.
19. Clint Jones, PhD (director of debate at Transylvania University, Lexington, KY), interview with the author, March 2014.
20. See "Welcome," National Educational Debate Association, http://www.neda.us/.
21. Thank you to my colleague Clint Jones, director of debate at Transylvania University in Lexington, Kentucky, for information about NEDA. Jones suggested that debate clubs interested in NEDA's styles of debate might be able to find a college debate team willing to visit a local middle or high school and hold a practice debate to show the debate club how NEDA's debate style works.

debate formats are probably the best options for you. All of these different formats can help you develop a variety of skills and interests.

If you would like to learn more about organized debate, check out the following organizations:

NEDA: National Educational Debate Association (Link 26-1)

NAUDL: National Association for Urban Debate League (Link 26-2)

National Speech and Debate Association (Link 26-3)

Review Exercises

Explain

Do you find the idea of formal debate appealing? Why or why not? Which of the previously mentioned types of debate do you find most appealing? Why?

Building Copiousness

Review

Review your old quotes.

Practice

Practice saying the quotes to someone in your class, or practice writing them down on paper.

Memorize

Memorize your new quote:

In the realm of the emotions, the real is indistinguishable from the imaginary. —André Gide[22]

Everyday Debate

Debate

Debate the following proposition: "Resolved: Consistent family dinners are a necessary component of a good family life." As you develop your argument for your side, use as many of the different argument types as possible that you have studied in this book. If you need to, consult the arguments and appeals chart in the appendix. Use appropriate eye contact, articulation, and gestures.

Learning from the Masters

Observe

Watch the third and final question-and-answer session from the Intelligence Squared immigration debate (Link 26-4). Then answer the questions that follow.

Moderator John Hockenberry asked, "How specifically can we be more secure?"

Discuss

Discuss at least two responses to Hockenberry's question.

22. Ratcliffe, *Oxford Dictionary of Quotations*, 147.

Explain

Explain which answer you thought was the most effective.

The Big Debate: Gun Control

Debate

Deliver your debate for which you have been practicing your arguments.

After you present your argument and complete the debate, answer the following questions:

1. What do you think you did well in your debate?
2. What would you like to improve for next time?

Conclusion

Debate Opportunities in Life

> SO MANY WORLDS, SO MUCH TO DO,
> SO LITTLE DONE, SUCH THINGS TO BE.
> —ALFRED LORD TENNYSON[1]

Now that you have reached the end of *Everyday Debate & Discussion*, you may be wondering how to take your skills to the next level. If you are interested in formal debate, consider starting a debate team at your school if it does not already have one. Talk to your principal or headmaster and tell him the kind of debate club you would like to have. Ask if there is a faculty member who can sponsor it. Even if no faculty members are available, don't let that discourage you. It is very likely that a parent in your school (one of your parents or a friend's parent) would be willing to sponsor a club. The exciting thing about developing your own debate club is that you can form a club to match your specific interests. For instance, maybe you are really interested in holding debates like the Intelligence Squared debates you watched in class. Public forum debates would be a good kind of debate for this. Or perhaps you want to get involved much more with the political aspect of debate. Congressional debate could be a good format if you wish to explore this aspect of debate.

If you desire to challenge *yourself* consistently to develop better debate skills, there are many local and national organizations that you can join which will allow you to participate in all sorts of tournament and debate competitions. The National Speech and Debate Association is the largest and most prominent debating organization for high school students in America. In addition, you may also enjoy participating in mock trial competitions, which simulate a courtroom trial experience. In this activity, you develop skills in legal debate. If you loved the process of participating in a debate during your studies of this book this year, formal debate and debate club might be a good option for you.

On the other hand, you may have found during your studies of this book that while you liked the process of research and writing and formulating arguments, you didn't like the public speaking and arguing aspect of debate. Or you may have enjoyed it when you could debate an idea one on one with someone but not when you had to debate a topic in front of everyone else. If so, you may be a person who will enjoy informal debate much more than formal debate. The good news is that there are probably all sorts of activities going on around you that contain an informal debate structure. For example, you may be aware that many people belong to book clubs, in which members read a book every month and then meet to discuss and critique the book. This type of discussion is certainly an informal debate, as club members must present and defend ideas and critique other ideas. However, these discussions are usually very nonthreatening and casual.

1. Susan Ratcliffe, ed., *Oxford Dictionary of Quotations by Subject*, 2nd ed. (Oxford: Oxford University Press, 2010), 203.

In addition, colleges and universities often hold lectures in which an academic or cultural leader presents a speech on a certain topic and then people have time afterward to ask questions. This cross-examination time is much like the cross-examination time of a debate, although not as intense. Furthermore, colleges will often hold panel discussions in which a various experts on an issue meet as a panel and each gives a short presentation on the topic, and a question-and-answer session follows. Though this is very similar to the Intelligence Squared debate format, it also may not be as intense. You may have realized that although you do not enjoy participating in public debates, you do enjoy hearing them and, possibly, participating by asking questions. Consider attending lectures like this or even organizing one at your own school.

No matter whether you continue to participate in formal debate or whether you prefer informal debates, remember that the skills of logic, listening, and questioning—the skills of dialectic or conversation—are skills that will help you in every area of life as you search for the truth and the answer to life's great questions. In closing, consider a famous quote by Socrates: "The greatest good for a man [is] to discuss virtue every day . . . for the unexamined life is not worth living."[2]

2. Plato, *Apology*, in *Plato: Five Dialogues: Euthyphro, Apology, Crito, Meno, Phaedo*, trans. G.M.A. Grube, 2nd ed. (Indianapolis, IN: Hackett Publishing, 2002), 41.

Review Exercises

Learning from the Masters

Observe and Explain

Watch the closing arguments from the Intelligence Squared immigration debate (Link 27-1), then explain which one you think is the most effective and why.

Glossary

Accent: Accent is a fallacy of ambiguity in which a change in emphasis (usually due to pronunciation or tone) within a statement distorts its meaning.

Acrostic: An acrostic is a list of items to remember, each line of which has a first letter or first word that makes a new word that acts as the memory device.

***Ad hominem*:** From the Latin phrase meaning "at the man," *ad hominem* is a fallacy committed when someone insults his opponent in an argument rather than disproving the opponent's argument.

Affirmative presentation: The affirmative presentation is the time in a debate when the affirmative side presents the arguments in favor of the resolution.

Affirmative side: The affirmative side in a formal debate is the side which argues for the proposition.

Alliteration: Alliteration is the juxtaposition of words which contain the same consonant, often at the beginning of the word.

Anadiplosis: Anadiplosis is the repetition of a word which is at the end of one phrase or clause and is at the beginning of the next word or clause.

Analogue: An analogue is one of the two items compared to something similar but different in an analogy.

Analogy: An analogy is an argument tool that compares an abstract idea to a similar, simpler concept that is more common and clear. The simpler concept illustrates the more abstract idea.

Anamnesis: Anamnesis is reciting past events or even the words of an authority from memory.

Anaphora: Anaphora is the repetition of words or phrases at the beginning of successive clauses or sentences.

Anomaly: An anomaly is an exception to a rule. It is an example that doesn't fit the pattern.

Antithesis: Antithesis is the balance and symmetry in a sentence created by the juxtaposition of two ideas which are similar in structure but opposite in meaning.

Antonyms: Antonyms are words that have opposite meanings.

Aposiopesis: Aposiopesis occurs when someone is silent after speaking or when he is deliberately silent for a short time as if to meditate or to quietly contemplate on the matter at hand.

Glossary

Apostrophe: Apostrophe occurs when someone addresses an inanimate object as though it had thoughts and emotions.

Appeal to illegitimate authority: This fallacy occurs when someone uses the authority of an expert in one field to prove a point in another field.

Appeal to novelty: Appeal to novelty occurs when someone argues that because something is new, it is good. Another way people commit this fallacy is when they argue that what is newer is always better than what is older.

Appeal to pathos: Appeals to pathos are argument techniques that stir emotion in relation to the subject under discussion.

Appeal to tradition: Appeal to tradition is a fallacy that occurs when someone argues that because something has always been done or believed, it is right to do or believe it.

***A priori*:** *A priori* beliefs are beliefs that are accepted at the outset of an argument. They are foundational beliefs in that they are accepted as given. Truths that are *a priori* are truths that are discovered without investigation into the world. They are true because they are a matter of reason.

***Argumentum ad ignorantiam*:** This is a fallacy that occurs when someone argues that a proposition hasn't been proven and then draws a conclusion from this premise—either that the proposition is true or false.

Assonance: Assonance is the repetition of initial vowel sounds at the beginning of words.

Authoritative source: An authoritative source is a source written by an authority on the topic.

Authority: An authority on a topic is someone who has expertise on that subject because of extensive research or professional or educational training.

Bandwagon: This fallacy occurs when someone reasons that because everyone is doing or believing something that it should be done or believed.

Bias: A predisposition in favor of or against something.

Burden of proof: "Burden of proof" is a term referring to the responsibility of someone arguing contra to the status quo to prove his point, rather than the person who is defending the status quo.

***Cacozelia*:** *Cacozelia* occurs when someone uses many difficult or foreign words that people do not understand. It also occurs when someone uses shocking or disgusting metaphors and similes that offend and disturb the audience, rather than helping them understand a point.

Causation: The term *causation* describes a relationship between two events (X and Y) in which X brings about Y.

Ceremonial discourse: Ceremonial discourse is a discourse which occurs whenever someone praises or blames another, highlighting their accomplishments or criticizing their failings.

Circumstance: Circumstance is the common topic we use when we look at what we can learn from the past to apply to current situations.

Comic relief: Comic relief is a moment of lightness or humor interjected into an otherwise serious or tragic movie or book.

Common topics: The common topics are a method developed by Aristotle for discovering all of the available arguments for a topic.

Comparison: Comparison is a common topic that develops an argument by examining similarities, dissimilarities, and degree of similarity or dissimilarity.

Conclusion: The conclusion is the part of the speech when the speaker wraps up his arguments, reemphasizes important points, and leaves the audience with a strong concluding idea. An arresting quote, story, or a call to action is usually the best choice for a strong conclusion. In a debate, this usually comes at the end of the main argumentation section. In a syllogism, the conclusion is the part of an argument in which the speaker states what she believes.

***Confirmatio*:** *Confirmatio* is the part of the speech when the speaker offers his proof for the case. The most effective way to do this is often by stating arguments in order of importance and significance, from the least important or significant to the most important or significant.

Congressional debate: Congressional debate is a debate format which focuses on issues like those debated in the United States congress.

Conjecture: Conjecture pertains to whether something happened or not. The first question in stasis theory, "Did he do it?" pertains to whether or not a supposed crime or wrongdoing happened or not.[1]

Consonance: Consonance is the repetition of consonants in adjacent words, especially when these consonants are at the end of the word.

***Copia*:** An abundant supply of quotes, stories, and other material you can use to prove your point.

Correlation: The term "correlation" describes a relationship between two events (X and Y) in which X and Y occur together, but X does not necessarily cause Y.

Corroboration: Further confirmation or secondary confirmation of a view or an idea.

Critical: The word "critical" comes from the Latin word *criticus*, which means "able to discern or judge." Someone who is critical is able to discern and judge the strength of the evidence and logic of an argument or idea.

Critical thinking: Critical thinking is the systematic evaluation or formulation of beliefs, or statements, by rational standards.[2]

Cross-examination: Cross-examination is the part of the debate in which both the affirmative and negative sides ask each other questions to clarify points and expose weaknesses in the opposition's arguments.

Debate: To debate is to turn over in one's mind; to contend in words; the formal discussion of a motion before a deliberative body according to the rules of parliamentary procedure; a regulated discussion of a proposition between two matched sides.

Deductive logic: Deductive logic is the branch of logic that draws out inferences from statements. It determines the validity of a formal argument in which the conclusion must, necessarily, be true if the premises used to support it are true. Arguments are said to be "black" or "white" and cannot be "gray." (See also **inductive logic**.)

Definition: Definition pertains to what kind of action a particular action is. The second question in stasis theory, "Did he do it?" pertains to the kind of action a particular action is.[3] Also, definition is an explanation or illustration of a word. It is the first of Aristotle's common topics and explores the meaning of a word in order to develop an argument.

Deliberative discourse: Deliberative discourse is the type of persuasion someone might use when she is urging someone to think about (or deliberate about) a specific action to take.

---

1. See Gideon O. Burton, *Silva Rhetoricae*, s.v. "stasis," Brigham Young University, page last updated February 26, 2007, http://rhetoric.byu.edu/.
2. Lewis Vaughn, *The Power of Critical Thinking: Effective Reasoning about Ordinary and Extraordinary Claims*, 2nd ed. (New York: Oxford University Press, 2008), 4.
3. See Burton, *Silva Rhetoricae*, s.v. "definition," http://rhetoric.byu.edu/.

Dialectic: Dialectic is conversation in which people pursue the truth by exploring ideas, finding limitations and problems with those ideas and replacing them with clearer, better reasoned ideas.

Dictionary definition: A dictionary definition is a definition for a word found in a dictionary.

Discussion: A discussion is a discourse or conversation between two people in which a specific problem or idea is explored.

***Enargia*:** *Enargia* is a vivid description or retelling of an event. This device can be very effective in evoking pathos, especially when the scene or event being described is extremely tragic or brutal or glorious and pleasant.

Epideictic rhetoric: This is another term for ceremonial discourse.

***Epimone*:** *Epimone* is the repetition of a phrase or question or a plea used to evoke emotions.[4]

***Epiplexis*:** *Epiplexis* is the use of a question to evoke shame rather than to seek for an answer.

Ethical appeal: An ethical appeal is an argument technique that builds the speaker's credibility with the audience.

Ethos: Ethos is a quality in a person that allows them to convince the audience that he is good, right, and moral.

Etymology: Etymology is the study of a word's origins.

Euphony: Euphony is the quality of something having a pleasant, good, or sweet voice or sound.

Examples: Examples are instances or illustrations of a larger group or concept.

***Exordium*:** The *exordium* is the introduction to the speech. The goal in this is to catch the audience's attention and preview what the speech is about. The most common way to do this is to start it with a story or quote.

External sources: External sources are sources outside of us like books, interviews, articles, and documentaries that we consult to gather arguments and knowledge.

Fallacy: A fallacy is a commonly recognized type of poor argument; an error in reasoning.

False analogy: A false analogy is a fallacy in which someone makes a generalization based on a comparison of two things that are so dissimilar that no comparison can be made.

False cause: False cause is a fallacy someone commits when he reasons that because A happened before B, A caused B.

Figure: Figure is the arrangement of the middle term in a syllogism.

Flowing an argument: When you flow an opponent's argument, you outline his arguments and the claims he makes to support those arguments.

Formal debate: Formal debate is a type of debate that takes place before a judge or some other deliberative body and proceeds according to a set of previously established rules. This kind of debate usually takes places in a classroom or a debate competition.

Generalization: Generalization is the process of extrapolating broad theories or ideas from consistent patterns we observe in life.

Hasty generalization: A hasty generalization is a fallacy that occurs when someone bases a generalization on too small a sample size.

High style: High style is a style that is focused on charming or moving the audience. This is a style of speech used in grand orations or major political speeches.

4. Ibid., s.v. "epimone."

Impromptu: Impromptu means off the top of your head, without previous preparation.

Induction: Induction is logic based on generalization. People make observations from everyday life and then generalize a theory based on these observations.

Inductive logic: One of the two branches in the study of logic, inductive logic deals with ordinary language arguments that tend to start with evidence that can be observed and compiled, and works toward generalizations that are reasonably accurate with more or less probability. Arguments are said to be either "strong" or "weak."[5] (See also **deductive logic**.)

Infer: To arrive at new information through the application of other axioms, postulates, or observed examples.

Informal debate: Informal debate is a type of debate that is often more like a discussion. It takes place between two or more people in an informal setting such as the home, the car, or a coffee shop. In this type of debate, two people discuss an idea to figure out truth or a plan or simply to entertain themselves intellectually. There is rarely any kind of deliberative body or previously established rules in an informal debate.

Internal sources: A person's logic and experience are her internal sources. These are sources inside of her from which she can formulate arguments.

***Ipse dixit* fallacy:** This is another name for the fallacy of appeal to illegitimate authority. It occurs when someone relies on the testimony of someone who is not an authority in the matter under discussion.

Judicial discourse: Judicial discourse is a discourse pertaining specifically to what laws should be made.

Layperson: A layperson is someone who is not an expert or who is not a member of a particular profession.

Lincoln-Douglas debate: This type of debate focuses on values such as justice and morality rather than policies.

Litotes: Litotes is deliberate understatement.

Logic: Logic is the art and science of reasoning.

Logos: Logos is a Greek word meaning reason, ground, or account.

Low style: Low style is a type of speaking style a speaker uses when she wants to deliver basic facts in a clear and efficient way. This is a style often used in teaching.

Major term: The major term is the predicate of the conclusion.

Method of *loci*: The method of *loci* is a memory strategy which uses association between objects and place as a memory device.

Middle style: Middle style is a style of speaking that focus primarily on persuading. This is a style often used in persuasive speeches or arguments.

Middle term: The middle term is the term in a syllogism that appears twice in the premises and connects the other two terms in the premises.

Minor term: The minor terms is the subject of the conclusion.

Mnemonic device: A mnemonic device is a memory strategy that uses a sentence to help you remember a list of words or something else you wish to remember.

5. Shelly Johnson, *The Argument Builder: Constructing an Argument Piece by Piece* (Camp Hill, PA: Classical Academic Press, 2008), 179.

Mood: Mood is the configuration of positive and negative premises in a syllogism.

***Narratio*:** *Narratio* is the statement of the key facts, definitions relating to the topic and its history. It helps the audience understand what the speech is all about. The most common things people put in this part are definitions of key terms, pertinent history, and facts about how this subject is important for everyday life.

Negative presentation: The negative presentation is when the negative side presents the arguments against the resolution.

Negative side: The negative side in a formal debate is the side which argues against a proposition.

Parallelism: Parallelism is the repetition of similarly structured words or phrases.

Parallel syntax: Parallel syntax is an arrangement of words, phrases, clauses, or sentences so that they have the same structure and arrangement of words.

***Partitio*:** *Partitio* (also known as *divisio* or division) is the brief outlining of arguments to come.

Pathos: Pathos is a quality that arouses feeling of sadness, sympathy, pity, or sorrow.

***Peroratio*:** The *peroratio*, also known as the peroration, is the conclusion of a speech, in which the orator wraps up her case. Often this involves a brief summary of points and leaving the audience with a strong image or anecdote that serves as a final emotional appeal.

Policy: Policy pertains to what kind of laws apply to a certain action. The fourth question in stasis theory, "Is this the right venue for this issue?" pertains to what laws relate to a specific action and what actions should be taken regarding it.[6]

Predicate term: The term in a proposition that follows the verb and renames or describes the subject.

Premises: Premises are the evidence or proof supporting a conclusion.

Principle of charity: This principle of debate and discussion requires you to assume that your opponent is an intelligent, rational, and moral person and that she has legitimate reasons for believing what she does.

Proposition: A proposition is a statement that can be proven true or false. In a debate, a proposition clearly states the issue being debated.

Public forum debate: A public forum debate focuses on topics that are in the current headlines.

Quality: Quality pertains to what kind of a thing something is or the nature of an action. The third question in stasis theory, "Was it just/expedient" pertains to the nature of the action someone did.[7]

Quantifier: A word in a proposition, such as "all," "no," "some," and "some not," which signals the amount of a class that a proposition discusses.

Rebuttal: The rebuttal is the time in the debate when both the affirmative and negative sides critique each other's arguments.

***Refutatio*:** *Refutatio* is the part of the speech when the speaker discredits the opposition's key arguments. In a debate, this is typically done in a rebuttal.

Relationship: Relationship is the common topic which looks at how one factor influences another.

Resolution: The resolution is the proposition that two people or teams will argue in a debate.

---

6. See Burton, *Silva Rhetoricae*, s.v. "policy," http://rhetoric.byu.edu/.

7. See ibid., s.v. "quality."

Rhetoric: Rhetoric is the art and science of public speaking.

Rhetorical devices: Rhetorical devices are techniques for arranging words and phrases to increase the beautiful sound of language.

Rhetorician: One who practices the art of public speaking.

Sample: A sample is the number of examples considered in a statistic.

Self-deprecating humor: Self-deprecating humor is humor that a person directs at himself. It can often be used to build rapport with the audience because people who are willing to poke fun at themselves are often viewed as being humble, which often earns an audience's respect.

Sibilance: Sibilance is the repetition of the letter *s* in adjacent words.

Skimming: Skimming occurs when someone reads material quickly, picking out the key themes and overall ideas, rather than reading every word or sentence.

Special topics: The special topics are another list of ways you can develop a topic for unique situations that require different development techniques than the ones you might use when you are using the common topics. The special situation in which a person usually uses the special topics are instances of deliberative, judicial, and ceremonial discourse.

Stasis theory: Stasis theory is an ancient rhetoric strategy that uses four questions to help a speaker develop a clear understanding of his or her topic. The questions pertain to conjecture, definition, quality, and policy. The questions are "Did he do it?" (conjecture); "What did he do?" (definition); "Was it just/expedient?" (quality); and "Is this the right venue for this issue?" (policy).[8]

Statistic: A statistic is a numerical representation of examples.

Status quo: The status quo is the current state of things, the norm.

Stipulative definition: A stipulative definition is a reasonable definition for a word which one or two people create on the spot to help them clarify their debate topic.

Straw man fallacy: The straw man fallacy occurs when a person draws a conclusion from a caricatured or otherwise distorted version of his opponent's argument.

Subject term: The term in a proposition, or the subject, about which the proposition is written. It is the first noun term in the proposition.

Syllogism: A syllogism is an argument that contains a conclusion that is implied by two premises.

Synonyms: Synonyms are words that have the same or a similar meaning to another word.

Syntax: Syntax refers to the particular way that words are arranged in a sentence and the rules that govern this arrangement.

Team policy debate: Team policy debate is a type of debate that centers on a specific policy that the government should or should not adopt.

Terms: Term are words or phrases that represent a class of related things.

Testimony: Testimony is one of the common topics. The different types of testimony are quotes from authority, examples, statistics, and personal testimony.

8. See ibid., s.v. "stasis."

Toulmin model: The Toulmin model is a type or argument structure developed by the philosopher Stephen Toulmin. It contains four parts of an argument: (1) claim, (2) evidence, (3) warrant, and (4) reservations.

Valid: Valid is a term used to describe an argument in which the conclusion is implied by the premises.

Bibliography

"2009–2010 National High School Debate Topic: Poverty." Economic Thinking: Understanding and Creating Prosperity. http://www.economicthinking.org/poverty/index.html.

"About Speech and Debate." National Speech and Debate Association. http://www.speechanddebate.org/.

Albright, Madeleine. "A Breakthrough Night for Obama" (blog). *Huffington Post*. Originally posted October 27, 2008. http://www.huffingtonpost.com/madeleine-albright/a-breakthrough-night-for_b_129786.html.

Allen, Erika Tyner. "The Kennedy-Nixon Presidential Debates, 1960." *Museum of Broadcast Communication*. http://www.museum.tv/eotvsection.php?entrycode=kennedy-nixon.

Almonte, Paul, and Theresa Desmond. *Capital Punishment (Facts About Series)*. Parsippany, NJ: Crestwood House, 1991.

Arnett, David. (Director of debate at the University of Kentucky, Lexington, KY.) Telephone interview with the author. February 3, 2015.

Atsma, Aaron J., ed. *The Theoi Project: Greek Mythology*. 2000–2011. http://www.theoi.com/.

Australian Media Pty Ltd. "Cat Quotes." 2001. http://www.catquotes.com/catquotes1.htm.

Avildsen, John G., Jerry Weintraub, R.J. Louis, Robert Mark Kamen, James Crabe, Bud S. Smith, Walt Mulconery, et al. *The Karate Kid*. Released in theaters 1984. DVD. Directed by John G. Avildsen. Culver City, CA: Columbia Pictures, 2005.

Barrabi, Thomas. "Martin Luther King Quotes: 21 Memorable Sayings for MLK Day 2015." *International Business Times*. January 19, 2015. http://www.ibtimes.com/martin-luther-king-quotes-21-memorable-sayings-mlk-day-2015-1783820.

Bedau, Hugo, ed. *The Death Penalty in America: Current Controversies*. New York: Oxford University Press, 1998.

Bedau, Hugo, and Paul Cassel, eds. *Debating the Death Penalty: Should America Have Capital Punishment? The Experts on Both Sides Make Their Case*. New York: Oxford University Press, 2004.

Black, Todd, Kate Forte, Joe Roth, Denzel Washington, Oprah Winfrey, Robert Eisele, Jeffrey Porro, et al. *The Great Debaters*. Released in theaters 2007. DVD. Directed by Denzel Washington. New York: Weinstein Co., 2008.

Blackman, Paul. "The Armed Criminal in America." NRA-ILA. September 9, 2003. https://www.nraila.org/articles/20030909/the-armed-criminal-in-america.

Bonner, Raymond, and Ford Fessenden. "Absence of Executions: A Special Report; States With No Death Penalty Share Lower Homicide Rates." *New York Times*. September 22, 2000.

Bonta, James. "Retributive Justice and Recidivism." Vol. 8, no. 1. January 2003. http://www.publicsafety.gc.ca/cnt/rsrcs/pblctns/jstc-rcdvs/jstc-rcdvs-eng.pdf.

Branagh, Kenneth, Julie Christie, Derek Jacobi, et al. *Hamlet*. Released in theaters 1996. Digital. Directed by Kenneth Branagh.

Burton, Gideon O. *Silva Rhetoricae*. Brigham Young University. Page last updated February 26, 2007. http://rhetoric.byu.edu/.

Cafe, Rebecca. "Does the Public Want the Death Penalty Brought Back?" BBC News. August 4, 2011. http://www.bbc.com/news/uk-14402195.

"Capital Punishment in Canada." CBCNewsCanada. Last updated June 7, 2010. http://www.cbc.ca/news/canada/capital-punishment-in-canada-1.795391.

Castiglione, Baldesar. *The Book of the Courtier*. London: Penguin Group, 1976.

Cicero. *Rhetorica ad Herennium*. Translated by Harry Caplan. Cambridge, MA: Harvard University Press, 1954.

Cohen, Stanley. *The Wrong Men: America's Epidemic of Wrongful Death Row Convictions*. New York: Carrol and Graf Publishers, 2003.

Copeland, James M. "Debate." In *World Book Encyclopedia*. Chicago: World Book, 1992.

Copeland, Lewis M., et al, eds. *World's Great Speeches: Fourth Enlarged (1999) Edition*. Mineola, NY: Dover Publications, 1999.

Corbett, Edward P.J., and Robert J. Connors. *Classical Rhetoric for the Modern Student*. 4th ed. New York: Oxford University Press, 1999.

Cothran, Helen. *Gun Control (The Opposing Viewpoints Series)*. Farmington Hills, MI: Greenhaven Press, 2002.

Cramer, Clayton E., and David B. Kopel. " 'Shall Issue': The New Wave of Concealed Handgun Permit Laws." Independence Institute. 1994. Footnotes 158–159. http://rkba.org/research/cramer/shall-issue.html.

CTV.ca News Staff. "Obama Apologizes for Special Olympics Gaffe." CTV News. March 20, 2009. http://www.ctvnews.ca/obama-apologizes-for-special-olympics-gaffe-1.381398

Curd, Patricia, ed., and Richard D. McKirahan, trans. *A Pre-Socratic Reader: Selected Fragments and Testimonia*. Indianapolis, IN: Hackett Pub. Co., 1995.

Day, Nancy. *The Death Penalty for Teens: A Pro/Con Issue*. Berkeley Heights, NJ: Enslow Publishers, 2000.

Davies, Sir John. "Hymn I: Of Astraea." Luminarium: Anthology of English Literature. Last updated February 13, 2012. http://www.luminarium.org/renlit/astraea1.htm.

Death Penalty Information Center (DPIC). http://www.deathpenaltyinfo.org/part-i-history-death-penalty.

Dieter, Richard C. "The Death Penalty Is Not an Effective Law Enforcement Tool." In *Does Capital Punishment Deter Crime?* Edited by Stephen E. Schonebaum. San Diego: Greenhaven Press, 1998.

Douglas, Michael, Steven Reuther, Fred Fuchs, Francis Ford Coppola, Matt Damon, Claire Danes, Jon Voight, et al. *John Grisham's The Rainmaker*, special ed. Released in theaters 1997. DVD. Directed by Francis Ford Coppola. Hollywood, CA: Paramount Home Entertainment, 2007.

Driscoll, Marcy P. *Psychology of Learning for Instruction*. 2nd ed. Boston: Allyn and Bacon, 2000.

Durang, Chris. "Barak Did Great, McCain Okay But Angry" (blog). *Huffington Post*. Originally posted October 27, 2008. http://www.huffingtonpost.com/chris-durang/barack-did-great-mccain-o_b_129802.html.

Erickson, Stephen A. "John Locke." In *World Book Encyclopedia*. Chicago: World Book, 1992.

"Fast Food Consumption Increases Obesity Risk." *FoodNavigator.com*. May 24, 2004. http://www.foodnavigator.com/Science-Nutrition/Fast-food-consumption-increases-obesity-risk.

Fins, Deborah. "Death Row USA." Fall 2013. A Quarterly Report by the Criminal Justice Project of the NAACP Legal Defense and Education Fund, Inc. http://www.deathpenaltyinfo.org/documents/DRUSAFall2013.pdf.

Foster, Richard. "Spiritual Formation Agenda." *Christianity Today* 53, no. 1 (2009): 29–32.

Fox, M. "Cats." In *World Book Encyclopedia*. Chicago: World Book, 1992.

Freidel, Frank, and Hugh Sidey. "The Presidents: Andrew Jackson." The White House. From *The Presidents of the United States*. The White House Historical Association. 2006. http://www.whitehouse.gov/1600/presidents/andrewjackson.

Gavin, Philip. "Great Speeches Collection: Patrick Henry, Liberty or Death!" *The History Place*. http://www.historyplace.com/speeches/henry.htm

Gibson, Mel, Glenn Close, Helena Bonham Carter, et al. *Hamlet*. Released in theaters 1991. Digital. Directed by Franco Zeffirelli.

Great Speeches of the Twentieth Century. (Various speakers.) Rhino, 1991. CD.

Greer, John Michael. "The Art of Memory." *Renaissance Magazine*. 1997. http://www.renaissancemagazine.com/backissues/memory.html.

Haffey, Deborah Bush, Jeffrey B. Molter, and Christy L. Shipe. *Argumentation and Debate: Taking the Next Step*. Percellville, VA: Home School Legal Defense Association, 2004.

Henry, Patrick. "Give Me Liberty or Give Me Death." Delivered March 23, 1775, at Henrico Parrish Church St, Richmond, Virginia, Second Virginia Convention. American Rhetoric Online Speech Bank. http://www.americanrhetoric.com/speeches/patrickhenrygivemeliberty.html

Hines, Lilian, and Ruth B. Howard. *Our Latin Heritage*. Book III. New York: Harcourt, Brace, and World, 1967.

Hobbes, Thomas. "Leviathan." In *Ethics: History, Theory, and Contemporary Problems*. Edited by Steven M. Cahn and Peter Markie. New York: Oxford University Press: 2012.

Hodge, Joelle, Aaron Larsen, and Shelly Johnson. *The Discovery of Deduction: An Introduction to Formal Logic*. Camp Hill, PA: Classical Academic Press, 2009.

Indiana University School of Medicine. "Violent Video Games Alter Brain Function in Young Men." *ScienceDaily*. December 1, 2011. www.sciencedaily.com/releases/2011/11/111130095251.htm.

"Introduction to the Death Penalty," Death Penalty Information Center, 2015, http://www.deathpenaltyinfo.org/part-i-history-death-penalty.

Janikowsky, Ralph. (Upper school principal, teacher, and debate coach at Rockbridge Academy, Millersville, MD.) In discussion with the author. Summer 2009.

Jay, Ilona. "Is It a Crime to Enter the US Illegally?" All Law. 2015. http://www.alllaw.com/articles/nolo/us-immigration/crime-enter-illegally.html.

Johnson, Shelly. *The Argument Builder: Constructing an Argument Piece by Piece*. Camp Hill, PA: Classical Academic Press, 2008.

Jones, Clint. (Director of debate at Transylvania University, Lexington, KY.) In discussion with the author. Fall 2013.

———. (Director of debate at Transylvania University, Lexington, KY.) Interview with the author. March 2014.

"Jury Duty Joke." In "Archive for Wife Jokes." Great Clean Jokes, 2015. http://www.greatcleanjokes.com/jokes/marriage-humor/wife-jokes/.

Kagan, Donald. "Demosthenes." In *World Book Encyclopedia*. Chicago: World Book, 1992.

Katzen, Mollie, and Walter Willett. *Eat, Drink, and Weigh Less: A Flexible and Delicious Way to Shrink Your Waist without Going Hungry*. New York: Hyperion, 2006.

Kelley, David. *The Art of Reasoning*. 4th ed. New York: W.W. Norton, 2013.

Kennedy, Robert F. "Remarks on the Assassination of Martin Luther King Jr." Indianapolis, IN. April 4, 1968. http://www.americanrhetoric.com/speeches/rfkonmlkdeath.html.

Keyser, Amy Marcaccio. *Does Capital Punishment Deter Crime? (At Issue Series)*. Farmington Hills, MI: Greenhaven Press, 2007.

Kraut, Richard. "Plato." In *Stanford Encyclopedia of Philosophy*. September 11, 2013. http://plato.stanford.edu/entries/plato/.

Krogstad, Jens Manuel, and Jeffrey S. Passel. "Five Facts about Illegal Immigration in the U.S." Pew Research Center. July 24, 2015. http://www.pewresearch.org/fact-tank/2014/11/18/5-facts-about-illegal-immigration-in-the-u-s.

LaFeber, Walter. *Inevitable Revolutions: The United States in Central America*. 2nd ed. New York: W.W. Norton, 1993.

La Mare, Walter de. "Silver." All Poetry. http://allpoetry.com/poem/8494557-Silver-by-Walter-de-la-Mare.

Langan, Patrick A., and David J. Levin. "Recidivism of Prisoners Released in 1994." *Bureau of Justice Statistics Special Report*. US Department of Justice. June 2002. http://bjs.gov/content/pub/pdf/rpr94.pdf.

Larsen, Aaron, and Joelle Hodge, with Christopher A. Perrin. *The Art of Argument: An Introduction to the Informal Fallacies*. Camp Hill, PA: Classical Academic Press, 2010.

Lindemans, Micha J. "Janus." In *Encyclopedia Mythica*. Modified August 28, 1999. http://www.pantheon.org/articles/j/janus.html.

Lockman, Diane. (Classical educator, author of several books, and debate coach.) Telephone interview with author. June 2009.

Lyon, Bryce. "Magna Carta." In *World Book Encyclopedia*. Chicago: World Book, 1992.

Manning, Kenneth F. "Florence Nightingale." In *World Book Encyclopedia* (Chicago: World Book, 1992), 424.

Magee, Bryan. *The Story of Philosophy*. New York: Dorling Kindersley, 2001.

McCuen, Gary E. *The Death Penalty and the Disadvantaged (Ideas in Conflict)*. Hudson, WI: Gem Pubns, 1996.

McGinnis, Sean. "Dogs." In *World Book Encyclopedia*. Chicago: World Book, 1992.

National Educational Debate Association. http://www.neda.us/.

National Speech and Debate Association. http://www.speechanddebate.org.

NewsOne Staff. "Barack Obama Quotes: His Most Memorable Lines." NewsOne. September 20, 2012. http://newsone.com/2044176/barack-obama-quotes/.

Noe, Alva. "What Is the Funniest Joke in the World?" NPR Cosmos & Culture. March 7, 2014. http://www.npr.org/sections/13.7/2014/03/07/287250640/what-is-the-funniest-joke-in-the-world.

Obama, Barack. "2004 Democratic National Convention Keynote Address." Delivered July 27, 2004, Fleet Center, Boston. American Rhetoric Online Speech Bank. http://www.americanrhetoric.com/speeches/convention2004/barackobama2004dnc.htm.

"Obama-McCain Presidential Debate Reaction: HuffPost Bloggers Weigh In" (blog). *Huffington Post*. Originally posted October 27, 2008. http://www.huffingtonpost.com/huffingtonpost/presidential-debate-react_b_129793.html.

Olivier, Lawrence, and Jean Simmons, et al. *Hamlet*. Released in theaters 1948. Digital. Directed by Lawrence Olivier.

Park, Alice. "Little By Little, Violent Video Games Make Us More Aggressive." *Time.com.* March 24, 2014. http://time.com/34075/how-violent-video-games-change-kids-attitudes-about-aggression/.

Passuello, Luciano. "Develop Perfect Memory with the Memory Palace Technique." On Litemind website. http://litemind.com/memory-palace/.

Paul, Richard, and Linda Elder. *The Thinker's Guide to The Art of Socratic Reasoning.* Dillon Beach, CA: Foundation for Critical Thinking, 2006.

Perrin, Christopher. *An Introduction to Classical Education: A Guide for Parents.* Camp Hill, PA: Classical Academic Press, 2005.

Plato. *Apology.* In *Plato: Five Dialogues: Euthyphro, Apology, Crito, Meno, Phaedo.* 2nd ed. Translated by G.M.A. Grube. Indianapolis, IN: Hackett Publishing Company, 2002.

———. *Apology.* Translated by Benjamin Jowett. http://classics.mit.edu/Plato/apology.html.

———. *Euthyphro, Apology, Crito, Phaedo: The Death Scene.* Translated by F. J. Church. Upper Saddle River, NJ: Prentice Hall, 1948.

———. *Phaedrus.* Translated by Alexander Nehemas and Paul Woodruff. Indianapolis, IN: Hackett Publishing, 1995.

———. *The Republic.* Translated by George Maximilian Anthony Grube and C.D.C. Reeve. 2nd ed. Indianapolis, IN: Hackett Publishing Company, 1992.

———. *Theaetetus.* In *Plato: Complete Works.* Edited by John M. Cooper. Indianapolis, IN: Hackett Publishing Co., 1997.

Plutarch. "The Parallel Lives." In *Loeb Classical Library.* Edited by Jeffrey Henderson. Cambridge, MA: Harvard University Press, 1913.

Poe, Edgar Allen. "The Raven." *Anthology of American Literature, Volume 1: Colonial Through Romantic.* Edited by George McMichael, 4th ed. New York: MacMillan, 1989.

Pojman, Louis P. *Classics of Philosophy: Volume I: Ancient and Medieval.* New York: Oxford University Press, 1998.

———. "A Defense of the Death Penalty." In *Contemporary Debates in Applied Ethics.* Edited by Andrew I. Cohen and Christopher Heath Wellman. Chichester, UK: Wiley Blackwell, 2014.

"Politics, Courage and Death." Opinion column. *New York Times.* May 18, 1982. http://www.nytimes.com/1982/05/18/opinion/politics-courage-and-death.html.

Polsby, Daniel D. "Private Ownership of Handguns Leads to Lower Rates of Handgun Violence." In *Gun Control: Opposing Viewpoints.* Edited by Tamara L. Roleff. San Diego: Greenhaven Press, 1997.

Price, Marty. "Personalizing Crime: Mediation Produces Restorative Justice for Victims and Offenders." *Dispute Resolution Magazine.* Fall 2001. http://www.vorp.com/articles/justice.html.

Pring, J.T. *The Pocket Oxford Greek Dictionary.* New York: Oxford University Press, 2000.

Rapp, Christof. "Aristotle's Rhetoric." In *Stanford Encyclopedia of Philosophy.* February 1, 2010. Edward N. Zalta, ed. http://plato.stanford.edu/archives/spr2010/entries/aristotle-rhetoric/.

Ratcliffe, Susan, ed. *Oxford Dictionary of Quotations by Subject.* 2nd ed. Oxford: Oxford University Press, 2010.

Reeves, Richard, "Seattle-Vancouver Figures Prove Gun Control Does Work." *Sun-Sentinel.* September 27, 1992. http://articles.sun-sentinel.com/1992-09-27/news/9201240223_1_colin-loftin-homicides-and-suicides-gun-control-laws.

Reiser, Paul. "Obama Underwhelms, McCain Patronizes" (blog). *Huffington Post.* Originally posted October 27, 2008. http://www.huffingtonpost.com/paul-reiser/obama-underwhelms-mccain_b_129818.html.

Riddle, Maxwell. "Pets." In *World Book Encyclopedia.* Chicago: World Book, 1992.

"A Right to Bear Arms?" Exploring Constitutional Conflicts. http://www.law.umkc.edu/faculty/projects/ftrials/conlaw/beararms.htm.

"The Right to Keep and Bear Arms: Report of the Subcommittee on the Constitution of the United States Senate Ninety-Seventh Congress, Second Session." February 1982. http://www.constitution.org/mil/rkba1982.htm.

"Robert Kennedy: Delivering the News of King's Death." Echoes of 1968. April 4, 2008. http://www.npr.org/2008/04/04/89365887/robert-kennedy-delivering-news-of-kings-death.

Schumacher, Joel, Arnon Milchan, Michael Nathanson, Hunt Lowry, Akiva Goldsman, Elliot Goldenthal, Sandra Bullock, et al. *A Time to Kill,* widescreen ed. Released in theaters 1996. DVD. Directed by Joel Schumacher. Burbank, CA: Warner Home Video, 2009.

Seelye, Katharine Q. "McCain and Palin's Interview with Couric" (blog). *New York Times.* September 28, 2008. http://thecaucus.blogs.nytimes.com/2008/09/29/mccain-and-palins-interview-with-couric/comment-page-28/?_r=2.

———. "Reaction in Scranton to Biden News" (blog). *New York Times.* August 23, 2008. http://thecaucus.blogs.nytimes.com/2008/08/23/reaction-in-scranton-pa-to-biden-news/comment-page-3/?_r=0.

Shakespeare, William. *Julius Caesar.* New York: Dover Publications, 1991.

———. *Romeo and Juliet.* New York: Dover Publications, 1993.

Shields, Christopher. "Aristotle." In *Stanford Encyclopedia of Philosophy.* July 29, 2015. http://plato.stanford.edu/entries/aristotle/.

Shuster, Kate, and John Meany. *Speak Out! Debate and Public Speaking in the Middle Grades.* New York: International Debate Education Association, 2005.

Silver, Steven. "Private Gun Ownership Is Protected by the Second Amendment." In *Gun Control: Opposing Viewpoints.* Edited by Tamara L. Roleff. San Diego: Greenhaven Press, 1997.

Silverman, Allen. "Plato's Middle Period Metaphysics and Epistemology." In *Stanford Encyclopedia of Philosophy.* July 14, 2014. http://plato.stanford.edu/entries/plato-metaphysics/#3.

Singer, Marcus G. "Philosophy." In *World Book Encyclopedia.* Chicago: World Book, 1992.

Spitz, Lewis W. "Reformation." In *World Book Encyclopedia.* Chicago: World Book, 1992.

Spurlock, Morgan, and Steve Horowitz. *Super Size Me.* Released in theaters 2004. DVD. Directed by Morgan Spurlock. New York: Hart Sharp Video, 2004.

"States With and Without the Death Penalty." *Death Penalty Information Center,* 2014. http://www.deathpenaltyinfo.org/states-and-without-death-penalty.

Straker, David. "Refuting Arguments." Changingminds.org. May 21, 2005. http: changingminds.org/disciplines/argument/making argument/refuting argument.htm.

Suetonius. "The Lives of the Twelve Caesars: Volume I: Julius. Augustus. Tiberius. Gaius. Caligula." In *Loeb Classical Library.* Edited by Jeffrey Henderson. Cambridge, MA: Harvard University Press, 1913. www.gutenberg.org/ebooks/6400.

Sweet, Lynn. "'Saturday Night Live' Third Debate Special" (blog). *Chicago Sun-Times*. October 17, 2008. http://blogs.suntimes.com/sweet/2008/10/saturday_night_live_third_deba.html.

Tebben, Joseph R. "Cicero." In *World Book Encyclopedia*. Chicago: World Book, 1992.

Trapp, Robert. *The Debatabase Book: A Must-Have Guide for Successful Debate*. 3rd ed. New York: International Debate Education Association, 2007.

Traupman, John C. *The New College Latin and English Dictionary Revised and Updated*. New York: Bantam Books, 2007.

Turner, William. "Sophists." In *The Catholic Encyclopedia*. New York: Robert Appleton Company, 1912. http://www.newadvent.org/cathen/14145c.htm.

"Unauthorized Immigrant Population Trend by States, Birth Countries and Regions." Pew Research Center. Hispanic Trends. December 11, 2014. http://www.pewhispanic.org/2014/12/11/unauthorized-trends/.

Vaughn, Lewis. *The Power of Critical Thinking: Effective Reasoning about Ordinary and Extraordinary Claims*. 2nd ed. New York: Oxford University Press, 2008.

Webster's Ninth New Collegiate Dictionary. Springfield, MA: Merriam-Webster, 1998.

Weir, William. *A Well-Regulated Militia: The Battle over Gun Control*. Hamden, CT: Archon Books, 1997.

Whitman, Glen. "Team Policy Debate." On author's *Debate* website. Page last modified September 5, 2000. http://www.csun.edu/~dgw61315/debformats.html#policy.

Williams, Jackson. "Joe the Plumber Meets Sarah the Energy Expert" (blog). *Huffington Post*. Originally posted February 28, 2009. http://www.huffingtonpost.com/jackson-williams/joe-the-plumber-meets-sar_b_135312.html.

Wunn, J. Scott. "Debate." In *World Book Encyclopedia*. Chicago: World Book, 2011.

Yates, Frances. *The Art of Memory*. Chicago: University of Chicago Press, 1966.

Zimring, Franklin E. "Capital Punishment." In *World Book Encyclopedia*. Chicago: World Book, 1992.

Appendix

Arguments and Appeals Chart

Common Topics

Definition

Comparison

Relationship

Circumstance

Testimony

Special Topics

Deliberative Topics

- Good and bad
- Advantageous and disadvantageous
- Worthy and unworthy

Judicial Topics

- What is it?
- Did it happen?
- What kind is it?

Ceremonial Topics

- Bravery and cowardice
- Self-control or indulgence
- Justice or injustice
- Generosity or selfishness
- Prudence or rashness
- Gentleness or brutality
- Loyalty or disloyalty

Deductive Arguments

AAA-1 Syllogism

EAE-1 Syllogism

AII-1 Syllogism

EIO-1 Syllogism

Appeals of Ethos

Anamnesis

Credibility

Litotes

Appeals of Pathos

Epimone

Enargia

Epiplexis

Apostrophe

Aposiopesis

Rhetorical Devices

Parallelism

Antithesis

Alliteration

Anaphora

Anadiplosis